CALAFIA
The California Poetry

PROJECT DIRECTOR: ISHMAEL REED
Y'BIRD BOOKS: BERKELEY 1979

PROJECT DIRECTOR: Ishmael Reed

CONTRIBUTING EDITORS: Simon Ortiz, Bob Callahan, Al Young, Victor Hernandez Cruz, Shawn Wong, Arl Young, Carla Blank, Marie Anderson

RESEARCH ASSISTANTS: Esta Anderson, Nancy Austin, Jackie Perret, Laura Ferguson, Alexa Garbarino, Kim Manfrin

DESIGN: Eileen Callahan

COVER: Betye Saar

Typeset by Barrett Watten. Paste-up by David Bullen

For Walter and Lillian Lowenfels, first citizens of the multi-cultures

This project was made possible by a grant to the Project Director from the California Arts Council. Thirty people were employed.

ISBN 0-931676-03-7
LC # 78-51132

O shining waterless rivers, orchards barren of grass,
Storms that disdain to thunder, seasons unseen as they pass!

From prairie and bayou and hillside long loved and bravely forsworn,
We come to woo you, enamored of your indolent smiling scorn.

California, lovely mulatto, your brown breasts fragrant with sun,
Your lovers are men who remember dear homes and old days that are
      done.

"Terra Nostalgia"
Robert Louis Burgess

ACKNOWLEDGMENTS

Grateful acknowledgment is made to each of the following for permission to reprint previously published selections:

ROBERT LOUIS BURGESS: "Terra Nostalgia" from *A Day In The Hills,* edited by Henry Meade Bland. San Francisco: private printing for Edwin Markham Chapter of English Poetry Society held at Villa Montalvo. Copyright© 1926.
SIMON J. ORTIZ: "An American Indian Vision: Indian Poetry". Copyright © 1977 by Simon J. Ortiz. Reprinted by permission of the author.
WAKAKO YAMAUCHI: "The Poetry of the Issei on the American Relocation Experience." Reprinted by permission of the author.
KEIHO YAMANAKA: Poetry included in "The Poetry of the Issei on the American Relocation Experience" by Wakako Yamauchi reprinted by permission of Keiho Yamanaka.
KEITH ABBOTT: "What You Know with No Name for It" from *Erase Words* by Keith Abbott. Blue Wind Press. Copyright © 1976 by Keith Abbott. Reprinted by permission of the author.
A.G.: "Composicion de doble sentido" from *La Voz De Mejico,* August 28, 1862. Translation by M.B. Anderson. Printed by permission of the author.
CHARLES ALEXANDER: "My Mother's Custard Pie," "It Matters Much," "My Kind of Man" from *The Negro Trail-Blazers of California* edited by Delilah L. Beasley. Los Angeles: 1919, 1st printing. 1968 reprint by R & E Research Associates, San Francisco.
ALTA: "Rewritten Letter from a Rejected Suitor." Copyright © 1977 by Alta. Reprinted by permission of the author.
ALURISTA: "Mojólogue." Copyright © 1977 by Alurista. Reprinted by permission of the author.
JEAN ANDERSON: "The Brown Girl" and "A Simple Tale" from *Poems* by Jean Anderson. Copyright© 1932 by Neal, Stratford & Kerr.
MAYA ANGELOU: "The Telephone" from *Oh Pray My Wings Are Gonna Fit Me Well* by Maya Angelou. Copyright © 1975 by Maya Angelou. Reprinted by permission of Random House, Inc.
JAIME DE ANGULO: "Indian fields over uplands" and "Land of many hues" from *Coyote's Bones* by Jaime de Angulo. Copyright © 1974 by Turtle Island Foundation. Reprinted by permission of the publisher.
ANONYMOUS: "Mining Localities peculiar to California" from *The Pacific Song Book* by John A. Stone (Old Put). San Francisco: D.E. Appleton Co., 1861. pg. 61-62.
JUANITA DE ARRANA: "Candle Flame" from *Poems From the Kernel.* Los Angeles: The College Press, 1939. "Semele" from *Westward,* International Magazine of Verse, edited by Hans A. Hoffman. Vol. 8, Nos. 9-10, October, 1939.
ANNE HARLEY AVILA: "Song from a Brown Throat" from *Land of Gold* (*Tierra de Oro*), edited by James Neill Northe. Copyright©1934 by James Neill Northe.
HERBERT BASHFORD: "Derndest Gal I Ever Knowed" from *At The Shrine of Song* by Herbert Bashford. San Francisco: Whitaker and Ray Company, 1909.
ROBERT BARLOW: "Tepuzteca, Tepehua" from *View From The Hill* by Robert Barlow. Copyright© 1948 by Robert Barlow.

ESTELLE BEASLEY TURNER: "The Devil's Garden,' "Feet," "Father," "He is on the Job," "Ecstasy" from mimeographed pamphlet prepared by Rev. Wm. A. Harris, Assoc. Minister, Beth Eden Baptist Church, Oakland, Ca., 1947. Reprinted by permission of William Beasley.

MARK TWAIN: "Lines" from *A Collection of Verse By California Poets* edited by A. MacDonald. San Francisco: A.M. Robertson, 1914.

VICTOR MANUEL VALLE: "Police Magazine." Reprinted by permission of the author.

PAUL VANGELISTI: "Event 24: John the Baptist." Reprinted by permission of the author.

ROBERTO VARGAS: "Mountain for November," "A," "B," "Moonsong 6," "Moonsong 5." Reprinted by permission of the author.

PEDRO VASQUEZ: "Oh Sister" from *Citybender*, Vol. 1, No. 1, 1977. Reprinted by permission of the author.

W.G.: "Angeles" from "The Poetry of the Argonauts" by James Miller Guinn in the Historical Society of Southern California, Publications Vol. 5. Los Angeles: 1903.

DERRAL DE RONDA WAGERS: "Solano Hills" and "Sleep" from *Westward*, International Magazine of Verse edited by Florence R. Keene. Vol. 1, No. 1. San Francisco: 1927.

WILLIAM ROSS WALLACE: "Columbia" from *The Negro Trail-Blazers of California* edited by Delilah L. Beasley. Published originally: Los Angeles: 1919. 1968 reprint by R & E Research Associates, San Francisco.

GLORIA WATKINS: "Janie." Reprinted by permission of the author.

MARIE DE LAVEAGA WELCH: "Words" from *The Dumbook*, 1925: "Littératrice" from *San Francisco Review*, 1926; "Jazz Dancers from *Poems* by Marie de LaVeaga Welch, MacMillan, 1933; "Camp Corcoran" from *This Is Our Own* by Marie de LaVeaga Welch, MacMillan, 1940.

LEW WELCH: "The Song Mt. Tamalpais Sings" from *Ring Of Bone*. Copyright © 1973 Grey Fox Press, Bolinas. Reprinted by permission of the publisher.

PHILIP WHALEN: "Absolute Realty Co.: Two Views" from *On Bear's Head*, Harcourt Brace: 1969. Reprinted by permission of the author and publisher.

JAMES M. WHITFIELD: "To Cinque" from *Early Black American Poets* edited by William H. Robinson, Jr., William C. Brown Co. Publishers.

J. RUTHERFORD WILLEMS: "Animals in the Fields" from *Amedamerica*, Tooth of Time: 1976. Reprinted by permission of the author.

DARYL WILSON: "Our Leaders," "Reflection,"'"Civilized," "Listen! The Beating Drums of the Gathering Nations," "The Shadow of the Castillion / The Tongue of the English." Reprinted by permission of the author.

WILLIAM J. WILSON: "The Coming Man" from *The Negro Trail-Blazers of California* edited by Delilah L. Beasley. Published originally in Los Angeles: 1919. 1968 reprint by R & E Research Associates, San Francisco.

FARICITA WYATT: "A Myriad of Images," "He is Black," "Ile de Gorée" from *By the Banks of the River* by Faricita Wyatt. Copyright © 1974 by Faricita Wyatt. All rights reserved. Reprinted by permission of the author.

KAREN YAMASHITA: "Obasan." First appeared in *Manuscript*. Carleton College, 1974 and in the *Rafu Shimpo* "Holiday Supplement," 1975. Reprinted by permission of the author.

AL YOUNG: "In Marin Again" and "Michael at Sixteen Months." Copyright © 1977 by Al Young. Reprinted by permission of the author.

TABLE OF CONTENTS

xxiii

xxiv

xxvi

Preface

Ishmael Reed

Is The Only Cultural Advantage To California That You Can Make A Right Turn On A Red Light?

The history of California is one that is scarcely documented. It is not written about the time the liquid mountains poured into the ocean, or when the fire swept across the northern part of California and the people lay in the damp sand in dried up river beds, in stagnant pools to survive. It is not written about the time the people clung to rocks when the world was rent and torn. The huge serpents that hung in deadly coils along the Sacramento River passed into extinction without the merest whisper of their existence, like the antelope and big cats. It is not written but it is very much a part of our history, our past.

—Andrea J. Kelsey

In his December thirtieth, 1977 broadcast on NBC, David Brinkley commented, "California, the unusual is the usual." She's never quite fit into the 'Union', though everybody seems to have lusted after her, especially the San Francisco Bay Area. Andrew Jackson wanted to buy it; it was offered to Texas. Early San Francisco must have possessed an eerie quality, all that fog, captured in Edward C. Kemble's Poe-like "Blowing Up The Wind." Rudyard Kipling said of San Francisco, once named Chrysopolis (City of Gold) "Recklessness is in the air. I can't explain where it comes from, but there it is. The roaring winds off the Pacific make you drunk to begin with . . . ."

The state was named for Calafia, a Negro Amazon. When she's in a good mood, we get those tremendous sunsets, so wonderful, people stand atop the hilltops applauding and shouting, "author! author!" When she gets mad, the land erupts. Eight-five to ninety percent of United States' earthquakes take place in California. San Francisco was the scene of an earthquake which registered eight point three on the Richter scale. Leslie Bates writes about "earthquake weather," in the poem "Premonition."

Californians have been warned that another one is due but people remain (one hundred thousand entered the state in nineteen seventy-six), get divorced for the fourth time, make movies, attend poetry readings, haul lumber, make wine, make love, and still build homes, sometimes over earthquake faults, which tells you something about Californians; they're gamblers. "The Fools of 'forty nine."

California became the home of the multi-cultures as soon as man arrived from the north, south, or from a "lost continent" which stretched across the Pacific to the California coast. Legend claims that the survivors of this continent hole up in buildings of Oriental design located on Mount Shasta, an Indian home of the gods. Not only were there physical differences between the groups of Indians— Salinan, Serrano, Morbo, Yokuts, Pomo, Wappo, Hato, Kajok, Costanoan, Maidu, Modoc, Wintun, Hupa, Yurok, Carmel, etc.— but linguistic ones as well. According to one source, "Only a part of the Sudan, and the Island of New Guinea offer as much language diversity" as found in the area extending from California to Oregon.

The Indians produced the first California poets: disputes were settled in the manner employed by some African tribes, through songs of lewd and insulting lyrics.

They lived off of "buckeye, manzanita, berries, wild raspberries, plums, grapes, elderberries, huckleberries, blackberries, thimbleberries, spearmint, sunflowers, wild oats, wild onions," and the diet staples, salmon and acorn.

They fought the invaders but couldn't withstand the diseases they brought: measles, smallpox, chicken pox, tuberculosis, malaria, typhoid, pneumonia and dysentery. By nineteen hundred the California Indian population had been reduced to sixteen thousand from an original population of about two-hundred-fifty thousand. Historians refuse to use the term "genocide" when describing what happened to the Indians, because their extermination wasn't "systematic" nor "government policy," as if their destruction were a mere matter of semantics.

Some historians tend to let the Spanish off the hook when writing about the treatment of Indians by the different invaders. It's hard to believe the Spanish didn't do their share of Indian massacring. In Haiti, sometimes called "The Mother of the Americas," since it was the site of early Spanish colonial experiments, the Indians were exterminated. Besides flogging, many Haitian Indians were used as dog food, just as the Chinese were in Utah later, in eighteen-twenty-four.

The Mexicans were just as bad. In eighteen-twenty-four, during the Mexican colonial regime of Governor Luís Argüello, Indians sucessfully captured missions at Santa Barbara and Santa Inez. Using cannons, a force led by Lt. Jose Matiano Estrada massacred the rebelling Indians at Purisima Concepcion.

The Indians of California fought each invader—often aided by maroon Negroes—until the last major California Indian war in eighteen-seventy-three when it took a half a million dollars and the government forces equipped with superior manpower and technology to subdue fifty-three warriors led by Modoc chief Captain Jack, who was hanged October third, eighteen-seventy-three. In that war, eighty-three whites were killed.

Until the eighteen-fifties, California government consisted of a string of feudal estates run on Indian labor, on which the invaders lived the good life. You see the monks' pictures on bottles in liquor stores. A long way from the Pope's authority, they abandoned their celibacy vows and used the Indian women they placed in "Nunneries." Absentee landlords, the Mexicans and Spanish didn't have the manpower to properly "rule" California, and so the Americans were able to obtain it through the comic-opera machinations of John C. Fremont and Robert F. Stockton.

Sixty-four Spanish soldiers and a priest "conquered" California, that is to say, missions were set up and down the coast within thirty miles from the coastline. When the Indians didn't work fast enough, cultivating the food supply, they were flogged, the accepted eighteenth-century manner of dealing with heathens. The cohabitation with the Indian population gave rise to a new race, part "Negro, Spanish and Indian" called Californios, "The Children of Light," who were fond of guitars, gambling and the fandango. They were a fiercely independent people who fought the Americans to an honorable peace at Guadalupe-Hidalgo. The American government violated their Spanish-Mexican land rights, guaranteed in Articles VIII and LX of the treaty, by encouraging its seizure by squatters and by prolonging suits the Californios brought against the squatters, in courts of squatter juries and squatter judges.

Those who believe that California history began in the nineteen-sixties might be surprised to learn that the Californios were a revolutionary people. The same charge made against the nineteen-sixties student revolutionaries was made against them. It was said that "In the Monterey area were many American and British businessmen who looked upon the Californios' impulse to constant revolution with disapproval." On April eleventh, eighteen-twenty-two, after the Mexican revolution, New Spain became New Mexico, and the Californios, between eighteen-twenty-two and eighteen-forty-five, expelled three governors Mexico sent to rule them. They ignored the ban against trading with the Russians, who raised a flag at Fort Ross, which had been set by the previous "conquerors" of California, the Spanish. In Francisco Carrillo Vallejo McGettigan's lovely "Ballad of California," a señorita and a Rusian sailor fall in love despite the hostility the Spanish family feels toward the Russian "heathen."

In the early eighteen-forties there were only about eight hundred Americans in California. They were ex-sailors, mountain men and trappers who were viewed by the Californios as "noisy, quarrelsome fellows and roustabouts." Exploiting the weaknesses of Mexican rule, Fremont, described by Bernard De Voto as "worse than a fool. An opportunist and adventurer, and a blunderer," captured Sonoma and set up a one month government called "The Bear Flag Republic." The "i" was omitted from the flag and it was made of a whitish-brown cotton cloth on which was painted "a grizzly bear and a red star, made of paint or pokeberry juice." It was supposed to have been designed by William L. Todd, Mrs. Abraham Lincoln's nephew. Fremont and Stockton went on to "capture" Santa Barbara, and Los Angeles without opposition, a feat immortalized in "Angeles" by "W.G."

On July fourteenth, eighteen-forty-six, John D. Sloat raised the American flag over Monterey making California a United States' possession one month after the Bear Flag Republic was born. There lingers in California history the dream of an independent white Republic. The dream foundered after California became part of the Union on September ninth, eighteen-fifty, only to re-surface after it appeared the Civil War would destroy the Union. Early maps depict California as an island. George Washington referred to it as a "country." In Ernest Callenbach's futuristic *Ectopia*, California secedes from the United States; demands of "black separatists" are granted; Negroes live in pogroms. The February 1978 issue of *Esquire* carried an article entitled "California vs. the USA."

When James Wilson Marshall discovered gold in eighteen-forty-eight, January twenty-fourth, while building a sawmill on the American River, the Gold Rush began. One hundred thousand people arrived from all over the world. (The pattern of world-wide immigration has not ceased; with the thousands of Asian immigrants from Laos and Vietnam, San Francisco airport takes on the appearance of a modern Angel Island.) For the Anglo-Americans the exploitation of California became a mission. Their zeal was captured in "Rallying Song for the Gold Diggers," penned by an anonymous Argonaut. People lived rough and ready. Life was cheap. The Argonauts sought to correct the rampant lawlessness through the Pioneers' Ten Commandments, whose first commandment was "Thou shall have no other claim than one." To encourage temperance the sixth commandment instructed: "Neither shall thou destroy thyself by getting 'tight,' nor 'slewed,' nor 'high,' nor 'corned,' nor 'half-seas over,' nor 'three sheets in the wind,' by drinking smoothly down 'brandy slings,' 'gin cock-tails,' 'whiskey punches,' 'rum toddies,' nor 'egg nogs.' Neither shalt thou suck 'mint juleps' nor 'sherry cobblers,' through a straw, nor gurgle from a bottle of the raw material...." It was a Bachelor society of lonely men. Susanna, you left behind, Sally Black, tired of waiting for you to come home rich, married the butcher. You came out here with very little. "A Shanghai rooster and one-spotted dog." Then as now, nobody was concerned about your background or "what was your name in the States?" It was with the coming of the Argonauts that American California's enduring values were set, so much so that Stephen Birmingham was able to write of contemporary San Francisco society "...as the arguments rise to battle pitch, a certain frontier flavor pervades the San Francisco air—an odor of saloons and gunsmoke—and, with several able-bodied contenders for top position, the fights are about as orderly as a Barbary Coast poker party. Beneath a veneer of politeness and gentility lurk the scruples and politics of the mining camp...."

> I soon shall be in Frisco
>> And then I'll look all round,
> And when I see the gold lumps there
>> I'll pick 'em off the ground;
> I'll scrape the mountains clean, my boys,
>> I'll drain the rivers dry,
> A pocket full of rocks bring home;
>> O! Susanna, don't you cry.

If the Indians were all but exterminated the other non-white groups were threatened with racist "laws," disenfranchised, and in the case of the Chinese, repeatedly massacred. The history of California is unique in another way. In California, one group was hated even more than the Negroes, who came first as royalty, second with the Spanish, and third as slaves and free Negroes.

Much debate concerning the exclusion of free Negroes from California took place at the Constitutional Convention of September, eighteen-forty-nine. Some delegates argued that if Negroes were admitted, "a black tide," would sweep over the land, "greater than the locusts of Egypt." Ummmm. Other delegates called for the exclusion of ". . . the degraded wretches from Sidney, South Wales, or the population of Chile, Peru, and Mexico," insisting that, ". . . most of them were as bad as any of the free Negroes of the North, or the worst slaves of the South." The Exclusion Act failed to pass in what has become known as the "legislature of a thousand drinks," but other legislation, reducing the Negro population to semi-slavery, got through.

The Chinese had come to California in ancient times when they named it Fusang. The eighteen-fifties' arrival of the Chinese overshadowed the question of Negro exclusion. Of the Chinese it was said, ". . . the Orientals had more vices and less virtues than Negroes, and they were too clanish and deceitful to serve a useful purpose in society." Bret Harte, under the pseudonym Truthful James, fueled the Anglo-Saxon imagination with his verse portraits of deceitful and sly Chinamen. Originally from New York, this is the same Francis Bret Harte who lost his job with a Humboldt County newspaper for denouncing the massacre of peaceful Indians at Gunther Island.

The Chinese settled in San Francisco and Los Angeles pogroms, where they were constantly set upon by hoodlums, a word coined in California. After passage of the Burlingame Treaty of eighteen-sixty-eight, guaranteeing unlimited Chinese immigration to the United States, riots occurred in Los Angeles. Hundreds were driven from their homes by mobs, twenty-two were killed.

Antagonism towards the Chinese led to the passage, in eighteen-eighty-two, of a bill which would declare a ten year moratorium on immigration from China. It was extended another ten years in eighteen-ninety-three. President Theodore Roosevelt, hero of Big Ten history departments, signed a bill prohibiting Chinese immigration forever. During World War II, the Japanese-Americans were placed in concentration camps; President Roosevelt, Theodore Roosevelt's relative, instructed the command of an Army camp to keep Japanese-Americans out of his sight when he came to visit. The Japanese-Americans were rounded up and guarded with shotguns.

Filipino, Japanese, Chileans would fare no better than the Negroes and Chinese in a land viewed by right-wing occultists as once having been inhabited by the citizens of Atlantis, which was said to have a city with a "golden gate."

The Vigilante committees were said to have grown from an incident in which some Chileans, at a place called "little Chile," were attacked by a gang known as The Hounds. The gang destroyed their homes and murdered them.

After riots against them at Watsonville in nineteen-thirty and at Salinas in nineteen-thirty-four, thousands of Filipinos were deported and forbidden to return.

In *Americans and the California Dream*, Kevin Starr writes, "Hatred of Mexicans is total—and totally in the service of American expansion. From Santa Fe to San Diego, the Mexican is depicted as a swarthy desperado, treacherous, cruel, cowardly."

Despite a history which reads like a shooting script for a "Dirty Harry" movie or gun fight at Kentucky Fried Chicken, California has produced a colorful gumbo culture. Between eighteen-fifty and eighteen-fifty-three, one thousand-two hundred people were murdered in San Francisco (in nineteen-seventy-four, one hundred-forty-four) but during the same period, according to Richard Miller, San Franciscans were served by "... twelve daily papers (one in German) two French tri-weeklies, a Chinese weekly, and a literary weekly counting more subscribers than any other journal on the coast. There were Jewish and Italian papers too. San Franciscans could choose among American, French, Spanish, German and Chinese theatres. The city had thirty-four schools, good bookstores and music stores, photography studios, a gymnasium, a music hall, two race courses and two bull-rings...."

Mark Twain called one of the literary journals, *Golden Era,* published during the gold-rush days, the best literary journal in the nation. Bret Harte later edited *Overland Monthly*. During this period, twenty-two of Shakespeare's plays were done in California; the San Francisco stage presented nine-hundred-seven plays and forty-eight operas in five languages; eighty-four extravaganzas; and sixty-six minstrel specialties." San Francisco was the west's biggest publishing center.

This cultural tradition continues unmitigated. According to testimony given at a January fourth, nineteen-seventy-eight White House Conference on the Arts held on the Berkeley Campus of the University of California, a congressional committee was told that by turnstile count more people attended museum shows in nineteen-seventy-seven than baseball games. In Los Angeles, the butt of many eastern jokes, five-hundred-thousand people belong to art-related industries. A poetry reading organized by Alan Soldofsky, and held at Berkeley's Greek Theatre, May, nineteen-seventy-seven, drew an audience as large as those which attend readings in the Soviet Union. Later that year, in November, large numbers also attended the Second Annual San Francisco Poetry Festival organized by David Moe. Afro-American music has found an audience in California since the California days of the founder of Jazz, Jelly Roll Morton.

California craftspeople influence the nation as well. Of California interior decorating, Erica Brown, in the January eighth, nineteen-seventy-eight New York Times, wrote: "The best interior design talents of the West Coast have created their own distinct environments, combining the openness of the California way of life with a sophisticated use of natural materials. It is a style that has become a major influence throughout America."

Poetry survives along with the bad headlines about Santa Cruz dogblood rites, mass murders and burials, revolutionaries shot in the back on San Quentin prison grounds.

This anthology attempts to bring together the poetry of different California cultures under one roof. We have not sought to segregate these cultures according to "race," "nation," or chronology. We agree with Simon Ortiz that "Poetry is an all-inclusive singular event and idea throughout time."

California poets have always written about reform, nature, "exotic" religions, the occult and revolution. Joaquin Miller wrote a "Cuba libre," and James Whitfield penned a "Cinque." The Frisco Bohemians of the early nineteen-hundreds dabbled in "jade, Japanese poetry, Esperanto, higher space, Bahaiism, and devil-worship." In those days you left the all night party, opium on the brain, an opera cloak wrapped about your neck; your wife put laurels in her hair, took cyanide while listening to Chopin. Society queens were whores or daughters of gold miners who got lucky.

In that famous legislature of a thousand drinks, someone described California culture as "a heterogeneous mass of human beings of every language and of every hue." And, though thirty people worked on this project, I was the lucky one who first saw this "heterogeneous mass" wriggling together between two covers: it was brilliant. I felt like the first man to enter Tut's tomb concealed in golden darkness all those years, and when someone asked what it looked like he said, "wonderful. It is wonderful."

Calafia is an anthology of poetry, but I'm sure that an anthology of Dance, Painting and Music would also show that, out of the high tides and pounding winds of its history, California has produced America's truly world state, and if, as they say, California is the United States' window on the future, then the prospects for a diverse, national poetry, instead of the various sects of the moment, are good.

And so what about the Woody Allen joke which goes, "the only cultural advantage to California is that you can make a right turn on a red light." Well, what about it?

January 22, 1978

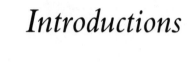

Introductions

Bob Callahan

Notes From The 21st Century

Restrained by local convention and limited populations in other areas of America, the full diversity of American culture breaks loose only in California. In California, more so than in any other state or region including New York, you will find yourself living & working in the same neighborhood with peoples from all over the world. Last night I attended an evening of Irish music, tomorrow I might go hear the Bali Orchestra. And for the weekend we talk about attending an exhibit of African Art out in Golden Gate Park. We are interested, not because of any feigned liberalism, but because neighbors are participating in all of these shows. My son David attends a Child Care Center called Nia House. On first glance Nia House looks like the back-up set for Sesame Street. Here is a story David, then just three years old, told us one afternoon:

"No school, tomorrow."

"Why, son?"

"Because it's Malcolm X's Birthday."

"Who was Malcolm X, David?"

"He was a great man who was shot by some thugs."

"And tomorrow is his Birthday?"

"Yes. We should buy some ice cream and cake. He might come over to our house for a party."

And if Malcolm did come over for a party, and the Staff at Nia House hosted it, I believe Malcolm X would be shocked and delighted at some of the not so insignificant changes which have gone on in American Culture during the last ten years.

California is then like a piece of the whole world now folded into these extraordinarily beautiful Pacific coastal mountains & valleys—the whole world, not in any stupid provincial sense—but in the truly cosmopolitan way you might be proud to raise your own child.

Diversity.

Diversity is the key.

The differences which can be easily found between California's ethnic & racial populations is more than matched by the differences which can be found within each of these so-called 'Mother Cultures.'

Today, traditional European coastal dwellers such as the Italians and the Portuguese can be found at work on the abalone trade off the Coast of Mendocino, while the elder farmers of Europe's aged grasslands, the Armenians & the Slavs, can now be found working sections of California's most famous Central Valley. There is no one European Culture, it becomes evident in California; the solidarity of European Culture, to cite one example, is a Myth.

And in this kind of cultural environment the opportunity for growth is enormous. A real education in American Culture awaits the average American, and many have journeyed to California just to learn.

Hence this anthology in the field that means so much to all of us. There is a brilliant gumbo baroqueness about contemporary American writing, and such gumbo is quite evident in this text. Here Asian-American writers bend spaces first realized by the Lake Poets of England, while young euro-American poets project their verse onto fresh grounds first opened by Charlie Parker. Listen, then, to the poems in this volume as the Editors listen to them, and hear how common political, social, and cultural themes become elaborated & made unique through the various languages & literatures which speak within the pages of this book. There is a grand anthropology being practiced in *Calafia,* a hall of mirrors if you will, and everyone who has participated in the creation of this landmark walked away with a sense of astonishment and great surprise.

Only from the point of view of Boston, we have learned, can California be considered the West. For those of us who live & work here it has long been a major world center, a vital intersection, where all of the world's cultures long ago came to meet.

Berkeley
Winter, 1977

xlviii

Victor Hernandez Cruz

Contemporary Hispanic Poetry from California

In a land where streets and cities and landscape have Spanish names, Hispanic peoples are bridges to the environment. Before this there was that. Now we see freeways out of towns, to edges of forests and spilling back towards city, boulevards and avenues on thru to downtown and real deal estate, contemporary avocado in nervous salad. To be mestizo is to have two floors, to have another is like Tresmosis and see even more, to what now we understand here as La Raza Cosmica, a home that has from other places fully developed its own even tone. Nothing loses in the gamble, criss-crossing and everyone gets to base full of more chances. The Chicano-Hispano peoples of California have pre-Washington D.C. roots to this land of the Redwoods. There are spectacular remnants of Spanish architecture throughout, interspliced with orange plastic looney-tune attempts at structure, like a heritage that made itself up at the beginning of its end. The new Disco-executives of the experimental arena are amuck with their own vocabulary, their symbols lead to no where. Destroy environment while you mispronounce the city you live in. The poets here express themselves in Spanish and English and a blend of the two, denial of neither language, using them both to form a circle; a storehouse of approaches to subjects and ideas, entering in one order in Spanish and another in English.

A land full of surprise and a solidness that is forming. Down there in San Diego you can drive past nuclear war heads while you listen to trio music coming from a Tijuana radio station. The poets are observers of these dynamics, they pop up everywhere, bringing furniture from one room to another, fitting all kinds of awkward things together, maintaining a good decor. Poems of desperation written in desperate peace. A tour of the sun falling on jails, hospitals, colleges and libraries, the edge of the ocean, the outskirts of vegetation. Something from that arrangement outside jumping through the shape of the language. They drive in automobiles atop the terrain, producing out of sensations words, ducking mind hustlers, freaks, religios, wine with arsenic in it (bad pluck), elements out of orientation. This is a great key to the content of the south, beyond the border, "the removal of borders" eloquently put by

Alurista from San Diego. A continuation of the spirit of Mexico, of Hispano America runs through the vision of the poets present here. Actually many things can come here and be themselves. We are recognizing here samples of what is being done, which is in constant evolution, later everyone might be out taking a ride, on the way back if they find parking, they will continue talking about Califoniasisa-phenominizlization.

San Francisco, 1977

Simon Ortiz

An American Vision: Indian Poetry

The poems written by Indian authors, mostly native Californians, in this book are all contemporary and they all speak of the past.

Except in a very limited sense, Indian poetry cannot be classified into Contemporary and Past. Or Before and After. Or Indian and Non-Indian. Or Alive and Dead. Poetry is an all-inclusive singular event and idea throughout time. A living people demands that perspective. We allow that a people's literature goes through a creative process, through stages, epochs, changes, so forth, but we cannot allow for its easy categorization when it is done to justify history and the literature that substantiates it. The intent and achievement of American society of which literature is an integral part has too often been to justify the process of Americanization. Poets, especially native poets of this land, must not provide America such an easy out. We must expect America to be responsible as we must expect ourselves to be responsible.

The living tradition of people includes a literature that is of the past and that is contemporary. Its poetry must be accountable to the immediate as well as bear upon the flux and changes that have occurred. When Indian people speak of the value of tradition they mean that the rituals, prayers, songs are not just ancient but that they are useful now—or can be and should be. When America has looked upon the past, especially upon "old Indian things," it has too often merely looked cursorily and refused to honestly investigate or analyze what is the true and actual value of what is past and traditional.

Americans look upon their ancestral traditions in the same way. They admit to their existence as necessary accoutrements but there seems to be no real sense of relationship with them because there is no real sense of responsiblity for them. It's nice to have a coat of arms on a living room wall or to sing a song an ancestral clan "used to sing," but they should be regarded as being more than just "nice." Those traditions should affect people in the same way that responsibility affects them, with a kind of fright because the responsibility for their continued usefulness—if they are useful—is large and sometimes awesome. Because of this responsibility, Indian people, especially the older people, have been reluctant in many cases to permit the publication of songs and stories which have been useful in their societies. They ask, "How will they be regarded?" That question indicates their concern for its value. The songs, stories, and poems have value of the context in which they have usefulness. The poems from this context express knowledge of, and a carrying out of, the responsibility of Indian people for each other, for the environment in which we live, for the earth upon which we thrive. Indian people want to be assured that the songs, poetry, and other forms of literature be regarded in the proper way—the sacred or truly responsible way. This concern has to reject the possibility of including it, without realizing its core value, into a body of literature which permits America to get away with continued uninformed definition of people.

I have been, on a number of occasions, confronted with the question "Is this the way that real Indians used to tell their history, or is this the way present-day Indians do it." I've been appalled, naturally—and rattled, although I've more often than not shrugged, and answered. I've seen older Indian people visibly flinch under such questions and commentary although they smile and answer politely anyway. Recently, a college art instructor described an Acoma woman's face as having become "suddenly stone faced" when he asked her to pose for photographs. What the question strikes upon is one's humanity. People in America have been particular victims of dehumanization. And it is not just those who are the victims who have been devastated, but it is those who propagate the history and attitudes who have been dehumanized more than anyone else.

We have been categorized, classified, and defined from the very beginning of the European "discovery" of the Western Hemisphere —when American history began to be recorded—as something other than human. Not just different people in the sense that there are different races of men but something *other* than human. Sometimes we were elevated to be some romanticized noble beings, but mostly we were derogated to a lowly contemptuous level of beings without emotion, intellect, and with morals which turned on conceptions of good and evil, and certainly no civilization. This was done in deliberate and fine conscience by the early day American thinkers, educators, writers, merchants, religious leaders, and it was done in order to justify what they did to the Indians they "discovered." And we know, though American history and literature doesn't make much of a public point of it, that Europeans Christianized the Indians, forced European education upon them, introduced them to alcohol and new disease, and unceremoniously killed them. As they "civilized" the Indians, they used them for their own purposes which, seen in an accurate historical light, was clearly for European economic motives rather than those intentions that American history has led us to believe—that it was mainly an exercise of religious freedom and the Christian purpose of saving souls (theirs and the Indians) which brought them to the American continents.

It was quite easy to deal with beings who were not like the colonizers and were accorded a lesser status than they. Anything could be done with the Indians. And, soon after, when patriots like Tecumseh, Osceola, Crazy Horse, Captain Jack, Geronimo were eventually killed or imprisoned—their people vanquished militarily and scattered—the "savages and heathens" became ghosts and lurked, as American history and literature has put it, in the shadows of American civilization. Indians became the very personification of evil— although it was the evil born of wrong done—in the American psyche. If the Fathers of American history had seen Indians as human beings, they would have had a chance. If the pilgrims had allowed themselves to remain human, not special precursors whose planned and chosen destiny was to manifest itself by "civilizing" the people they came into contact with and the land which was occupied by them, they would have had a chance. But, of course, they did not allow knowledge of themselves as human people. Perhaps they were not able. We must allow ourselves this chance because indeed we are human.

Indian people were never savage heathens nor lurking ghosts. They loved their land, their people, the social structures they developed, their history, literature and religion. Ever since European people first came into contact with those native to this hemisphere, Indian people have wanted to be known as human. That's what they want to be known and accepted as. That is why they are still continuing to fight so determinedly against the image that American history and literature has presented of them. Indian people insist on correcting the image, not to revise American history, but to teach other people that the only way they can be human is to recognize the humanity of others. We insist that America know our humanity and we resist dehumanization. Indian America's knowledge of that, and further direction towards it, does not divide conveniently into Past and Contemporary. It remains in vibrant motion through Indian people because that vital event and idea of humanity is what keeps us alive, makes us responsible to that knowledge, and allows us vision by which to continue knowing ourselves as people in relationship with all other beings in the universe. That, above all, is what we want to be. That is the vision that Indian people and their poetry require that America know: our humanity.

Shawn H. Wong

Longtime Californ'

"We wanted to learn from the men who they were... they would reach into their vest pockets as they began, take out a soft plastic folder with the photograph of a young man, black hair combed back, eyes looking straight ahead: an alien registration card. The old men keep these rare pictures of themselves as youths. "Yeah, that's me! 1951. I was sixteen years old when I came in!" They talk of coming off the steamer with a father or an uncle who had already been working here for a long time. "Me longtime Californ'," the oldtimers would say to the immigration officials.
—from *Longtime Californ'*, Victor G. and Brett deBary Nee

Today I said to an Indian friend
Who had been in the seige of Alcatraz,
"We're going to take all the islands in the Bay."
We shook on it, laughing,
But his eyes were knots,
Knowing as I do
An island is the saddest kind of land there is.
—from *Angel Island* by Connie Young Yu

When the fog in San Francisco Bay moves back out towards the sea it looses its grip on the Berkeley hills, lowers down over the water, moves out through the Golden Gate Bridge leaving a halo of fog around the island standing in its path. On the northeastern corner of Angel Island State park at Winslow Cove is Building 317, in a state of decay from water erosion and natural deterioration. Building 317 is the only building left of the Angel Island Immigration Station, "the Ellis Island of the West Coast." From 1910 to 1940 Angel Island Immigration Station processed and interrogated Chinese and Japanese immigrants and returning Chinese-Americans and Japanese-Americans. All of the immigrants were detained in barracks that resemble prisons. Some were imprisoned for up to three years waiting to hear whether or not they could settle in the land they could see out their windows. Bribery and corruption ruled the Immigration Station, women were sold into slavery or into prostitution. An investigation brought indictments to nine immigration officials from the director down to the clerks. All nine finally confessed to bribery, selling women, altering records, and selling immigration records and were given presidential pardons for being their own witnesses.

For 30 years, Chinese and Japanese immigrants carved poems on the walls of Building 317.[1.]

> The small building with 3 beams is just sufficient to shelter to body
> It is unbearable to relate the accumulated true stories on the slopes
> of the island
> Wait until the day I am successful and fulfill my wish
> I will not be benevolent and will level and uproot the immigration
> station.
>
> —Written by one from Toishan

> I left my village behind me and bade farewell to my father and my
> mother
> I stare at the faraway clouds and mountains and tears well in my
> eyes
> The wandering son was longing for the wealth of Tao Chu
> Who could have told that I will be imprisoned on this island?
> I beat my breast as I think of China and cried bitterly like Juan Chih
> Our nation's rights are flowing out and lost to others and in
> addition there are national humiliations
> My fellow countrymen should recognize the occasion and plan to
> be determined
> Vow to take over the U.S. to avenge previous wrongs.
>
> —Written by a Wandering Son of Heungshan

> From this moment on, I bid farewell to this building
> My fellow villagers here are rejoicing like me
> Say not that here everything is western style
> Even if it were built of jade, it has turned into a cage.

There are dozens of other poems carved into the walls describing the frustrations and despair of waiting on Angel Island. The Exclusion Acts of 1882, 1888, 1892, 1904 and 1924 were meant to make immigration as difficult as possible for Chinese men and women. In the midst of all this exclusion and the violent anti-Chinese movements that led to the laws, America went wild popularizing the hate in songs. The plea for exclusion was direct in the song "California As It Is and Was" (*Put's Original California Songster*, 5th edition, 1868):

> I remember, I remember, when the Yuba used to pay,
> With nothing but a rocker, five hundred dollars a day;
> We used to think 't would always last, and would with perfect
> ease,

If Uncle Sam had only stopped the coming of the Chinese.
If Uncle Sam had only stopped the coming of the Chinese.

In the same book are songs about Joaquin Murrieta raiding Chinese camps:

Joaquin, just before he was taken,
Killed a Chinaman, and then stole his bacon;
Then he went to Sonora, where he killed eleven more,
                    —"Joaquin, The Horse Thief"

No matter who was robbed or killed, 'twas all laid to Joaquin,
His band out in the chapparal not long ago was seen;
With pick and shovel on his back, as though out on a tramp,
An honest miner might have seen, robbing a Chinese camp.

        Chorus—
As he pulled them around by the tails,
They scratched with their long finger nails;
A tom iron round his body was bound,
So of course it must be Joaquin.

From *The Gold Digger's Song Book* (1856) "John Chinaman's Appeal" tells the story of a Chinese immigrant:

American now mind my song
If you would but hear me sing,
And I will tell you of the wrong,
That happened to "Gee Sing"
In "fifty two" I left my home—
I bid farewell to "Hong Kong"—
I started with Cup Gee to roam
To the land where they use the "long tom."

In forty days I reached the Bay,
And nearly starved was I, sir,
I cooked and ate a dog one day,
I didn't know the laws, sir.
But soon I found my dainty meal
Was 'gainst the city order,
The penalty I had to feel—
Confound the old Recorder.

By paying up my cost and fines
They freed me from the lcoker,

And then I started for the mines—
I got a pick and rocker.
I went to work in an untouched place,
I'm sure I meant no blame, sir,
But a white man struck me in the face
And told me to leave his claim, sir.

Twas then I packed my tools away
And set up in a new place
But they would not let me stay—
They didn't like the "cue" race.
And then I knew not what to do.
I could not get employ.
The Know Nothings would bid me go—
'Twas tu nah mug ahoy.

I started then for Weaverville
Where Chinamen were thriving,
But found our China agents there
In ancient feuds were driving.
So I pitched into politics,
But with the weaker party;
The Cantons with their clubs and bricks,
Did drub us out "right hearty."

I started for Yreka then;
I thought that I would stay there,
But found for even Chinamen
The "diggings" wouldn't pay there.
So I set up a washing shop,
But how extremely funny,
The miners all had dirty clothes,
But not a cent of money.

I met a big stout Indian once,
He stopped me in the trail, sir,
He drew an awful scalping knife,
And I trembled for my tail, sir.
He caught me by the hair, its true,
In a manner quite uncivil,
But when he saw my awful cue,
He thought I was the devil.

Oh, now my friends I'm going away
From this infernal place, sir;
The balance of my days I'll stay
With the Celestial race, sir.
I'll go to raising rice and tea;
I'll be a heathen ever,
For Christians all have treated me
As men should be used never.

Frank Chin wrote in "Confession of A Chinatown Cowboy," "... America picked up the Charleston, big bands, ragtime jazz and put to music, the agony of our old men doomed here without women or a hope of returning to China and danced to it. The songs of the old '49ers about 'John Chinaman,' were updated and civilized in New York's Tin Pan Alley to become 'Little Chinky Butterfly,' 'China girl,' 'Chinese Lullaby,' and a song that must have been sung a lot around the piano, for I've heard bits of it sung by Chinese-Americans—mothers of grammar school friends—who sung it in their school days in talent shows. I found the sheet music and remembered hearing it, a song featured by Fred Schmitt and his Rialto Orchestra called "Hong Kong Dream Girl":

China boy is very sad because he went away,
From his little China maiden,
China boy feel very sad and only yesterday
He wrote a note to her to say:

My little Hong Kong Dream girl
In every dream you seem, girl,
Two almond eyes are smiling,
And my poor heart is whirling
Like a big sail round my pigtail
I dream of you till dawning,
But early in the morning
Oriental dream is gone,
China boy is so forlorn.,
Hong Kong Dream Girl goodbye.[2]

Famous California writers watched the immigration of the Chinese into California and wrote about and encouraged an end to immigration and the passage of exclusion laws. The poet Bret Harte wrote in *The Latest Chinese Outrage*,"

> 'Are we men?' says Joe Johnson, 'and list to this jaw,
> Without process of warrant or color of law?
> ...'Shall we stand here as idle, and let Asia pour
> Her barbaric hordes on this civilized shore?
> Has the White Man no country? Are we left in the lurch?
> And likewise what's gone of the Established Church?'

One of Bret Harte's most famous poems was a long poem called "Plain Language From Truthful James":

> "Which I wish to remark,
>   And my language is plain,
> That for ways that are dark
>   And for tricks that are vain,
> The heathen Chinee is peculiar,
>   Which the same I would rise to explain."

Jack London wrote an essay, '*The Unparalleled Invasion*,'' predicting that by 1975 China would overtake America since America allowed Chinese to immigrate, and that the sheer number of Chinese in China combined with those in America that would reproduce would smother America. In a short story called "The Chinago" (1914) he wrote:

> Between the western nations and China there is no common psychological speech. Their thought processes are radically dissimilar. There is no intimate vocabulary. The Western mind penetrates the Chinese mind but a short distance when it finds itself in a fathomless maze. The Chinese mind penetrates the Western mind an equally short distance when it fetches up against a blank, incomprehensible wall. It is all a matter of language. There is no way to communicate Western ideas to the Chinese mind...the Chinese mind cannot thrill to short, Saxon words; nor can the English speaking mind thrill to heiroglyphics. The fabrics of their minds are woven from totally different stuffs. They are mental aliens.

And Mark Twain wrote in *Roughing It*:

> Chinamen make good house servents, being quick, obedient, patient, quick to learn, and tirelessly industrious. They do not need to be taught a thing twice, as a general rule. They are imitative. If a Chinaman were to see his master break up a center table, in a passion, and kindle a fire with it, that Chinaman would be likely to resort to the furniture for fuel forever afterward.

There were dozens of books describing the fall of America to Chinese immigration, among them were, *Almond Eyes* (1880), *The Chinese Invasion* (1873) and *The Yellow Peril in Action* (1907). F.M. Pixley stated before a joint congressional committee investigating Chinese immigration:

> The Divine Wisdom has said that He would divide this country and the world as a heritage of five great families: that to the Blacks He wouild give Africa; to the Red Man He would give America; and Asia He would give to the Yellow race... The White race is to have the inheritance of Europe and America and... the Yellow races are to be confined to what the Almighty originally gave them and as they are not favored people, they are not to be permitted to steal from us what we have robbed the American savage of... (1876).

In the nineteenth century the California magazine "*Land of Sunshine*" published the short stories of Sui Sin Far, an English-born Eurasian. The editors of *Aiiieeeee! An Anthology of Asian American Writers* point out that "she was one of the first to speak for an Asian American sensibility that was neither Asian nor white American. And, interesting enough, in her work, there is no cultural conflict between East and West. "... Working within the terms of the stereotype of the Chinese as laundryman, prostitute, smuggler, coolie, she presents 'John Chinaman' as a little more than a comic caricature, giving him a sensibility that was her own."[3]

In 1896 *Land of Sunshine* said her stories' characters "... are all of Chinese characters in California or on the Pacific Coast; and they have an insight and sympathy which are probably unique. To others the alien Celestial is at best mere 'literary material': in these stories he (or she) is a human being."

In 1912 Sui Sin Far published a collection of 37 short stories under the title *Mrs. Spring Fragrance* (A.C. McClug and Co.). The stories are remarkable in their description of California Chinese in the midst of exclusion laws and writers encouraging stronger exclusion laws.

Around the time Sui Sin Far was publishing her stories in *Land of Sunshine*, Japanese immigrants began coming into California in large numbers. Later in 1921, over 20,000 "picture brides" landed at Angel Island Immigration Station. In the Twenties and early Thirties there was a wealth (by today's standards) of Japanese poets from Japan publishing small volumes of poetry and essays. *Tanka Poems in Exile* by Jun Fujita was published in Chicago by Covici-McGee Co. in 1923. Bunichi Kagawa, who spent at least 10 years living in Palo Alto, California from 1921 to 1931, published two books of poetry, *Silent Intimacy and Other Poems* and *Hidden Flame* (1930). Yone Noguchi, the most famous of the three poets, spent a lot of time travelling around America from about 1895 to 1905. After his return to Japan he published a collection of his speeches and essays titled *Japan and America* (Tokyo: Keio University Press, 1921). In one essay, "Literary Co-operation Between America and Japan," Yone Noguchi takes a break in the middle of the essay to describe the California he lived in and travelled through:

> The million miles of blue waves of the Pacific Ocean are guarded by those two awe-inspiring but kind mountains, awe-inspiring like kings, kind like queens, Fuji Mountain in Japan and Mount Shasta in California, whose white-crowned heads reach the sky and exchange a salutation of voiceless words with God... here the scenic wonder of California is begun with Mount Shasta, a northern guardian tower, through which you can step in the richest bosoms of the valleys crawling like dragons. Behold the solitude of Mount Shasta silently scorning the forest below, by which Klamath River in north and Sacramanto River in south run carrying her divine shape that is nothing but the deathless castle challenging against Eternity. She is the mountain of snow and light, a glorious pyramid out-standing beyond the seasons and age. And behold, turning your head to the other side, how the Yosemite Valley with El Capitan, that monster of granite of three thousand feet high, and with the Merced River whose mirror-white breast decorates itself with wonderful trees and flowers, is competing with Mount Shasta. Here are several waterfalls, as I once wrote, with the "tempestuous song of Heaven's organ throbbing wild peace through the sky and land"; there are cedars and sequoias sending out the sweetest odours to accentuate the rhythm of nature.

Professor Sam Solberg of the University of Washington notes, "Noguchi was a pioneer in the introduction of Western poetry and literature to Japan—wrote poetry in Japanese apparently as out-landish for its day as what he did in English, and pursued a long and honored career as Professor of English at Keio University. There is no doubt in my mind that he was seriously concerned with bridging the gap between Japanese and Western cultures, but there is an element of play, irony (even put-on if you will) behind his early English poetry at least . . . I think this is what Earl Miner overlooks when he dismisses him as a 'pseudo-oriental' poet. When Noguchi transferred those 'pseudo-oriental' elements from his English poetry to his Japanese they created something new and exciting for younger Japanese poets, if nothing very great in themselves."[4]

Bunichi Kagawa is the most interesting of the immigrant poets because he spent so much time in California and lived in Palo Alto for ten years and gained enough fame to be included in *California Poets: An Anthology of 244 Contemporaries* (New York: The House of Henry Harrison, 1932). Kagawa published two collections of poetry in California, *Silent Intimacy and Other Poems* (1932) and *Hidden Flame* (1930). The note in *Hidden Flame* by the publisher stated that the book "was published by Ruth Mantz of Half Moon Press (Stanford, California), sponsored by Margery Bailey, completed third week of July MCMXXX. Two hundred numbered copies on Alexandra Japan Book, bound in Japan parchment." Yvor Winters wrote the forward to *Hidden Flame*:

> (Kagawa) fairly well-known to the literary member of the large Japanese population on the Pacific Coast, has been confronted with the cultural dilemma of that population, which, unable to return to Japan for economic reasons, must try either to keep its culture alive more or less artificially in an alien environment or to assimilate that alien environment and in turn be assimilated by it. The dilemma can be eliminated by time alone, and by a good deal of time; the attitude toward it is for the present, I gather, a trifle bewildered; and tentative efforts are being made in both directions. Mr. Kagawa is, for the time being, a bilingual poet; a few of his English poems have appeared in magazines, but this is the first considerable collection of them. It is likewise the first collection of English poems by a Japanese, that, to my knowledge, has endeavored to stand on its own merits as poetry rather than as an illustration of a foreign state of mind. Mr. Kagawa's style is certainly not in th English tradition, but neither, so far as his more recent work is concerned, is it in the Japanese; he is a writer cut off from tradition. His severance from tradition is all too real; it is not, as in the case of so many contemporary American poets, a sentimental or rhetorical pretense; and this makes his position peculiarly difficult. The difficulty should not lead us to overlook or condone his faults—for poetry, after all, is poetry—but a realization of the difficulty may enable the reader to understand those faults more

exactly, as well as more accurately to evaluate his virtues.

Mr. Kagawa's rhythmic tempo is very slow and somewhat elaborate. A slow and elaborate rhythm must never be allowed by falter, for if it does falter, the entire performance collapses. Mr. Kagawa is not always, it seems to me, successful in preserving his somewhat precarious metrical integrity, but I believe that he is successful a fair part of the time....

Another trait that may cause difficulty—and that is, I suspect, a racial trait that cannot be eradicated, of which he is in all likelihood unconscious—is his penchant for elaborate symbolism. Mr. Kagawa is, I think, very seldom deliberately ornate or decorative, but he sometimes appears so, for the reason that his symbols, to the occidental reader at least, now and then seem to lose their anchorage and drift. The fault, however, is usually one of perception on the part of the reader or of execution on the part of the poet; it does not reside in the poet's concept of poetry.

The reader acquainted with modern poetry will find in these pieces a few familiar phrases. As a foreigner, learning the language, Mr. Kagawa has sometimes picked up phrases as one might words; in other instances he has deliberately selected phrases from other writers as central themes, and built new poems about them. Little damage has been done to his poetry either way, and the values of the borrowed expressions have usually been pretty thoroughly altered by the time he has done with them.

...Mr. Kagawa is creating and endeavoring to master a definite rhetoric, and because the peculiar quality of that rhetoric may be overlooked by the reader who has not had time to accustom himself to it, unless he is forewarned and rendered especially wary. It would be a pity; I believe, to overlook Mr. Kagawa's poetry; its modest, but nevertheless valid and penetrating introspective wisdom, and its elaborately hesitant precision, possess values not duplicated in contemporary poetry.

Winters, in his forward to *Hidden Flame*, becomes "elaborately hesitant" himself in describing Kagawa's style. Winters describes the process of creating new language but never saying so and makes the use of symbolism by Kagawa a racial trait (something English poets must have borrowed from the Japanese). Or perhaps Kagawa was getting too close to mastering, instead of "borrowing," phrases. "Identity" is a poem from *Hidden Flame*:

> When, one by one, as the leaves turn
> Yellow, turn yellow and fall

Quietly to the whisper we came after,
And cold winter twigs hold the liquid
Moon in their delicate fingers
Of memory, the toothless laughter—
Of indifference that touches not you.
Nor me, combs our mind at last patient
As the aimless clatter of clay—

And there is a certain rest for you
When the stillness of wind released
From our foreseen death wraps, binds,
Thin trees and moon in its icy hair;
When the shadowy pain half awake
In your surrendered eagerness picks
Its way drifting slowly as the drifting
Sea-weed upon the pale ocean floor.

Ah, when the frost seals the bare
Winter earth, and dreams deeply
Through the crooked humor of frozen night,
We, whose heritage is tried, who are
Identified mostly by what we could not
Attain, nail our sleep utterly with what
Strict permanency we could not keep.

In the early Thirties, the laws regarding interracial marriages
between "Mongolians" and "Negroes" were altered to include people of the "Malay race." Joaquin Legaspi came to America in 1917 at
the age of twenty-one and began writing and publishing here. Carlos
Bulosan immigrated into Seattle, Washington in 1930 at the age of
seventeen and moved to California where he spent most of his life.
Bulosan, in his autobiography, *America is in the Heart* (1946), stated,
"I came to know afterward that in many ways it was a crime to be a
Filipino in California. I came to know that the public streets were not
free to my people: we were stopped each time these vigilant patrol-
men saw us driving a car. We were suspect each time we were seen
with a white woman. And perhaps it was this narrowing of our life
into an island, into a filthy segment of American society, that had
driven Filipinos like Doro inward, hating everyone and despising all
positive urgencies toward freedom..."

Carlos Bulosan's poem "The Surrounded" is an unpublished
poem which was written in Los Angeles County Hospital. He died

of tuberculosis in 1956. In *America is in the Heart* he wrote:

> I bought a bottle of wine when I arrived in San Luis Obispo. I
> rented a room in a Japanese Hotel and started a letter to my brother
> Macario, whose address had been given to me by a friend. Then it
> came to me, like a revelation, that I could actually write under-
> standable English. I was seized with happiness. I wrote slowly and
> boldy, drinking the wine when I stopped, laughing silently and
> crying. When the long letter was finished, a letter which was
> actually a story of my life, I jumped to my feet and shouted
> through my tears:
> "They can't silence me any more! I'll telll the world what they
> have done to me!"

Lawson Inada points out that the title to his collection of poetry,
Before the War, comes from an expression you hear all the time if you
listen to older Japanese-Americans—"Before the war I was living in
California . . . " It's an expression full of the land, of land being taken
away, and, in California, it means Manzanar or Tule Lake Relocation Centers. Inada wrote about this kind of land in "Japanese Geometry":

> "Hey, you ever been over to Tule Lake, Mary Ann?
> You know, over by Alturas...
> Well, did you know
> there was a Camp over there?
> Well there was—
> over 18 thousand of us there, man.
>
> And I go there all the time, whenever I can,
> just because it's so damn beautiful,
> but whenever I'd get there
> I'd practically freak out, you know,
> because it's just like
> where *I* was, you know—
> way out in nowhere, man,
> nothing but sand—
>
> and so I'd be out there, you know,
> kicking the shit out of dust,
> kicking the shit out of snow,
> throwing rocks,
> kicking the shit out of

what's left of fences and foundations,
and it would really get
kind of scarey, you know,
because there I'd be, man,
all alone,
because I'd leave my family at home, you know,
and I'd be out there,
with nothing but
duck hunters and potato farmers
and, man, it wasn't them so much
as me, you know,
like that time I was cruising
over what's left of roads,
everything all laid out in neat rows you know,
you can still see em,
trying to make some sense
out of structure—
where the ball field was,
the sewer plant, mess halls, headquarters—

well, so then there's this road crew
doing something, hell, I don't know,
so slow down, cruise
on by, you know,
and this dude hollers at me, man,
"Where the hell you think you're going!'
and man, bam!, that's it,
shit I'm outa the car
while it's still rolling, man,
screaming right into this dude's throat, man,
and there's 2 of them
standing there
in hard hats, with pick and shovels,
and shit I don't give a damn, man,
quivering, screaming
'What the fuck did you say!
What the fuck did you say, buddy!'
and he's going 'uh, well, uh,
didn't you see that sign, uh..."
and the other dude's going
'uh, yeah, the sign, well uh, maybe...
and man, man,
well, it's just so fucken ridiculous, you know,

these 2 dudes out here, shitting,
and so I kinda start laughing
inside, you know,
but then flash on
'Well, look buddy,
I don't mind you trying to fix up the road,
but don't just be hollering, that's all.
Not at me.
Because this is
my land, man. *My* land, buddy.
And you better
remember that. This is *my* land, man.'
And you know, the wild thing is,
later that day
I began to find
a lot of things, like they were left for me, you know:

faucet handle, half
a Japanese teacup, piece of wood
with numbers on it, nails,
little bits of tarpaper,
part of a mirror, green
glass to look through,
an old ink bottle
that when you blew into it
went hhhhhhwwwwhhhhooooo
or sounded in your ears
like the ocean hhhhhhrrrrrrr

and I got all these things at home
because they're *mine*, man,
and one of these days
I'm gonna arrange em in frame
to pass on through the family...

Literary magazines and journals filled with short stories and poetry were published in these camps: *Trek* was published at Topaz, Utah and featured the artist Mine Okubo who later published a book of her drawings and narrative on camp life in *Citizen 13660* (1946), short story writer, Toshio Mori, whose book of short stories *Yokohama, California* (1949) was supposed to be published before the war, and the poet Toyo Suyemoto. There were other magazines like *All Aboard* or *Pulse* published at the Amache, Arkansas camp. At

Manzanar Relocation Center it was the *Manzanar Free Press*, a start-ling collection of essays, articles, poetry and short stories. In an essay about camp poetry printed in the *Journal of American Folklore*, "Senryu Poetry as Folk and Community Expression," by Marvin K. Opler and F. Obayashi, is significant in its subtleties. The authors present the three principal forms of Japanese poetry and their metric composition. While trying to connect the poetry written at Tule Lake, California with the heritage of Senryu poetry in Japan we see the obvious experience emerge in merely reading their list of verbs of "topic 1":

> "Topics Expressed by Verb, Adverb, Adjective and Preposition: Too, or Again; Probably, or Seemingly; Then; Against, or Op-posing; Spring Comes; Above All, or Further; Until Arriving; Given Up; Doubled; Worrying; While Awaiting the Downpour; Being Obedient; Peeping; Giving Up; Home Coming; Getting Ready; Careless; Worthless.

The authors note that 48% of the topics were expressed by abstract nouns. Although few of the words in topic 1 are abstract, the authors state that in translation they would be abstract, therefore they in-clude these words with the previous 48% to get 68% "of all topics may be said to be rather abstract in type." We see the contradiction in their own translations of the poems:

> The taste of rice-wine,
> Even there, to the place of exile
> Clinging around.

Wakako Yamauchi states in her essay "The Poetry of the Issei on the American Relocation Experience: "Under the surface of these spare lines are the intensely personal and emotional nature of the poet dealing with the situation."

The editors of *Aiiieeeee! An Anthology of Asian American Writers* point out in their introduction, "The critics have forgotten that the vitality of literature stems from its ability to codify and legitimize common experience in the terms of that experience and to celebrate life as it is lived ... the literary establishment has never considered the fact that a new folk in a strange land would experience the land and develop new language out of old words ... (the Asian-American writer's) task is to ... legitimize the language, style, and syntax of his people's experience, to codify the experiences common to his people into symbols, cliches, linguistic mannerisms, and sense of humor that emerges from organic familiarity with the experience."[6]

Asian Americans have been here for seven generations and still, to date, a major publisher has not published a novel or a collection of poetry by an American-born Chinese-American man. The writing is there, the writers are there. Read these California writers because they own California, it belongs to them. Read Lawson Inada's poem "At the Stronghold" where he says:

> What land we had
> we must have back again.
> This is the stronghold,
> the heart, the spirit
> in the land, the heart

Or Carlos Bulosan when he says, "We are America!" There is Yone Noguchi's seizure of California in his lyric description. The poetry of the Issei:

> Clasping a photograph, asleep...
> awakened by a dream
> Missoula is cold
> winds from the snows

They are all saying, "We are old enough to haunt this land."

FOOTNOTES:

1. Information on the Angel Island poetry was given to me by Him Mark Lai who has compiled various translations and re-edited them.
2. Frank Chin, "The Confessions of a Chinese Cowboy," *Bulletin of Concerned Asian Scholars*, Special Issue: Asian America, Fall 1972, pp. 58-70.
3. Frank Chin, Jeffery Chan, Lawson Inada and Shawn Wong, *Aiiieeeee! An Anthology of Asian American Writers* (Washington, D.C.: Howard University Press, 1974), p. xxi.
4. Letter from Sam Solberg, January 12, 1976.
5. Lawson Inada, "Japanese Geometry," *Yardbird Reader Volume 3,* ed. by Shawn Wong and Frank Chin (Berkeley: Yardbird Publishing Co., 1975), pp. 130-182.
6. *Aiiieeeee!*, p. xxxvi.

Wakako Yamauchi

The Poetry Of The Issei
On The American Relocation Experience

I have been asked to prepare a paper on literature in camps, and how that period of incarceration affected the thinking of writers. I suppose I can labor through dusty documents and old bulletins and come up with something semi-literate, maybe a graph or two, but that's not the kind of writer I am. I write stories of people, stories of hurts, stories of love... mostly stories of love. "Variations of very ancient themes..." And I shall have to tell this in my own way.

The Sansei accuse us of not wanting to talk about the evacuation experience. And it's true. I speak for hundreds of Nisei like myself, or perhaps just *people* like myself, who are sometimes overwhelmed by a current of events we can neither understand nor stem, and from self-defense cope with only what directly applies to the self... political, social, or economic. Sure, the times affected us, moved us here or there, shaped our attitudes, our destinies, but how many of us know why or how?

Or maybe we do know, intuitively, but deep inside something tells us we could have been braver, or stronger, and what has happened is past history and what good does it do to bring back those events that might prove we could have, should have, behaved more courageously.

And when we do see those old photographs of the mass evacuation, we search the faces of our brothers and sisters, and in that backward look, in those old faces, young faces, we can see the mirror of our tragedy. Few of us can hold back the tears that most often smack of self-pity, but maybe somewhere behind those tears we know that this is the event that changed the course of our lives, and though there were those among us who had more insight, more courage, whatever path we chose, we have survived—whole. Maybe that's why so many of us remain silent about our camp experience. Maybe in our silence we ask you to honor us for that—survival. We ask that you not indulge us with pity, neither then nor now. The fact of our survival is proof of our valor. And that is enough.

Now I'd like to talk about some people who did speak about the experience.

While looking through the literary edition of the *Amerasia Journal* of 1976, I came across poems by Issei poets on the American Relocation experience. These poems were written then—while it was happening. I think that's important. These are not backward glances. Now, more than thirty years later, I read them and I look backward and I am moved. I see again the scenes, feel again the emotions of then. The poet Yamanaka Keiho and Constance Hayashi bring some of these poems to us in the *Amerasia Journal*.

The poems are Haiku, Tanka, and Senryu, a most disciplined form of poetry. The Haiku with syllables of 5–7–5, deal with nature, the seasons, the land. Tanka, with the combination of syllables, 5–7–5–7–7, has a broader scope of subjects. The Senryu with the 5–7–5 rhythm, deal with personal, philosophical, religious, and social subjects.

It is said in the days of the war lords and *samurai*, commoners and peasants were greatly suppressed, and freedom of speech meant generally and literally freedom from the head: *Kubi*. There was a wise poet named Kerai Senryu who devised a way to convey his thoughts through the limited use of words and syllables, expressing only the germ of his feelings. Those that related to his feelings understood his poetry. Those that didn't, the oppressors, went along with what they thought was a new form—a fad, perhaps.

These are the poems I shall read today, the Senryu that the Issei poets wrote on evacuation. You will notice there are no words like constitutionality, illegality, economic expediency, etc. Under the surface of these spare lines are the intensely personal and emotional nature of the poet dealing with the situation.

I will try to reveal them to you.

Zaibei no
sanjunen wa
yume to nari
  —*Sasabune*

Thirty years
in America
become a dream

The thirty years that I have labored and loved in this country have returned to that unreal world. Gone—like phantoms... Did they actually occur? Can thirty years of hopes, defeats, joys, really come to this? And in thirty more years will *this* experience too become only an illusion?

> Minzoku no
> hitori to shite
> ni o matome
> > —*Keiho*

> > As one
> > of the Japanese
> > I gather my belongings

If I were not Japanese, I would not have to go. Only because, especially because I'm Japanese, I am selected to be imprisoned in a camp. While packing my worldly goods, I think if that is the reason, I go proudly.

> Gaman shite
> gaman shite iru
> hifu no iro
> > —*Kikyo*

> > Enduring
> > and still enduring
> > the color of my skin

In the country we come from, this is the color of all skin. It's the proud yellow of a proud race. Here, they say it's not the proper color. They heap us with abuses, they put us behind barbed wire. Well, I will endure. I will at elast endure, because this *is* the color of my skin. And I take *all* that comes with it.

> Nokoshita wa
> kimi dakede nai
> Karifonia
> > —*Shocho*

> > I leave behind
> > not only you,
> > my California

I cared for you, my California, you took care of me. You bound to me, I to you. And the sunrise, the sunset, the friends, the loves, the sorrows implicit in life, I leave behind with you. And the loyalties . . . Have you betrayed me?

In camp there was an enormous number of people—thousands —all Japanese, and we were unaccustomed to this type of mass dwelling. When we stood in line for anything: innoculations, food, clothing rations, bureaucratic red tape, there was a danger of children getting lost. Some parents tied their children to them with rope. This is an observation of that:

> Nawa tsukete
> moratte kodomo
> inu no mane
> —*Keiho*

> Tied by ropes
> the children
> imitate dogs

These innocent children don't understand why they're here. Tied by ropes, in pulling distance from their parents, they feel safe. Caught in the excitement of the milling crowd and in the spirit of fun, they bark, they paw the ground, imitating dogs. *Kawaiso.* What do they know? I feel sad.

> Taikutsu e
> hikoki moji o
> kaite mise
> —*Keiho*

> In boredom observed
> an airplane writing
> letters for me

I am a happy man most of the time. But in camp, you know, I'm cooped up—can't get beyond the fence, you know. I sit in the sun bored, you see, nothing to do. I look up in the sky and see a plane. He writes letters. How carefree, I think. People at war, dying, and he writes letters in the sky . . . Maybe it's some propaganda about the war . . .

Here is a love poem:

Senta no
jimusho ni koi o
sasayaite
      —*Bonsai*

In an office
at the Center, love
is whispered

Love is tender. And in this office where people mill around curiously, lovers are careful to keep it close between them—whispered.

Kojo no
yo ni haka doru
kurinikku
      —*Suikyo*

Like a factory
the line-up
at the clinic

In camp times lies heavy. There's nothing to do but attend to our bodies. We run to the clinic with small injuries, a scratch, a rash, an itch, a bump, a cold. We line up at the clinic and doctors swab us, sew us, clean us . . . like items on an assembly line.

Sekitan no
yama mo kodomo no
asobi basho
      —*Keiho*

A coal heap
becomes
the children's playground

Trucks come and dump mountains of coal at convenient areas. Carrying out buckets and cardboard cartons, we scurry to get there first, picking the largest and the best pieces for ourselves, our families . . . scavenging animals savagely protecting our own. What have we come to? Children teach us that even in this land of grey and black there is joy to be found. They play in the dust of our coal heap, the residue of our pickings.

This poem concerns the loyalty questionaires evacuees were required to answer:

> Chu, fuchu
> hito moshi kikaba
> nanto kotaen
>   —*Toshu*

> Loyalty, disloyalty
> if one should ask
> I cannot answer

They ask me to take a stand. I can only divide myself. The ancestral land that could not provide for me still holds all those things dear to me: the ashes of my father, my mother, memories of my boyhood, *Yamato Damashi*—the spirit of Yamato. My brother is a soldier in the Imperial Army. They ask me to deny these. They ask me to commit myself to a country that will not accept me. And yet... and yet in these years here, I have found a measure of happiness and comfort. I have invested my children here. I stand divided.

Many men were separated from their families and imprisoned in separate detention centers. The loneliness of this experience is recorded here:

> Sashin daite nete
> yume mite samete
> Misora samui yo
> yuki no kaze
>   —*Sasabune*

> Clasping a photograph, asleep...
> awakened by a dream
> Missoula is cold...
> winds from the snows

This dear photograph assures me that we once had a life together in another place. I see the stand of trees behind you that we had grown from seed. I remember why you laughed as I pressed the shutter. The children stand by, embarrassed by our intimacy. Dreams of those pleasant days come and go. The winds of chance, politics, economics, separate us and blow cold over the snows of Missoula. I wake and find we are indeed apart.

Another instance where the man was separated from his family:

> Tachinoki no
> shirase o nigiru
> haru no yo ni
> haha no mite toru
> tsuma omoinu
> —*Sojin'*

> Of the spring night
> that I clutched
> the evacuation orders
> the image of my wife
> holding my mother's hand
> comes to mind

I stood with rage as I read the evacuation orders. Yet I could not sustain that rage as I saw the face of my mother and wife cloud with anxiety. They rely on my manhood, yet I cannot protect them. They hold each other for strength. What will happen to them while I am away? Their faces remind me of my helplessness... my impotence.

When people were permitted to leave the centers for relocation in eastern cities, friends and families were again faced with separation:

> Kondo wakare rya
> aware mo sumai
> nakoka tomodomo
> namida no tane ga
> tsukite kawaite
> nakenumade
> —*Sasabune*

> This time if we part
> we might not meet again
> shall we weep together, friend?
> the seeds of our tears
> cling and dry
> until we cry no more

We are faced with yet another goodbye. And you go now to still another alien land. Old friends have scattered—the securities of the past have vanished. I am afraid. *Osoroshii.* This may be our last goodbye; we may never meet again. Shall we then cry together, you and I? It's all right... there is a time when even men must cry. The tears will come until the well dries.

This is the final poem:

> Iminshi wa
> owareri akikaze
> mata samishi
>   *—Kikyo*

> The immigrants' story
> has ended
> autumn winds are
> lonely again

I would like to repeat the poem by Keiho:

> Sekitan no
> Yama mo kodomo no
> asobi basho

> A coal heap
> becomes
> the children's playground

So if you ask me what I experienced in camp, I would have to say I was one of the children playing in the coal heap... in the residue of my own selfishness.

Al Young

Afro-California Poetry : Some Notes

In his marvelously insightful book, *California: The New Society*, published in 1963, author Remi Nadeau had this to say about his native state: "There is in California a sense of individuality but little sense of community... Like the early Spanish Californians with their Christmas *piñata*, the modern Californians have taken a stick to life itself and are beating it till the last goody falls out."

And like countless other peoples, men and women of African and part-African descent have played essential roles in the settling and development of the Golden State. Under Spanish, Anglo and corporate rule, California blacks and mulattoes—for better or for worse—have fought against and sided with Native Americans, and have blazed trails, pioneered, homesteaded, farmed, fished, lumberjacked, cattle ranched, rustled, robbed, traded, invented, manufactured, marketed, administrated, governed, cajoled, politicked, legislated, gambled, mined, dueled, run guns, cooked, ironed, kept house, gardened, waited tables, bootblacked, blacksmithed, sheriffed, portered, longshored, architected, taught, entertained, patrolled, preached, doctored, lawyered, organized, rebelled, reported, broadcasted, published, and even founded whole cities. The majority of the settlers who founded Los Angeles in 1781, for example, were what we would now call black.

As social and political history, all of this may be perused at length in such diverting volumes as Delilah L. Beasley's *The Negro Trail Blazers of California*, Russell E. Belous's *America's Black Heritage*, Arna Bontemp's and Jack Conroy's *Anyplace But here*, Martin E. Dann's *The Black Press: 1827-1890*, Philip Durham's and Everett L. Jones's *The Negro Cowboys*, Jack D. Forbes's *Afro-Americans in the Far West*, William Loren Katz's *The Black West*, I. Garland Penn's *The Afro-American Press and Its Editors*, Kenneth Wiggins Porter's *The Negro on the American Frontier*, Sue Bailey Thurman's *Pioneers of Negro Origin in California*, and Richard R. Wright's *The Making of Black America*.

Poetry and imaginative writing in all of its varieties is also a form of history. Poets are, after all, only people, and people are rooted, however uncomfortably, in particular times, places, cultures, and myths. Each of us is born, grows, hungers, struggles, dreams, suffers, enjoys, despises, fears, clings, rejoices, deceives, learns, sings, ripens and leaves. The stuff of poetry, which is life itself, belongs to everyone and to no one. Poets sing the dreaming that nourishes us all. They dream what we cannot see and often see what we would never have dreamed. "Since California's actual history has so often resembled romantic fiction," writes Walton Bean in his *California: An Interpretive History*, "it is not entirely inappropriate that it got its name from a novel."

You will not find much evidence of the existence of black poets in most officially-sanctioned California literary journals or anthologies published prior to Great Society days. This should come as no surprise to anyone, for it has only been in recent years that the deeds and achievements of black Americans—to say nothing of black Westerners—have been recognized or recorded, even grudgingly, by our nation's blindfolded historians.

As quiet as it is kept, though, black Californians have been writing and publishing poetry for as long as there has been a California. Their work appeared occasionally in the pages of some of the earliest black California weeklies—*Mirror of the Times*, a forerunner first published at San Francisco in 1855, *The Pacific Appeal, The Elevator, The Vindicator, The California Eagle, New Age, The Los Angeles Post, The Cactus*. "In pioneer days," Delilah L. Beasley reminds us in her 1919 landmark study, *The Negro Trail Blazers of California*, "the Negro press in California was highly respected by the opposite race and much valued by the Negro race. The Negro press championed the race in all its severe fights for the privilege to live in California."

Among the pioneer Afro-Californians whose poems appear in this section are: James Madison Bell, Edward Cain, Jeams (*nom de plume* for a certain Captain Ferguson of the Brannan Guards), Mrs. Priscilla Stewart, William Ross Wallace, and William J. Wilson. Their characteristic patriotism and the quaint 19th century eloquence of their pleas for social justice will be readily recognized.

All told, this abbreviated selection of poems represents an historical span of over one hundred years. It cannot be denied that, during that time, California's citizens of color have made visible social, political and material advances. It is also reasonable to speculate that restrictive social conditions have forced them to retain more of a sense of community than the majority of Californians. Whether they will ultimately get a fair swing at what might be termed The Golden State Piñata is another matter altogether.

By way of acknowledgement, I must state that I have relied rather heavily upon Delilah Beasley's invaluable book for information regarding early black California poets. I would also like to extend my heartfelt thanks to the following organizations and individuals without whose advice, guidance, assistance, resources and encouragement this modest project could never have been realized: The African-American Historical Society of San Francisco; Mr. and Mrs. Fred Brown of Palo Alto, native Californians of several generations; Prof. Charles Davis of Yale University, esteemed historian and Afro-American scholar; Dr. St. Clair Drake, Professor Emeritus of Sociology and Anthropology, Stanford University; Mr. and Mrs. Eugene P. Lasartemay of the East Bay Negro Historical Society who gladly opened their archives to me; and, of course, to Arl Young, my research assistant and wife.

I assume full responsibility for all serious omissions and errors.

Palo Alto, 1977

The Poetry

The name "California" was taken from the Spanish writer Ordonñez de Montalvo's imaginative story, *Las Sergas de Esplandian* (first published in Madrid in 1510) which told of black Amazons and their Queen Calafia who ruled an island of this name located "at the right hand of the Indies . . . very close to that part of the Terrestrial Paradise." This thriller, written as a sequel to the more famous *Amadis de Gaula,* was one of the most popular pieces of early 16th Century Spanish fiction. It has also inspired us to title the collection CALAFÍA.

—*Al Young*

Keith Abbott

What You Know With No Name For It

> *"But name is only*
> *the guest of reality—*
> *will I be doing it*
> *so I can play*
> *the part of the guest?"*
> —*Chuang Tzu*

What you know with
No name for it

Two unused water faucets
Between the book shelves
One presumably hot the other cold

Mother and daughter talking
In the next room
Over the telephone

My wife temporarily gone
Into someone
Who I vaguely know
A daughter a sister another woman

I sit here surrounded by a dark
That I only have to open the door
To penetrate

An unknown light slightly yellowish green
Like a gas lamp in a Lautrec poster
Barely seen through the storm window
The plastic puts a glossy sheen on the darkness

Buying big black plastic cubes
Of night in the supermarkets
A record which causes silence
A drug which lets you see

That strange feeling
When a chemical is inside you
Like a leftover 12X6 beam
For a house that was never built

I can't wait until a drug is done
So I can go back to being
Someone who isn't already known

Though it's a relief
To step into a puppet of sensations
All the strings are attached
To a highly usable past

There's no worry except
When the strings begin
To go slack

Like the time I staggered out onto the railroad tracks
To go take a piss
And forgot to look and see if
There was a train coming

And by the time I had thought of it
I was already 50 yards out on a trestle
"I'll just swing down and hang there,"
I thought, "until the train goes past,"
As I took out my prick and the yellow stream
Dissolved into the green valley
Several hundred feet below me

Illustrating
The magic
Of absentmindedness

And then there are the times I can't forget
Like the jeweller in North Beach
Little black moustache
Patiently fitting Lani with her wedding ring
As I stood idly by
The sound of the hammer
And her eyes intent on the gold ring

2

But there are those other
Moments
Of huge emotions

So large I can't understand them
Or recall them exactly

The strange black dressed woman
In the Pacific Grove library

The gaunt face
Caved into a ripple
Of wrinkles

The little black hat with a feather
Slightly obscuring her white skin
And blonde hair

I stared at her thin legs probably
Very elegant at one time
And waited for her
To speak to me

I was sure
She would a vast
Restless cloud
Of emotion seemed to

Fill my chest
She read
And got up and left

I watched from the library window
She seemed even thinner outside
Wondering what I had missed

*

Sometimes the world narrows
Down to one point

And I laugh
As my daughter asks for a "hankersniff"

It all seems to clear then
And not what I wanted
But did want
Secretly

Sometimes people see
That what they just told me
I didn't hear
Or didn't bother to understand

The moments when I'm no one

The moment when your ears clear
After the gong is rung

Not to be measured along a parallel line
With your life

"I first understood..."
"From then on I knew..."

What I think I have known
Has never been unknown

The child laughs
Hearing his voice for
The first time
And tries it out again

My first memory
I think

CODA

The white stone
In the ditch
Hidden by the frozen grass

4

I'd look at it
When no one else was around
While waiting for the school bus

Every summer I lost it
Couldn't find it in the tall grass
And then each winter it would reappear

A round white stone
In my imagination marble
And infinitely valuable

I would reach down
Through the cold water
And touch it year after year

A.G.

Untitled

Translated by M.B. Anderson

Composición de doble sentido,
comenzando por la cabeza y
luego por el rabo.

Si crees, China que te quiero,
Crees muy bien; y crees muy mal
Si crees que no soy formal,
Si crees que soy embustero,
Crees, China lo verdadero
Si crees que te amo de veras,
Estás creyendo tonteras
Si estás creyendo al revés.
Es mentira; y muy bien crees
Si cierto mi amor creyeras.

     Cuarteto de igual clase.
Si te han dicho que te quiero

Te han dicho bien y han mentido
Si te han dicho por descuido
Que solo amo tu dinero.

28 de agosto de 1862.

Composition with a double
meaning, beginning at the
start (by the head) and
then at the end (by the tail)

If you think, Girl, that I love you,
You believe correctly; and you believe wrongly
If you believe that I am not serious,
If you believe that I am deceitful,
You believe, darling, the truth
If you believe that I love you truly,
You're believing nonsense.
If you're thinking the opposite.
It's a lie; and rightly you believe
If true you believe my love.

Quatrain of the same type
If they have told you that I love you
They have told you correctly and they have lied
If they have told you by mistake
That I only love your money.

Charles Alexander

My Kind Of Man

I like the man who will go to the bat,
And will take off his coat, and throw off his hat;
Who will roll up his sleeves, and spit on his hands,
And hit at the ball just as hard as he can.

Hit at it, I say, never mind if he miss;
Never mind if the crowd will hollow and hiss.

I like the man who will enter the race
Unwavering, resolve shining out of his face;
Who will shirk not, not falter, but will strive for the goal,
Showing courage and patience when nearing the shoal;
For courage and patience are big bits of grace,
And the man who will claim them may yet win the race.

I like the man who will pick up his load,
Who will start with a rush on his way up the road;
Who will risk every peril he finds on the way,
And say in his heart: "Every debt I will pay."
For that sort of a man unheeds the world's lust—
But that sort of man is worthy of trust.

I like the man who is gentle and kind,
Who will show by example the true master mind;
Who knows of the feeling of poverty's pinch
And will stand out for right, every foot, every inch.
For that sort of man is the man of the hour;
He has in his soul God's fire and power.

My Mother's Custard Pie

You may talk about the cooking
    They do in Italy;
And the kind the Frenchman
    Sets before his company;
Of the German's toast and "weenies,"
    Or the English mutton-chop.
But there is one thing to remember
    That will start you on the hop;
It's delicious, it is luscious,
    It will brighten up your eye;
It is like a view of heaven —
    That is mother's custard pie.

7

You have had poetic dreaming,
    With its rapturous vision rare;
You have known the potent blessing
    Of that swiftly-vanished care;
You have felt ecstatic heavings
    In your big and noble heart,
And have felt the pangs of sorrow
    When your dearest friend would part.
But your joys are without number –
    You can stand the severing tie,
If you know you'll have a portion
    Of my mother's custard pie.

It will take one slice, I tell you,
    To dissipate the gloom,
And to start an agitation,
    Like the buzzing of a loom.
It will bring delights and pleasures
    You have never known before;
It will make you feel like hanging
    'Round about our kitchen door.
Yes, indeed, I know the feeling,
    You'll be ready then to die,
If, for once, you get a-plenty
    Of my mother's custard pie.

It Matters Much

It matters little where I was born,
Or if my parents were rich or poor;
Whether they shrank at the cold world's scorn
Or walked in the pride of wealth secure.
But whether I live an honest man
And hold my integrity firm in my clutch,
I tell you, brother, plain as I am,
It matters much.

Alta

Rewritten Letter From A Rejected Suitor

if yr a Real Woman,
wheres yr hot pants?
how come you got fat thighs?
your sposed to be demure, yr sposed
to wait for men & wiggle yr ass.
yr lovers are sposed to be older, not younger,
taller, not shorter. yr sposed to want character
in a man, not stamina. (stamina
                                    stamin)
if yr a Real Woman,
what the hell is yr last name?

Alurista

Mojólogue

swoosh, swoosh, swoosh clinkclinkclink.. swoosh, swoosh
swoosh clinkclinkclink ... clak! pócatelas! ahí vá otra copa que-
brada, chinacatlán con el vidrio. agarra l'onda esse.. 'we can't
afford all this broken glass!' chinga, malcolmo don't go for no more
overhead. heady cat, pinche vato, haciéndole pedo a la carolina con
su rollo. si supiera lo que la carnalita has had to stomach sin saber
quien violó la noche de su furor huelgista, o de sus días de monja
cuerpo-e-paz en bolivia.. pa'dale lo' santo'leo' al ché.. carajo, cara
ajo, rajo, jocar, joker!
                        "time is slippin'
                                    slippin'
                                        slippin'
intoo the future".....là rola, rola..
no entiendo porque rayos el malcolmo anda'ciéndole la segunda al
mañaco de daleygas.. es más a mí se me hace que'l sindicated rat

running down the mazas of his guilt..
                    "maybe i'm amazed at the way you love me all
the time
            or maybe i'm afraid of the way i love you"...swoosh,
swoosh, swoosh clinkclinkclink...swoosh, swoosh, swoosh clink
clinkclink...i wouldn't put carolina's rape beyond el pedodale, dale
pedo...chut up, esse. chut up. no eres la mama de tarzan, i chita ni
te pela. en este neon jungle, ni on ni off...only the juglares get a
chuckle out of frankenstein, einstein frank? or was it albert? beto-
stein? chut up mon an'wach thee glass. look at'em get down
an'bump. water beds are in, if you ain't too limp after so much
firewater. se salen, chit they cain hardly bump let alone git down or
stay in, mon..two güey out...no foun ta in at this parke, no parke,
no liga, no ligazo, no lazo...no l az o polque no tiene cuelda.
                    "time keeps on slippin'
                              slippin'
                                  slippin'
into the future"...discotime
mojo's bar gettin' on my case. i si de casos hablamos, mine ain't got
no plata no gas no coco for the pla,pla,pla. swoosh, swoosh,
swoosh clinkclinkclink...swoosh, swoosh, swoosh clinkclinkclink
        .."fly like an eagle
                          and be free
let the spirit carry me"...
órale, ora lé, le ora, leo ora, or ale...ginger, ginger who got thee
bread? panadero, panadero... wha'kind of pang carri tu hoi...
        ..."wha'happen' mon
                  i don' know...
me dicen que pol bolacho po'en la'cera cayó"...
...ya no quiere trabaja'llá en la panadelía"...
        sin embalgo te pasa to'o'l día flente' la licorelía"...órale matus,
que tú e' lavaplatus. chin, chin el tepurochu pinche mal. pinche mal
e'lcolmo con su welder siñoriti, and thee qualití of his methane cuete.
        people steel afraid o'bein' born, bean bearin' ol'e time thee
weight. paleface dailygas. he say they carry the burden cuando los as
nos ni siquiera se lavan las má nos. i te dang bonos an' blu' chip es
tamps reed.. reedamable, derramable when redemption cum's
a'round, roun'an'roun' we go, gallo. mi jor mi callo. si mon. mi jor
mi callo...polque tulnin' down a roach clip'steel a vetelano. vete'l
ano pride.

10

"time keeps on
                slippin'
                        slippin'
                                slippin'
                                        slippin'
        in
to the
        future . . . there
's a solution . . ."
i la luna move al daleygas mañaco. i el juñion malcolmo think he got
thee busy nezz to gether, to gather all thee guzzlers in thee ziti an'
make some doe . . . 'deer' . . . with his own enterprise, u know what
a'mean bubble eyes
git down an'inter prize, neve'mine ice an'soul, truck out blues an
chuckle in walls, chit we take master charch . . . what a dreamer this
methane tank's all a bout. ni pedo esse, 'garra l'onda. this here yo'
camello, i la panza e' plimelo. what would malcomo know'bout
calolina's agoní, an'her well meaning smile que no crackea con el
oro, ni se in barra con el toro. chuck the bull fights and the swords in
the world of cloak and dagger, cum petition and thee like. mon
against nature on the ring, too much sand for the likes of caro who
don' like to kick no dust, or cloud nobodies eye balls . . . calla. calla té
mat us que las neon black lit walls es tiran las orejas i las man o tas del
es tate depart'men'tappin'el enjuage de tus dedos en el swoosh,
swoosh, swoosh clinkclinkclink, swoosh, swoosh, swoosh clink
clink clink de las copas. no hagas pedo, matus, swallow bitter wine,
dig the contract. 'boss sai yo's doin' fine . . !' . . . u heard thee line . .
'let's keep the over head down mat. it's for real now, blood. just
got laid off, u know'.
                "shoe the children
                        runnin' in bare feet
feed the people
                who don't got enough to eat
                house the people
                        living in the street
time keeps on slippin'slippin'slippin
                into the future . . .
                        . . . there's a solution . . ."
an'then he lick the chops of daleygas pa'que 'respete malcom's siñor-
ití'. su pen dejada tá' fuera de control. el way que ofrece, el güey

que ofrece? . . . too way out, two güey out en la com pañia del mayor
to b sellin' his color tv too caro, to carol? tuck'n'roll? pinche vato,
pullin' rank with his shoechine daze . . . 'what's wrong wichu, girl?
what's wrong wi'chu, girl, this is ame rica, u know? save?' save?
kimo, kimono, ki mono nó? pelo que sabe'te bruto e papay a. quele
juga' con olivoil pelo wimpy really lookin' for the ham burguesa.
tonto mal i su long daily pinchi gas.

       "matus, I want to go home now. take me home now."
"no the agüites carolina. ya son las dos i estos dos'tán más pa'llá que
pa'cá, i pa'caca ni a pedo controlado llegan."
        "time keeps on slippin'
             slippin'
                slippin'
   in
   to
   the
   few
   chure . . ."
wachin' diches . . . swoosh,swoosh,swoosh clinkclinkclink
        swoosh,swoosh,swoosh clinkclinkclink
to the future. can i b? can malcomo z? g but then there is mr d all so
noun ass mister may or tu b. and what we gonna do 'bout miss c i su
babi?
      "soar like an eagle
         an'b free
  let the spirit carry me . . .
      there's a sol u chón, solo u chón
        in
           revol u chón
        in
           revolt u tio chón
bola de cachigranizos rocanroleros. cachin' hail all the time from the
führers of this here yan kilo n d. a? o? say kan u sea? sí, que nó? no,
pos seemon. . . .

Jean Anderson

The Brown Girl
(A Love Story)

She was satin wood from the topmost crown,
Of her elegant smooth coifed head,
To the tip of her slender pointed toe;
One piece of satin, sleekly, richly brown,
With pretty undulations where her arteries sped
The flow of the warm pulsating blood,
That fed and watered all this loveliness.
You would have said she was cast in bronze unless
You had seen her swiftly, swiftly go
To meet her expected lover: then down, down
From her enchanted pedestal she flew to his embrace.

One lazy August afternoon I was gently floating
In less than a dream, when suddenly I saw her:
I had been greedily swallowing air, fond eyes doting
On the cloud shadowed turquoise of the bay;
In this luxurious repose a swift premonition
Of a greater loveliness, to crown all nature came
To me: quickly I turned my eyes to where
A headland jutted sharply out; the day
Was waning, and the sunset flame
Outlined her, as some radiant apparition
Is poised against a lustrous curtain rare.

And when she dived from her high promontory
She was an arrow that never missed a mark;
But when she sharply clove the dark
Engulfing waters I was shaken, and momentary
Tremors had me in their grip until she rose,
And nymph-like shook the water from her hair.
Oh but her fresh laved human-ness was fair;
Jewels of ocean covered her; you might suppose
That she was Neptune's mistress and bedecked
With gems of his bestowing. Here she poised for air
Wind kissed, and water washed, and sunshine flecked.

13

Often I sought the charmed spot where she
Transported me to a world so pagan fresh;
And I would gladly wait long hours to see
Her perfectness that was something more than flesh:
For was she not a gull fleet winged and roving,
Or a fawn that poised against the sunset flush,
Or a silky hare at home in the bracken's hush?
Still as a leaf when not a breath is moving
She was the crown of visible nature, and yet she
Had given herself to nature unreservedly.

You would have said that she could never utter
A word that was not simple, free, and pure.
Her lip's fine bow was never curved to flatter;
Hers no idle evasions; no, for as rightly sure
As her body was her brain, and this
An uncorrupted servant fed her lips
With wholsesome, natural words: no finished miss
Was she, but ever growing: her finger tip
Itched expectantly for tasks from the bidding mind;
And she could run all day and not be fagged;
For nothing of futility in the years behind
Haunted her yet. Her spirit never lagged.

Someone that loved her as she should be loved,
Got her; and in my heart I could not grudge
Him happiness: he was plainly mad about her.
She might, for love, have turned a shabby drudge:
She was that kind; with her it was all or nothing.
But the powers ordered wisely, once, this time.
Just think—if one had tasted her to flout her
I would have strangled him for utter loathing,
Although she never guessed my thought of her.
Naturally, naturally I am deeply moved
When I hear those pealing bells—their wedding chime.

A Simple Tale

When I was younger than I am
My singing heart was light
And scornful of the love of man,
That spell as black as night.

"The sable grapes of passion",
I said, "are only trod
By such as wish to fashion
For their own backs a rod".

Then my lover came to me,
And shook my house of life,
Bruising my equanimity:
The kettle drum and fife

Rang in his laughter; and his lips
That left my own, so firm
Crumbled my heart; his finger tips
Were to my blood a fever germ.

"You will be lost", I said, "Put on
The straight stays of your pride,
So much of you the thief has won,
Your soul had almost died".

So I was proud, and he was proud,
And then he went away:
The heart within my breast was loud
With grief that dreadful day.

It knocked against my slender side,
As if to burst the wall:
I thought I surely would have died,
But I was not sick at all;

Only that grief like a small file
Kept turning in the wound:
The sound of laughter was more vile
Than any other sound.

It seemed so coarse that folk should eat,
So coarse each cheerful commonplace:
I only sought a far retreat
In some dark quiet place.

I could be happy now, nor grieve
That my dear love has gone,
If I could only have the sleeve
Of his old coat to weep upon.

Maya Angelou

The Telephone

It comes in black
and blue, indecisive
beige. In red and chaperons my life.
Sitting like a strict
and spinstered Aunt
spiked between my needs
and need.

It tats the day, crocheting
other people's lives
in neat arrangements
ignoring me
busy with hemming
of strangers
overlong affairs or
the darning of my
neighbors' worn-out
dreams.

From Monday, the morning of the week
through mid-times
noon and Sunday's dying
light. It sits silent.
Its needle sound

does not transfix my ear
or draw my longing to
a close.

Ring. Damn you!

Jaime de Angulo

Indian Fields Over Uplands

Indian fields over uplands
sky azure
and vultures flying,
mountains, mountains, abysses.

Indians singing together,
flute sad; the low flute,

and the horse walking, walking
strong under foreign saddle
and the bent rider. He shakes with fever;
with a girl riding pillion.

And the indians say:
"See that poor dago,
poor dago, high fever."

Holy shrine up aloft,
heap of stone, rather
where the indian porters pray to the Lake-Snake;
steady their loads with a head-band,
and every man adds a stone to the pile.

And the stranger gets down from his horse:
"I'm done, kid, get home without me."

The horse a good walker, good walker,
The indians inside their huts say:

"Look at that gal there, alone, going alone.
Dago's gal, with a face proud, proud,
That's what our chiefs were like in the old days."

And on the ridge under the blue air the vultures
with their elegant huge wings circling,
circling:
"Indian, dago, horse, jackass, cattle
all come to our table."

Land Of Many Hues

    land of many hues
    California of the climes
    wide valleys parched in the sun

!   tsho, anda ganado, ye, tsho   !

    indios, and dead towns
    where the coyotes howl
    with the yellow moon

!   tsho, anda ganado, yeh, tsho   !

    buckaroo from the north
    take your turn at the rear
    I lost my neckerchief in whoretown last night

    sheepherder in the mountains
    crazy with solitude
    land of redwoods
    land of spring flowers
    sweet land of dead indians
    land of ghosts

!   tsho, anda ganado, yeh, tsho   !

    toll the mission bell
    for the dead indian
    for the friar in hell

conquistador, gambler,
whore and forty-niner

! tsho, anda ganado, tsho !

howl, coyote, howl to the yellow moon

Anonymous

What Was Your Name In The States?

Oh, what was your name in the States?
Was it Muggins or Buggins or Bates?
Did you murder your wife
And fly for your life?
Say, what was your name in the States?

Anonymous

A Rallying Song For The Gold Diggers

To the mines! to the mines! away to the mines,
Where the virgin gold in the crevice shines!
Where the shale and the slate and the quartz enfold,
In their stony arms the glittering gold.

'Tis in vain that ye seek any longer to hide
Your treasures of gold in your rivers so wide,
In your gulches so deep, or your wild cañon home,
For the Anglo-American race is come.

And the noise that ye hear is the sound of the spade,
The pick, the bar, and the bright shining spade,
Of the knife and the shovel, the cradle and pan,
Brave adjuncts of toil to the laboring man!

Far up in the mountains, all rugged and steep,
Far down in the cañon, all foaming and deep,
In the bars of the river, the small mountain plains,
Lies the wealth that ye seek for, in numberless grains.

Turn the stream from its bed—search the bottom with care,
The largest, the richest, the finest is there;
Dig deep in the gulches, nor stop till the stone
Reveals there its treasures, or till there's none.

Nor be thou disheartened, dismayed nor cast down,
If success should decline thy first efforts to crown;
Go ahead! Go ahead! Since Creation began,
"No wealth without toil" is the record to man.

              *   *   *   *

To the mines! to the mines! away to the mines!
Where the virgin gold in the crevice shines!
Where the shale and the slate and the quartz enfold,
In their stony arms the glittering gold.

March 22, 1850
Pacific News

Anonymous

Arrival Of The Greenhorn

AIR:—*"Jeanette and Jeanot"*

I have just got in across the plains, I'm poorer than a snail,
My mules all died, but poor old Clip I pulled in by the tail,
I fed him last at Chimney Rock, that's where the grass gave out,
I'm proud to tell, we stood it well, along the Truckee route.
But I'm very weak and lean, though I started plump and fat,
How I wish I had the gold machine, I left back on the Platte;

And a pair of striped bed-tick pants, my Sally made for me
To wear while digging after gold; and when I left says she,
"Here, take the laudanum with you, Sam, to check the dia-a-ree."

When I left Missouri river, with my California rig,
I had a shovel, pick and pan, the tools they used to dig;
My mules gave out along the Platte, where they got alkalied,
And I sick with the "di-a-ree," my laudanum by my side;
When I reached the little Blue, I had one boot and a shoe,
Which I thought by greasing once or twice, would last me nearly
    thro';
I had needles, thread and pills, which my mammy did prescribe,
And a flint-lock musket loaded full, to shoot the Digger tribe,
But I left them all on Goose Creek where I freely did imbibe.

I joined in with a train from Pike, at Independence Rock,
The Indians came in that night, stampeded all their stock,
They laughed at me, said "Go a-foot," but soon they stopped their
    fun,
For my old mule was left behind, so poor he could not run.
So I packed my fancy nag, for the rest I could not wait,
And I traveled up Sweet Water, till I came to Devil's Gate;
When my mule gave out in sight of where I started in the morn,
I'd have given all my boots and shoes, if I had not been born,
Or I'd rather stripped at New Orleans, to swim around the Horn.

I arrived at Salt Lake City, on the 18th of July
Old Brigham Young was on a "bust," he swore they'd never die;
I went to see the Jordan, with a lady, God forgive her,
She took me to the water's edge, and shoved me in the river;
I crawled out and started on, and I managed very well,
Until I struck the Humboldt, which I thought was nearly h——l,
I traveled till I struck the sink where outlet can't be found,
The Lord got thro' late Saturday night, he'd finished all around.
But would not work on Sunday, so he run it in the ground.

The Peyouts stole what grub I had, they left me not a bite,
And now the d——l was to pay, the Desert was in sight;
And as the people passed along, they'd say to me, "You fool,
"You'll never get through in the world, unless you leave that mule."
But I pushed, pulled and coaxed, till I finally made a start,

And his bones, they squeaked and rattled so, I thought he'd fall
    apart,
I killed a buzzard now and then, gave Clip the legs and head,
We crossed the Truckee thirty times, but not a tear was shed,
We crossed the summit, took the trail, that to Nevada led.

When I got to Sacramento, I got on a little tight,
I lodged aboard the Prison brig, one-half a day and night;
I vamosed when I got ashore, went to the Northern mines,
There found the saying very true, "All is not gold that shines,"
I have dug, packed and chopped, and have drifted night and day,
But I hav'nt struck a single lead, that would me wages pay.
At home they think we ought to have gold on our cabin shelves,
Wear high-heeled boots, well blacked, instead of rubbers No.
    twelves;
But let them come and try it, 'till they satisfy themselves.

Anonymous

The Fools of '49

AIR:—*"Commence you Darkies all."*

When gold was found in '48, the people said 'twas gas,
And some were fools enough to think the lumps were only brass.
But soon they all were satisfied, and started off to mine:
They bought their ships, came round the Horn, in the fall of '49.

CHORUS

> Then they thought of what they'd been told,
> When they started after gold,
> That they never in the world would make a pile.

The people all were crazy then, they didn't know what to do.
They sold their farms for just enough to pay their passage thro':
They bid their friends a long farewell; said, "Dear wife don't you
    cry,
I'll send you home the yellow lumps a piano for to buy."

Then they thought, &c., &c.

The poor, the old and rotten scows, were advertised to sail
From New Orleans with passengers, but they must pump and bail.
The ships were crowded more than full, and some hung on behind,
And others dived off from the wharf and swam till they were blind.

Then they thought, &c., &c.

With rusty pork and stinking beef, and rotten, wormy bread,
And captains, too, that never were up as high as the main-mast head.
The steerage passengers would rave and swear that they'd paid their
    passage;
And wanted something more to eat besides Bologna sausage.

Then they thought, &c., &c.

Then they began to cross the plains with oxen, hollowing "haw;"
And steamers they began to run as far as Panama:
And there for months the people staid that started after gold,
And some returned disgusted with the lies that had been told.

Then they thought, &c., &c.

The people died on every route, they sicken'd and died like sheep;
And those at sea, before they were dead, were launched into the
    deep:
And those that died while crossing the plains fared not so well as
    that,
For a hole was dug and they thrown in, along the miserable Platte.

Then they thought, &c., &c.

The ships at last began to arrive, and the people began to inquire,
They say that flour is a dollar a pound, do you think it will be any
    higher?
And then to carry their blankets and sleep outdoors, it seemed so
    droll;
Both tired and mad, without a cent, they d————d the lousy hole.

Then they thought, &c., &c.

23

Anonymous

Days of Forty-Nine

1

Here—you see old Tom Moore,
A relic of by-gone days;
A bummer, too, they call me now,
But what care I for praise?
For my heart is filled with grief and woe,
And oft I do repine
For the Days of Old, the Days of Gold,
And the Days of 'Forty-Nine.

2

I had comrads then—a saucy set,
They were rough, I must confess,
But staunch and brave, as true as steel,
Like hunters from the West;
But they like many another fish
Have now run out their line,
But like good old bricks they stood the kicks,
Of the Days of 'Forty-Nine.

3

There was Monte Pete—I'll ne'er forget
The luck he always had,
He'd deal for you both night and day,
Or as long as you had a scad.
One night a pistol laid him out,
'Twas his last lay-out, in fine;
It caught Pete sure, right bang in the door,
In the days of 'Forty-Nine.

4

There was New York Jake, a butcher boy,
So fond of getting tight;

Whenever Jake got full of gin
He was looking for a fight.
One night he ran against a knife
In the hands of old Bob Kline—
So over Jake we had a wake,
In the Days of 'Forty-Nine.

5

There was another chap from New Orleans,
Big Ruben was his name—
On the plaza there, with a sardine box,
He opened a Faro game—
He dealt so fair that a millionaire
He became in course of time
'Til death stepped in and called the tune
In the Days of 'Forty-Nine.

6

There was Kentucky Bill, one of the boys
Who was always in for a game—
No matter whether he lost or won.
To him 'twas all the same.
He'd ante a slug, he'd pass the buck;
He'd go a hatful blind,
In a game of death, Bill lost his breath,
In the Days of 'Forty-Nine.

7

There was North Carolina Jess, a hard old case
Who never would repent,
Jess was never known to miss a meal,
Or ever pay a cent.
But poor old Jess, like all the rest,
To Death did at last resign,
And in his bloom, he went up the Flume
In the Days of 'Forty-Nine.

8

There was Rackensack Jim, who could out-roar

A buffalo bull, you bet!
He roared all night, he roared all day,
He may be roaring yet.
One night he fell in a prospect-hole—
'Twas a roaring bad design—
For in that hole Jim roared out his soul
In the Days of 'Forty-Nine.

9

Of all the comrades I had then
There's none left now but me,
And the only thing I'm fitting for
Is a senator to be—
The people cry, as I pass by—
"There goes a travelling sign;
"That's Old Tom Moore, a bummer
"Of the Days of 'Forty-Nine."

10

O, since that time how things have changed
In this land of Liberty!
Darkies didn't vote nor plead in court
Nor rule this coun-to-ry.
But the Chinese question, the worst of all,
In those days did not shine
For the country was right, and the boys all white.
In the Days of 'Forty-Nine.

Anonymous

California Stage Company

Here's - no respect for youth or age,
On board a California stage;
But pull and haul about for seats
As bedbugs do among the sheets

Chorus:
They started as a thieving line
In eighteen hundred forty-nine;
All "opposition" they defy,
So the people must root hog or die.

2

You're crowded in with Chinamen,
As fattening hogs are in a pen,
and what will more a man provoke,
Is musty plug tobacco smoke.

3

The ladies are compelled to sit
With dresses in tobacco spit;
The gentlemen don't seem to care,
But talk on politics and swear.

4

The dust is deep in summer time,
The mountains very hard to climb;
And drivers often stop and yell,
"Get out, all hands, and push—up hill!"

5

The drivers, when they feel inclined,
Will have you walking on behind,
And on your shoulders lug a pole,
To help them through some muddy hole.

6

They promise, when your fare you pay,
"You'll have to walk but *half* the way;"
Then add *aside,* with cunning laugh,
"You'll push and pull the *other half!*"

7

They have and will monopolize

The business, 'till the *people rise,*
And send them "kiteing" down below,
To start a line with Bates and Rowe!

Anonymous

Sweet Betsey From Pike

Oh, don't you remember sweet Betsey from Pike,
Who cross'd the big mountains with her lover Ike,
With two yoke of cattle, a large yellow dog,
A tall Shanghai rooster and one spotted hog.

Chorus:
Singing too-ral lal loo-ral lal loo-ral lal la,
Singing too-ral lal loo-ral lal loo-ral lal la,
Singing too-ral lal loo-ral, Sing too-ral lal la,
Singing too-ral lal loo-ral lal loo-ral lal la.

2

One evening quite early they camped on the Platte,
'Twas near by the road on a green shady flat,
Where Betsey, sore-footed, lay down to repose—
With wonder Ike gazed on that Pike County rose.

3

Their wagons broke down with a terrible crash,
And out on the prairie rolled all kinds of trash;
A few little baby clothes done up with care-
'Twas rather suspicious, though all on the *square.*

4

The shanghai ran off, and their cattle all died;
That morning the last piece of bacon was fried;
Poor Ike was discouraged, and Betsey got mad,
The dog drooped his tail and looked wondrously sad.

5

They stopped at Salt Lake to inquire the way,
When Brigham declared that sweet Betsey should stay;
But Betsey got frightened and ran like a deer,
While Brigham stood pawing the ground like a steer.

6

They soon reached the desert, where Betsey gave out,
And down in the sand she lay rolling about;
While Ike, half distracted, looked on with surprise,
Saying, "Betsey, get up, you'll get sand in your eyes."

7

Sweet Betsey got up in a great deal of pain,
Declared she'd go back to Pike County again;
But Ike gave a sigh, and they fondly embraced,
And they traveled along with his arm round her waist.

8

They suddenly stopped on a very high hill,
With wonder looked down upon old Placerville;
Ike sighed when he said, and he cast his eyes down,
"Sweet Betsey, my darling, we've got to Hangtown."

9

Long Ike and sweet Betsey attended a dance;
Ike wore a pair of his Pike County pants;
Sweet Betsey was covered with ribbons and rings;
Says Ike, "You're an angel, but where are your wings?"

10

A miner said, "Betsey, will you dance with me?"
"I will that, old hoss, if you don't make too free;
But don't dance me hard; do you want to know why?
Dog on you! I'm chock full of strong alkali!"

11

This Pike County couple got married of course,

And Ike became jealous—obtained a divorce;
Sweet Betsey, well satisfied, said with a shout,
"Goodbye, you big lummux, I'm glad you've backed out!"

Anonymous

Joe Bowers

My name it is Joe Bowers—I've got a brother Ike;
I come from old Missouri, yes, all the way from Pike;
I'll tell you why I left thar, and how I came to roam,
And leave my poor old mammy, so fer away from home.

I used to love a gal thar, they call'd her Sally Black;
I axed her for to marry me, she said it was a whack;
"But," says she to me, "Joe Bowers, before we hitch for life,
You'd orter have a little home to keep your little wife."

Says I, "My dearest Sally, oh! Sally, for your sake,
I'll go to Californy, and try to raise a stake."
Says she to me, "Joe Bowers, oh, you're the chap to win,
Guv me a buss to seal the bargain," and she threw a dozen in!

I shal ne'er forgit my feelins when I bid adieu to all;
Sally cotched me round the neck, then I began to bawl;
When I sot in, they all commenced—you ne're did hear the like,
How they all took on and cried, the day I left old Pike.

When I got to this 'ere country, I hadn't nary red,
I had sich wolfish feelins I wish'd myself most dead;
But the thoughts of my dear Sally soon made these feelins git,
And whispered hopes to Bowers—lord, I wish I had 'em yit!

At length I went to minin', put in my biggest licks,
Come down upon the boulders jist like a thousand bricks;
I worked both late and airly, in rain, and sun, and snow,
But I was working for my Sally, so 'twas all the same to Joe.

I made a very lucky strike, as the gold itself did tell,
And saved it for my Sally, the gal I loved so well;
I saved it for my Sally, that I might pour it at her feet,
That she might kiss and hug me, and call me something sweet.

But one day I got a letter from my dear, kind brother, Ike—
It come from old Missouri, sent all the way from Pike;
It brought me the gol-darn'dest news as every you did hear—
My heart is almost bustin', so, pray, excuse this tear.

It said my Sal was fickle, that her love for me had fled;
That she'd married with a butcher, whose *har* was orful red!
It told me more than that—oh! it's enough to make one swar,
It said Sally had a baby, and the baby had red *har!*

Now, I've told you all I could tell about this sad affar,
'Bout Sally marryin' the butcher, and the butcher had red *har.*
Whether 'twas a boy or gal child, the letter never said,
It only said its cussed *har* was inclined to be a *red!*

Anonmymous

The Ragged Coat

Oh, what a world of flummery—there's nothing but deceit in it—
    So you'll find, if you'll mind, as through life you travel on;
Old and young, rich and poor, every one you meet in it,
    All judge you by appearances, and I'll prove it in my song.
Eight years ago I left New York—I hadn't nary red, sirs;
    My folks were rich, but wouldn't lend a single dollar note;
So I started off across the plains, and was really almost dead, sirs—
    I had no hat, no shirt, no boots, and this very ragged coat.

But being in the land of gold, my spirits soon got lighter—
    I got a pick and shovel, and I started off to work;
I made a very lucky strike—my prospects soon got brighter—
    I made a handsome fortune, though I worked like any Turk.
And then I thought that I'd return, and see my friends at home, sirs;

So I bought a first class passage on board of a steamboat.
I had a heap more cash then than when I 'gan to roam sirs,
   But to fathom out deception I kept on my ragged coat.

The boat was very crowded, but I got a first rate berth, sirs,
   And tried to make myself at home with the passengers on board;
But their behavior oftentimes it caused me lots of mirth, sirs—
   I'd commence a conversation, but they wouldn't say a word.
When I heard a silly puppy say, though lowly he did breath it,
   "It's a shame to let a ragged man in this part of the boat;"
Said I, "You foppish rascal, there's a good heart beats beneath it—
   So don't despise a man because he wears a ragged coat."

My journey being ended, I put my foot on shore, sirs,
   Glad enough, indeed, I was of them to get relief.
I walked up to my cousin's, and straight knocked at the door, sirs,
   But he banged it in my face again, as though I was a thief.
I told him plainly who I was—my *face* he didn't know, sirs.
   I told him I had made a pile—he quickly chang'd his note;
He wanted then to borrow, but, said I, "Oh, dear me, no sirs,
   For you despised the *man* because he wore a ragged coat."

Then I called on a young lady, who I thought I'd like to marry,
   And settle down in handsome style, but I'll tell what occurred;
When I popped the question to her, said she, "Oh, dear, Lord Harry,
   The idea of such a thing as that is perfectly absurd.
My beau must be a handsome man, dressed in the heighth of
      fashion—
   But you, with your long hair and beard, look like some ugly goat;
My husband must have lots of cash for me to cut a dash on,
   And I couldn't think of wedding one who wore a ragged coat.

I soon got quite disgusted with the fashionable throng, sirs,
   And quickly left the city, although it gave me birth.
To California back I came, and wrote this little song, sirs—
   I love its hills and valleys—'tis the fairest spot on earth.
Here, if an honest man's in want, a stranger will relieve you;
   I'm very sure you'll allow it's true now what I've wrote.
You don't judge us by appearances, which ofttimes will deceive you,
   And you don't despise a man because he wears a ragged coat.

Anonymous

Mining Localities Peculiar To California

Jim Crow Cañon,
Happy Valley,
Ground Hog's Glory,
Red Dog,
Hell's Delight,
Jackass Gulch,
Devil's Basin,
Bogus Thunder,
Ladies' Cañon,
Dead Wood,
Last Chance,
Miller's Defeat,
Gouge Eye,
Greenhorn Cañon,
Loafer Hill,
Puke Ravine,
Shanghai Hill,
Mad Cañon,
Plug-head Gulch,
Shirt-tail Cañon,
Guano Hill,
Slap Jack Bar,
Skunk Gulch,
Rattlesnake Bar,
Quack Hill,
Coon Hollow,
Murderer's Bar,
Whiskey Bar,
Pepper-Box Flat,
Poor Man's Creek,
Poverty Hill,
Nigger Hill.
Humbug Cañon.
Greasers' Camp,
Seventy-Six.

Snow Point.
Wild Cat Bar.
Paradise,
Nary Red,
Dead Mule Cañon
Blue-Belly Ravine,
Gas Hill,
Dead Man's Bar,
Wild Goose Flat,
Sluice-Fork.
Ladies' Valley,
Brandy Flat,
Shinbone Peak,
Graveyard Cañon,
Gridiron Bar.
Seven-up Ravine.
Gospel Gulch.
Hen-Roost Camp.
Loafer's Retreat.
Chicken Thief Flat.
Lousey Ravine,
Humpback Slide,
Hungry Camp,
Lazy Man's Cañon,
Swellhead Diggings,
Mud Springs,
Logtown,
Cayote Hill,
Skinflint,
Git-up-and-git,
Poodletown,
American Hollow,
Gopher Flat,
Yankee Doodle,
Gold hill,

Bloomer Hill.
Christian Flat,
Piety Hill,
Grizzly Flat,
Rough and Ready,
Hog's Diggings,
Rat Trap Slide
Ragtown.
Brandy Gulch.
Pike Hill.
Sugar-Loaf Hill,
Liberty Hill,
Port Wine.
Poker Flat,
Paint-Pot Hill.

Stud-Horse Cañon,
Horsetown,
Pancake Ravine,
Bob Ridley Flat,
Petticoat Slide,
Centipede Hollow,
One Eye,
Chucklehead Digging
Nutcake Camp,
Push-Coach Hill,
Mount Zion,
Seven-by-nine Valley,
Puppytown,
Barefoot Diggings,

Anonymous

Californios Poem

This is one of the few poems of the early California period which has surfaced. It was printed in Monterey and the date is given as 1836. It can be seen in the Bancroft Library on the Berkeley campus of the University of California. Translated by M. B. Anderson.

En Recuerdo del Glorioso Grito:
Dado en el pueblo de Dolores,
En el año de mil ochocientos diez.

La Religion con la Union,
E Independencia segura;
Formaron una hermosura,
Que ama nuestra corazón.

La paz sin alteración
Siempre en *Mexico* resida;
Y los bienes sin medida,
Con los de fortuna estable

Sean caudal interminable
De esta PATRIA tan querida.

In Memory of the Glorious Shout:
Raised in the town of Dolores,
In the Year 1810.

Religion with Union
And Independence secure;
Molded a beauty,
Which our heart loves.

May peace without disturbance
Dwell in Mexico always,
And may riches without measure,
Along with steady good fortune
Form an unending current
From this homeland so beloved.

Juanita de Arrana

Candle Flame

I sat and watched a candle flame one night
Burn mystically toward its life's decline,
And thought of taper blaze in holy rite
Of Christian church and Asiatic shrine.
I mused the esoteric symbolism
Of flame — the secret paracelsus learned
Of myth, and mystery, and cabalism.
And conning so, I gradually discerned
A salamander, phoenix-like arise,
Above the taper's death-becooling pure
Attired in nebulous spirit guise,
Trans-muted from the dying ray of fire!

Ah, skeptic, look upon the candle's flame
And doubt no more the spirit's deathless claim!

Semele

Too late—In her Cadmean bower burned
To death by blaze of Zeus' supernal light—
Sad Semele the fatal lesson learned
Of truth too blinding-stark for neophyte.
For she had made demand, while yet a maid
Of mortal flesh, to see the godly guise
Of him whose deific array conveyed
But holocaust to unaccustomed eyes.

For so it is: Each one must wait the span
Of his required novitiate, until
The tardy truth, released of curbing ban,
Descends, at last, the learner's quest to fill.
      And thus, no soul before its rightful time
      May comprehend the way of laws sublime!

Anne Harvey Avila

Song From A Brown Throat

When the night from spools of shadow
Girds my brown rebellious feet,
Slumber lurks beyond the silence,
Strong and venomously sweet.

Slumber is a tilted goblet
Slyly pressing dulcet sips
Of a necromantic fluid
To my frail, defenceless lips.

Slumber frees the cloistered image
Buried by repentant qualms
Of a face white and forbidden
Shyly pressed between dark palms.

36

Robert Barlow

Tepuzteca, Tepehua

We do not even know when their
    eyeballs were eaten by time,
The Copper People, the Hill-Lords.
The roof of that century has fallen in,
    corn is dried on its floors.
They may have examined ginger-jars
    under resinous torches,
Before the end of that night they
    people like stars;
Their flute-accompanied corteges may
    have held up the muleteers
Ascending the Camino Real under the
    Caves, with bundle of Cantonee silk.
We do not find written anywhere
    when the last old man or old
    woman complained last,
And was packed into the grotto of the
    dead with his bundle of food handy.
In 1580 Philip II read the
    report which said, "this town
    is called Fallen Star,
"Because of a King they had, who
    was called the Star-King. They
    speak Tepuzteco".
In 1750 the Viceroy of New Spain
    read the report which said,
"It is difficult to suppress
    the growing of contraband tobacco,
"For these hills are unoccupied".
We have a word of their
    language—it means "god"
    (or, possibly, "devil"),
And a paper bagful of
    potsherds we think they made.
These pieces of dishes are petals

From one of the many flowers
    which here and there on the
    mountain of Time,
In summers of a different sun and
    winters of a different rain,
Have unfolded beyond the reach
    of our gathering.

Herbert Bashford

Derndest Gal I Ever Knowed

Derndest gal I ever knowed,
Neatest gal I ever seen,
Lived down in the Red Ravine
Jest below the county road.
Guess she wuz about sixteen—
Sophy wuz her name an' she
Wuz ez cute ez cute kin be.

When I'd go t' town I brung
Her the biggest lot o' stuff,
Pop corn, likrish, 'n' enough
Candy fer t' fill a room.
Once she hit me with a broom
Cuz I kissed her on the cheek,
An' the midget wouldn't speak
T' me fer, perhaps, a week.
When I'd raise my eyes to hern
Jeminny! my cheeks 'ud burn
An' git redder 'n' a beet.
Oh, she looked jest powerful sweet!
When I'd try to call her dear
Why I'd feel so doggoned queer
That I'd lean ag'in th' fence
Zif I didn' hev no sense
Twist th' buttons on my vest,
Ast her who she liked th' best,

Ast her if it wuzn't Bill
Er old Jones thet run th' mill,
Keep a hintin' 'round yuh see
Till she'd up an' say twuz me.
I wuz jellus o' Jim Pike
Jellus ez th' very deuce
Though there didn't seem much use
Fer his freckles wuz so thick,
An' his hair wuz so like brick
Thet a feller one day said
Yuh could toast a hunk o' bread
Ef yuh'd hold it nigh his head.
He wuz awkarder 'n' sin,
Never fished along the crick
But he'd hev t' tumble in.
Sophy 'peared t' pity Jim
While I thought if I wuz him
I'd go off 'n' hide somewhere
Else put plaster on my hair.
But this homely, lantern-jawed
Lookin' cuss stood 'round 'n' chawed
On a plug o' terbacker
Half his time 'n' talked t' her
Of his love till I jest told
Him to' mosey an' he rolled
Up his sleeves 'n' landed me
Plumb betwixt th' eyes, then he
Went to Sophy an' sir, she
Married him! The pesky mule!
Wuzn't she a reg'ler fool?
I wuz jest tetotally blowed—
Derndest gal I ever knowed!

Leslie Bates

Out Of Chinatown

Along the shady Chinese alley-ways
They drowsed, the market-men, with slitted eyes,
And nodded by their loaded rattan trays,
Sleek-bellied, unperturbed, content, and wise.
The air was hot and heavy and the flies
Hummed in the dust or settled on blue dishes
Or swarmed on shining strings of drying fishes.

Indifferent to time they dream and wait.
This surging San Francisco calls in vain.
They muse and dream beside the Golden Gate
Of temple songs slow-booming in the rain.
Ghosts of old China drift along the brain.
And so they watch the cable cars clang by,
Waiting, impassive, for the world to die.

Premonition

Hot and humid,
San Jose droops under sultry skies.
"Earthquake weather," people call it.

Squatting, sprawling, on the cool, park lawns,
Weary men, their shirts open at the throat,
Dream open-eyed dreams
And learn the courtesy of still moments.
All races,
In semi-circles,
Lean on blanket rolls;
Harvest wanderers,
Fruit tramps,
Talking softly in broken tongues.

Young cannery girls hurry by,

Their minds intent on apricots and peaches
And on their pretty selves.

It is earthquake weather.

James Madison Bell

Poem

Wherefore half-mast and waving sadly,
    And seeming ill-disposed to move,
Are those bright emblems which so gladly
    Were wont to wave our homes above?
And why is this all glorious nation
    Thus in her hour of hope bowed low?

Wherefore those marks of grief and sorrow
    So visible on every face?
To what foul deed of bloody horror
    Do all those gloomy signs retrace?
Aback to the walls and lofty spire,
Back to your country's bleeding sire,
    Black to your dying Magistrate.

We know not why God has permitted
    This tragic scene, this bloody deed;
An act so seemingly unfitted
    In this auspicious hour of need.
Though none perhaps may the intention
    Or the wondrous purpose tell,
Of this direful life suspension—
    Yet God, the Lord, doeth all things well.

Our Nation's Father has been murdered;
    Our Nation's Chieftain has been slain
By traitorous hands most basely ordered;
    And we, his children, feel the pain.
Our pain is mixed with indignation,

Our sorrow is not purely brief,
And nothing short of a libation
    From Treason's heart can bring relief.

And we, in spite of earth and heaven,
    On bended knee with lifted hand,
Swear, as we hope to be forgiven,
    To drive foul Treason from the land.
And that fair land so long polluted
    By the sweat of unpaid toil,
Shall be by Liberty uprooted
    And thickly spread with freedom's soil.

Thus we'll avenge the death of Lincoln,
    His noble principles maintain,
Till every base, inhuman falcon
    Is swept from freedom's broad domain;
Until from tower and from turret,
    From mountain height and prairie wide,
One Flag shall wave—and freedom's spirit
    In peace and love o'er all preside.

Bill Berkson

Election Day Fog

the perfect roundness (halo?)

and density of headlights

coming from behind

as I walk up hill

heading towards a house

where warmth may freely spread

its muted grace-notes

like pork chops

cooking

it's been a short day
just the right number
of decisions
two
"everything else
has everything else"
says the light
of another stripe
it looks like
that one is going
up in smoke
meanwhile
the past is calling
it all comes back
more or less amusing
like the anatomy of melancholy
a studied look
into the not too distant
winning
flame

To Lynn

The wind is blowing hard, and you walk
through its force to loose this morning's lost bunny
in a field of scrub. It's like everything is adangle
from this earthy grip. You watch patiently. The rabbit runs off.
I watch you. You are bigger than the bushes, and like them, not
to be bowled over, unlike me, by a whim. Head up,
you are fully aware of the clouds, and when there aren't any
you take in a lot of light. You give off a lot of heat in
the form of color. Today you are wearing white.

Duane Big Eagle

My Father's Country

In the morning light
My father's form
Against a mountain on the horizon.
Woolen trousers and smart leather shoes,
At thirty-two, a handsome man
Standing in the backroads
Of a country as open as his shirt collar.
There the silence of a moonless night
Had purity and breath
But that is almost gone.
Now the night, never dark nor silent,
Dazzles our certainty,
Rumbles loudly through fading dreams of spacious warmth.

Father, let us walk again
As our grandfathers did.
If need be we will make new bodies of this earth,
Eat only memories,
Drink only the liquid spilt in our dreams,
Take shelter
In our love.
In the vastness of this land
We need only the songs its spirits teach us
And to sing!
Always to sing!

White Sugar

I just saw your face
On a woman in a supermarket in Oregon.
She bought a ten pound bag of white sugar
To make pastry –
So that her children would still love her,

So her husband maybe wouldn't go see
The divorcée he knows uptown.

She had that same fixed expression
Which sadness follows around like a hungry cat.
That holds trouble like a life
Desperate to be filled up with something –
Anything.

And I was glad then
That we didn't get married,
That after all this time
And maybe at the end of this journey,
You'll be there for me
For a day
Or a couple of days,
And glad too, that you don't any longer use
White sugar.

Paris Perspectives

I might as well be here as anywhere,
Leaning against a tree
By a narrow Paris street-
Rue de l'amour perdu.

We journey a thousand kilometers
Into the country
Enter an abandoned farmhouse,
Now reclaimed,
And hear Charlie Parker-
"Scrapple from the Apple"
(Radio Jugoslavia).

We visit the Chateau de George Sand
Her death house now.
A young man whose voice has just changed
Shows us around.
In her bedroom

A bee springs against the window
Trying to get out.

Common things occupy my mind,
Taxi cabs, the sign for the lost and found.
There is no sculpture on this corner
And your face does not appear
In the leaves of trees.

The streets I know could be anywhere,
The child I know is mine and not mine.
I see him for the first time–
Feel for a moment in the warm streets
A young father feed his son
Ice cream in a sidewalk cafe.

The Wanderer

"I live in a jungle!
Piss drunken wino,
Take your daughter
And get out!"

4 A.M. The streets of Bandon, Oregon,
Glisten with the night's rain.
Small clouds race to the hills in the east.
The little girl and I
Cast no shadow
Under a moon with no edges.

Black Bart

Lines Dedicated To Wells, Fargo & Co.

Here I lay me down to sleep,
    To wait the coming morrow,
Perhaps success, perhaps defeat,

and everlasting sorrow.
Yet come what will—I'll try it on,
    My condition can't be worse,
And if there's money in that box,
    'tis money for my purse.

James Washington Blake

Lucca

for Eda Giampoli

The center of all is age:

When a woman's skin
crusts from time, the young panic
because ugly is the belief;
not knowing
that beauty is standing
with the future before you, old people,
roots embedded in history.

Branches span tribulations to the meristems
like an aged watchful eye
that yearns the fate of the old.

Her springs are dry, as water has moved
with succeeding generations
into an oasis of youth
highlighting an illusion of barrenness.

Senility is having experience
too much to articulate;
having familiar landmarks disappear
into memory
as the aphorisms of the young
pain a slowing heart.

The generosity of the aged

is not a childish whim.
It is the spirit of knowing
that boundaries are mistakes
in the minds of men;
a superficial dam
against the flow of time.

Peter Blue Cloud

America 1976

Pencil poised to analyze inherent hate,
the whys of my people still being killed
the wherefores of torn and tattered treaties
    pieces drift by my window
shadow-bent thoughts my hatred contains
and the elements of my thinking
interrupted by dog barks across moist fields
    the messages fireflies dare
the mind to new beginnings.

Ears laid flat to skull to question
    a season's pain in the cycle
to watch a nation fold crumple wings
dryrot in the marrowbone of spirit
   —sing me no freedoms.

America, the futile product
of endeavors shriveled by greed
inability to truly dream.
That yours was and is the potential
of a learning of a better lifeway,
but you chose to create kingdoms
    instead of kinships
and your hypocrisy appalls
the very Creation.

There are no secrets to divulge,

we are all of the mystery,
                          life,
the seeds of good and evil
are possessed by each.

But you don't see, ever,
                      do you?

Therefore, America, I mourn
you, but for a moment
      and now
that moment passes.

I come of strange singers
of bedrock foot dancers
children of turtle,
      I sleep
and wake up many tomorrows
later, I have been given
      dreams
to pass on to you,
      when
                  will you listen?

Autumn Morning

Full moon and the whispering leaves   She
of dry corn stalks touched by wind,   sings
a low mist swirls the river's surface   us
in gentle dance, like visions lent   sweetly,
by starlight the owl's eyes reflect,   touches
and moon path on water is a walking   our
murmur of soft questions   feet
      only a child will ask.   with
and maple's shadow is a pattern   dance,
woven by the Creation in a balance   hands
of earth and sky,   us
                  then softly   golden
again the owl's call, an inner   fruit,

sound of warm feathers,   hums
then sudden gust of wind   us
announces day with a shower   night
of falling leaves which dance   songs
a frantic, short-lived race.   we

and dawn is a praise of silence   ever
to be respected   taste.

For Ace

I cannot summon a tear
or feel badly just now
it's not my loss so much
as it is all our losing.

There won't be a journey
to the pueblo where he was born
or any tracings of childhood
there in red clay dust where
he might have sketched pictures
with a twig,

and no anger at his being taken
from family and home, away
to government school like
so many others,
    no one really cares or understands
or even wants to — .

He learned to read and to think
and to drink and to smoke dope
and to make love,
just all the usual things,
    except
that he had a talent, Wow!
    Imagine that! Talent!

So talented was he that
he was beaten to death

in a Chicago barroom,
	Wow! Talent!

So what is it I want to say
or want to remember?
The drunk parties when
we had to carry him home,
or the time he was so depressed
at being turned down by a girl?

No, none of these, but all of them,
all the rage, frustration and confusion,
all the love, tenderness and desperate wanting,
all these things which we all carry
within us, but in him
surged with such energy
from brain to fingers to pigment
to living canvas,
			there, and then,
in those moments I was held,
like a child witnessing my first view
of the stars, the frightening and wondrous
	universe.

His energy was overpowering as he
sketched or painted,
I see him standing before a canvas
half as large as the room
buffalo and ghost dancers emerging
alive, moving, demanding more space,
	what'll happen, I wondered in panic,
	when he paints the walls
	and crashes through the window
	and begins painting the streets,
	the houses, the billowing clouds,
		the very air?

And his dancers leaped at me
with a loud cry grabbing me,
forcing me into the dance
	and I danced

51

not gladly, but still frightened
I danced
    as buffalo pawed earth
and blew and snorted
and blizzards swept the plain
leaving me a naked, ice-coated tree,
eyes frozen open, forced at last to see.

I danced
        as a nation was slaughtered
and lay broken and bleeding
I danced
        among angered ghosts
who would not lie down gentle
    to death.

I see him at this moment, sketching,
sitting at a littered table,
creating four universes of thought
in as many years,
            fingers in frantic haste
as if tasting the shortness of his life.

I am bitter now, at this moment,
I would reach and pull him from sleep
and make him dance
    with his own dancers,
              with me,
tears streaming down faces,
limbs jerking in sanity gone fallen,
and falling into the void of space
we would clutch and grasp at
each and every one of you
and force you into the dance,
and rub your faces into the gore
so proudly you helped create.

And what's the use, and what's the use
my mind screams to the shadows,
so many of our youth

gone into death,
                    so much dying,

and all the blame and blood
and all the justifications
and explanations, add up
to a loss we share the deed of—
        yes, it's true,
it is us, the runaways,
the self-made outcasts
it is to our grief
that we are forgetting
                        the dance.

Arna Bontemps

Golgotha Is A Mountain

Golgotha is a mountain, a purple mound
Almost out of sight.
One night they hanged two thieves there,
And another man.
Some women wept heavily that night;
Their tears are flowing still. They have made a river;
Once it covered me.
Then the people went away and left Golgotha
Deserted.
Oh, I've seen many mountains:
Pale purple mountains melting in the evening mists and blurring on
    the borders of the sky.

I climbed old Shasta and chilled my hands in its summer snows.
I rested in the shadow of Popocatapetl and it whispered to me of
    daring prowess.
I looked upon the Pyrenees and felt the zest of warm exotic nights.
I slept at the foot of Fujiyama and dreamed of legend and of death.
And I've seen other mountains rising from the wistful moors like the
    breasts of a slender maiden.

Who knows the mystery of mountains!
Some of them are awful, others are just lonely.

*   *   *

Italy has its Rome and California has San Francisco,
All covered with mountains.
Some think these mountains grew
Like ant hills
Or sand dunes.
That might be so —
I wonder what started them all!
Babylon is a mountain
And so is Nineveh,
With grass growing on them;
Palaces and hanging gardens started them.
I wonder what is under the hills
In Mexico
And Japan!
There are mountains in Africa too.
Treasure is buried there:
Gold and precious stones
And moulded glory.
Lush grass is growing there
Smirking before the wind.
black men are bowing.
Naked in that grass
Digging with their fingers.
I am one of them:
Those mountains should be ours.
It would be great
To touch the pieces of glory with our hands.
These mute unhappy hills,
Bowed down with broken backs,
Speak often one to another:
"A day is as a year," they cry,
"And a thousand years as one day."
We watched the caravan
That bore our queen to the courts of Solomon;
And when the first slave traders came

We bowed our heads.
"Oh, Brothers, it is not long!
Dust shall yet devour the stones
But we shall be here when they are gone."
Mountains are rising all around me.
Some are so small they are not seen;
Others are large.
All of them get big in time and people forget
What started them at first.

Oh the world is covered with mountains!
Beneath each one there is something buried:
Some pile of wreckage that started it there.
Mountains are lonely and some are awful.

* * *

One day I will crumble.
They'll cover my heap with dirt and that will make a mountain.
I think it will be Golgotha.

Natasha Borovsky-Hidalgo

On Seeing The Documentary HEARTS AND MINDS

A row of graves dug in the yellow earth.
    A young wife kneeling, all in white.
"For the Oriental, life has little worth,"
Says the Commanding General, square jaw tight.
    The people are so small, so thin,
    All eyes and bones and yellow skin,
        Yet we can't win.

The helicopter blades long grasses churn.
    Machine-guns chatter. All is stilled.
Flame-throwers spew. The straw-roofed hamlets burn.
A puddle where a little child was killed.

The father's face is full of hate.
What will it take their will to break?
    What will it take?

A pile of rubble where a kitchen stood.
    Three sisters lived there. One is dead.
For coffins, in the North, there is no wood.
One sister cries; the elder stares ahead.
    The bombs like orange blossoms burst;
    Amidst the green, in puffs they burst,
        And we're accursed.

The coffin-maker's eyes with hatred glare.
    Tall soldiers stroll, their faces blank.
Drink Coca-Cola, the city billboards blare.
"Big sister at cheap price for handsome Yank."
    Little boy pushers, beggars, pimps,
    And amputees with plastic limbs,
        With plastic limbs.

For hash and whores, on leave, the bored Yanks shop.
    Dissenters are in cages penned.
"In ambush, all my buddies have been shot."
The countryfolk from camp to camp are sent.
    A girl draws water from a well.
    Rice paddies turned a flaming hell;
        Still, they rebel.

On her black hair, a pointed yellow hat.
    The Saigon whores with big brown tits.
The rich officials in the club are fat.
A small Viet-Cong is by a large boot kicked.
    The fat officials are obscene,
    And God is absent from the scene,
        God is unseen.

Why are we there? What is our cause, our claim?
    Our leaders sent us. Why? To win.
To win for whom, what for, and in whose name?
    How soon will they give in?
    How many tons of dynamite,

How much defoliant and napalm,
Infra-red sensors, radar, tanks,
Anti-personnel weapons, shells?
How many missions must be flown,
How many pilots captured, lost?
How many soldiers maimed and dead
 Before they yield? How long?
  Can they fight on?

"Orientals do not prize a human life,"
 The General says, jaw square and tight.
Over the row of graves, a kneeling wife
With long black hair, so slender, all in white.
 Above the yellow earth, blue sky.
 I hear it still, her wailing cry,
  And I ask why?

Lillian Boss

Forgetting

Through the fading years I have forgotten,
Forgotten your eyes, and your unforgettable hair.
Down halls of days I lost your smile—
And I can scarcely care.
Where a rose should bloom on my breast
Is a silver, long-healed scar.
I see it. I never pause to wonder where you are.
But as long as life shall last
And hours are tossed out like dice,
I shall never walk again on the path
Of moonlight across ice!

I Asked The Sea
Conversations at Mendocino

I asked the Sea how deep things are.

O, said She, that depends upon
how far you want to go.

Well, I have a sea in me, said I,
do you have a me in you?

I'll look, said the Sea,
but that's apt to go rather deep.

And she broke a wave over my foot.

                *   *   *

I asked the Sea
how to cope with my life.

Yes, She said, Yes...

No no, said I,
I want to know
how to be strong like you.

Yes, She said, Yes...
kissing the arms of the cove.

                *   *   *

I took a morning glory
down to the Sea at sunrise
and laid it at her feet.
But the day darkened and stormed.

A gift should not be niggardly.
Remember that imperiled mariner

who chopped off his finger
and tossed it overboard?

Tomorrow I must take my heart.

* * *

The world, I said,
chirps a roaratorio
of meaningless questions
and wrong answers.
Isn't there somewhere
a quiet place?

Yes, said the Sea.
In the eye of the hurricane.

* * *

Why are you so restless?
said I to the Sea.

I'm calmer than you, said She.
The wind and the moon
like to toss me about
but myself I do nothing at all.
I accept whatever comes
and everything comes to me.
How do you manage that? said I.

Oh, She replied, I have
rather a good digestion.

* * *

Why are you always going
in and out?
I asked the Sea.
Why don't you just
stay put?

I'm not a puddle

or a bush, she said.
Furthermore
I only go out
in order to come in again.
Nothing goes forward
without first going
back.

*   *   *

Old Mother Sea, I pray you,
you who absorb and reflect
all the collected ponders,
have I another think coming?

I confess the wrongs of my head.
I repent its thoughtless notions.
Have you a tonic brain wash?
I am ready to mind my change.

O Lady of Another Think Coming,
have you a fresh profundity
to help me launch and pilot
the homeward voyage of my ark?

*   *   *

Let's talk of my dead,
        the Sea said.

Let's not, said I,
        I'm dry on my dune.

But what of the drowned?
        The Sea boomed.

Their ghosts I know,
        said I on the sand,
as I know my own doom.

        Then, said the Sea,

when I wash up the dead
    will you wade in?

I'll swim, I said.

*   *   *

Wading into the surf
I saw in the oncoming wave
a coal of fire ablaze
like the very eye of the deep.

I plunged and reached out.
When I found my feet again
I clutched in the dripping air
a rose-colored tennis shoe.

Said the Sea in my ears:
Love is the element, flowing
and burning, is the fire
in which you swim.

I Heard In The Shell

    I heard in the shell
    all the hymns of hell,
I heard all the angels crying,
    I heard the earth
    in pangs of birth
and all the galaxies dying.

    I heard in the shell
    the resounding well
of all humanity's voices,
    I heard every shout
    of laughter and doubt
in the crashing war of choices.

    I heard in the shell
    the throb of each cell

from flower and rock and feather.
   But loudest of all
   rang the quiet call
of Yes and No singing together.

Eva Carter Buckner

What Constitutes A Negro?

When the first slave-ship was landed
   With its cargo on this side,
There was then no vexing question
   As to which race he's allied;
Just a Negro, pure and simple,
   And as such might have remained,
But — well, here we drop the subject,
   For there is nothing to be gained.

Years have passed, and now we see him;
   On him's turned the strongest light;
Every race is represented —
   Black, brown, yellow, red, and white;
And they call him now a problem,
For there's One not been consulted
   And in it He is involved.

There's rise and fall of Nations,
   But, dispute it if you can,
There is just one God and Father
   And the brotherhood of man.
Ten-tenths blood of pure Caucasian,
   This it takes to make you white.
But one drop of Negro blood is
   Just the same, as Black as night.

For this stamp was put upon him
   And so let it thus remain.
For what is the use contending?

All contentions are in vain.
It is said ten million Negroes
    On this firm free land doth stand.
God inspires him to mount upward
    Though chains bind both foot and hand.

Read his crimes in boldest letters,
    Negro, and no question then;
And we own him, our heads bowing,
    Grieved to know we have such men.
On the other hand turning,
        We can point with pride to those
Who thought it worth while in striving,
    And to fame and honor rose.

Dumas, known as the French novelist,
    He his Negro blood could trace;
Tanner, artist known so widely,
    Who has won himself a place.
Yes, and there is the "Black Napoleon,"
    Brace "Toussaint L'Ouverture,"
And the great Edmonia Lewis,
    Sculptress, whose work will endure.

And we claim S. Taylor Coleridge;
    Dunbar, though he's dead still lives;
Booker Washington we all know,
    For the race his best thoughts gives;
Bishop Grant, in sermons, lectures;
    DuBois, John H. Jackson, true;
Chesnutt, Vernon, trace 'em; Pushkin,
    Browning, many others, too.

Great Rome had her gladiators,
    And of them was very proud;
We care nothing for the prize-ring
    But, since it has been allowed,
Why not then applaud the winner,
    Whether white or dusky man?
The survival of the fittest
    Is the rule, and it will stand.

Call him Ishmaelite or Arab,
   Paraphrase him, if you will;
Say Egyptian, if more pleasing,
   But he is a Negro still.
This would be a grander Nation
   With the goodness that's innate.
It would be a perfect haven —
   But the prejudice — too great.

But there, friends,
   Join us in life's great combat,
Though your skin be dark, what matter?
   You're a man, e'en for all that;
And we are using every effort
   To make good where e'er we trod,
One hand with the flag a-waving,
   And the other stretched to God.

Carlos Bulosan

The Surrounded

Try this if you can; try to walk under
The winter rain. Try this and if you can't
Feel the pain, O try again and again.

It is hard to sleep in the cold night.
It is harder to think before sleep comes
In like a steam of burning alcohol.
(I can't even dream; the whiteness of the land
Skulks in my sleep, stifling my dream...)
Hundreds starve in the snow, the radio announces;
And this husbandless middle-class woman smiles
A beautiful wish on her tubercular face.
(Here in my basement room I listen to the wind
Sweeping the tenement houses...) A baby cries.
Her mother shouts and hums a lullaby,
"Stop that darling now", and goes to sleep

Under the sputtering rain. *Try again!*
If this be love why not love life? the radio weeps
Above the lynch trees. O sing a song of love where
Patriotic citizens mock him because he is dark:
Here is your innocent negro dripping with blood:
See him well, the broken limbs, the scratched eyes.
You must try again! (I can't even think. I try
To remember something. I must look through the window
And dance my eyes on the wideness of the snow.
But I am hungry, if you want to know.
I tell you I will eat the snow and eat you too...)
And so the radio bleeds above the death trees,
If this be love why not love life?

Try this if you can; try to walk
Under the rain. I swear to you —
You want to love life again.

Letter In Exile: I

Hourly the planes scour the skies to chart
The uncharted defenses of their loved country.
It is summer and the waiting steamers will
Unload by the sounding sea, to fill the needs
Of cities falling in the hunger of working men;
While the green hills widen their luxuriant
Shoulders of sharp glades, caught in the palm
Of the determinate sun, born of the islands.

All seems to concentrate on their way.
They make millions and their sons enter night clubs.
Bright virgin girls moan and bleed in their beds.
They close banks and their daughters throw money
To titled foreign gentlemen and cynical waiters.
Their bourgeois homes are wrecked. Into the streets
They pursue the course of their passion. They hold
Life in bubbles of drunkenness and fancy.

Knowing the tremendous web of this mistake,
I think of our favorite little islands

Cupped in those dovelike moving seas,
And our paternal homestead where exuberant
Brothers and silent sisters met every morning
To exhibit all ways of courtesy.
We were passionate in those days. Our parents
Condoned no dishonesties and personal indecencies.

Recalling all this before the hour of midnight,
I remembered you, brother, and hoped you
Could watch with me the splendid glide
Of limousines in this street, and in that other,
The long parade of hungry working men
That approached my window at dawn to remind
Me once again of the coughing orbit of life
In this strange land, their loved country.

We didn't have the poet's vision of the hangman's
Dream to twist the whole of living on our finger,
But in those islands, under familiar trees we spoke
Of the littlest things with the simplest joys.
There were no books and hard intellectual thoughts,
But we grew into manhood with the music of trees
In our hearts that would not break, breaking
At last to the barrenness of hard city streets.

Gelett Burgess

Ballad Of The Hyde Street Grip

A San Francisco Rhapsody

Oh, the rain is slanting sharply, and the Norther's blowing cold,
When the cable strands are loosened, she is nasty hard to hold;
There's little time for sitting down and little time for gab,
For the bumper guards the crossing, and you'd best be keeping tab!
Two-and-twenty "let's go's" every double trip—
It takes a bit of doing, on the Hyde Street Grip!

Throw her off at Powell Street, let her go at Post,
Watch her well at Geary and at Sutter, when you coast,

Easy at the Power House, have a care at Clay,
Sacramento, Washington, Jackson, all the way!
Drop the rope at Union, never make a slip—
The lever keeps you busy, on the Hyde Street Grip!

Foot-brake, wheel-brake, slot-brake and gong,
You've got to keep 'em working, or you'll soon be going wrong!
Rush her on the crossing, catch her on the rise,
Easy round the corners, when the dust is in your eyes!
And the bell will always stop you, if you hit her up a clip—
You are apt to earn your wages, on the Hyde Street Grip!

North Beach to Tenderloin, over Russian Hill,
The grades are something giddy, and the curves are fit to kill!
All the way to Market Street, climbing up the slope,
Down upon the other side, hanging to the rope;
But the sight of San Francisco, as you take the lurching dip!
There is plenty of excitement, on the Hyde Street Grip!

Oh, the lights are in the Mission, and ships are in the Bay;
And Tamalpais is looming from the Gate, across the way;
The Presidio trees are waving, and the hills are growing brown,
And the driving fog is harried from the Ocean to the town!
How the pulleys slap and rattle! How the cables hum and whip!
Oh, they sing a gallant chorus, on the Hyde Street Grip!

When the Orpheum is closing, and the crowd is on the way,
The conductor's punch is ringing, and the dummy's light and gay;
But the wait upon the table by the Beach is dark and still—
Just the swashing of the surges on the shore below the mill;
And the flash of Angel Island breaks across the channel rip,
As the hush of midnight falls upon the Hyde Street Grip!

The Peculiar History Of The Chewing-Gum Man

O Willie, an' Wallie, an' Huldy Ann,
They went an' built a big CHEWIN'-GUM MAN:
It was none o' your teenty little dots,
With pinhole eyes an' pencil-spots;
But this was a terribul big one—well,

'T was a'most as high as the Palace Hotel!
It took 'em a year to chew the gum!!
And Willie he done it all, 'cept some
That Huldy got her ma to chew,
By the time the head was ready to do

*　　*　　*　　*

Well, Willie he chewed it for days 'n' days;
They brung it to him in gret big drays;
An' fast as he got it good an' soft,
Then Wallie he come and carried it oft.
Then he'd roll it into a great big ball,
An' he made a-more 'n a MILLION in all!
Then Huldy Ann she spanked 'em flat
An' pinched an' poked, an' the like o' that.
Till she got it inter a gret big hunk—
My! did n't Huldy have the spunk!
And then she sliced one end half-way
To make the laigs ('cause they never stay
When you stick 'em on in a seprit piece—
Seems like the ends was made o' grease);
And she slit an arm right up each side,—
I could n't a done it if I'd a tried!
O' course, her brothers they helped her, though,
An' rolled the arms an' laigs out, so
They all was smooth with roundin' bends
An' *chopped* the fingers inter the ends!
An' when their mother had chewn the head,
She went an' *stuck* it on, instead!
An' then, when the man was almost done,
They had an awful lots o' fun.
A-walkin' down his stummick was best
To make the buttons onter his vest!
They struck big cartwheels in him for eyes;
His eyes was both tremendous size;
His nose was a barrel—an' then beneath
They used a ladder, to make his teeth!
An' when he was layin' acrost the street
Along come their daddy, as whit 's a sheet,—

He was skeert half outer his wits, I guess,
An' he did n't know whatter make o' the mess,—
But Huldy she up an' begun to coax
To have him down town, to skeer the folks!
So her dad he grabbed him offen the street,
An' Willie an' Wallie they took his feet,
An' they dragged him clean down to the Cogswell fountain,
An' stood him up as big as a mountain!
You 'd orter seen him a-standin' there,
A-straddlin' Market street in the air!

Well, he stood up straight for a week 'n' a half
An' the folks, Gee! did n't they yell 'n' laff:
The boys clum up his laigs quite bold—
The gum was so soft they got good hold;
The cars run under him day an' night,
An' the people come miles to see the sight!
Well, after he'd stayed as stiff 's a post,
With his head on top o' the roofts almost,
The sun come outer the fog one day
An'—well, I guess you can see the way
That gret big feller begun to melt;—
Imagine how Willie and Wallie felt!
For first he cocked his head out some,
An' when the heat got inter the gum
He slowly waved his arms ahead
An' slanted forred, just like he was dead!

Edward Cain

Forget-Me-Not

To flourish around my native bower
    And blossom around my cot,
I cultivate a little flower
    That's called forget-me-not.

The ocean may between us roll,
    And distance be our lot,
I hope that we may meet again;
    I pray, Forget-me-not.

So adieu! Some happy day
    When we shall meet again,
May the fragrant breeze of summer bear
    The fragrance of the glen.

May every bright-winged, singing bird
    Plume themselves in song;
So short would seem our summer's day,
    We wish it still more long.

Adieu, adieu! your little stars
    Are twinkling one by one,
When the moon comes out to take the place
    Left vacant by the sun.

When all the stars grow dim
    They cannot pierce her light;
How proud and beautiful she is,
    My dearest friend, good-night.

Sadie H. Calbert

The Dog And The Cat

The dog said to the cat, "I don't like you."
Said the cat to the dog, "same from me to you!"
Said the dog to the cat, "you run around the house,
Trying to catch a poor little mouse."
Said the cat to the dog, "*you* have a bad habit,
Of chasing after a frightened rabbit."
So they had a cat and dog fight,
With each one insisting that he was right,
Each putting on the other the blame,
And explaining his own fault by another name.

The Pig

This is a greedy little pig,
    His appetite is very big.
When in the trough he puts his snout.
    He really hates to take it out!

The Elephant

I'm a great big wrinkled elephant,
This long thing is really relevant;
For it doubles as a nose,
And sprays out water like a hose.

When its tip is going south,
It will put food in my mouth.
And if it is transportation you lack,
Will put you safely on my back.

Bob Callahan

The Dream

I awoke this morning
with a sense of another world
a world where my heart
had started beating again.

It was a sweet world
a Moonlit world where a beautiful
Welsh girl with short red hair
flashed her eyes, laughed,
flashed her thighs
and bid me into the moonlit forest

I awoke this morning
with a sense of a sweet world

a world where my heart
had started beating again
and bid me to the enchanted forest.

Faith

> What is the meaning of number?
> What is the measure of rhyme?
>
> How many feet to a pyramid?
> How many megaliths to an inch?
>
> Who is Pythagoras, and why?
> Who is actually counting the years.

Go ask your Father, Boy, the Elders say, he's the only Irish in these here parts who knows how to play those old scales.

He sees his Old Man moving in the den. Six times six. Ten times ten. Pure motion. Reels and Airs are singing through the Philco. A sound wall becomes a snow storm. It swirls. The ghosts of all their ancestors join his father in his room.

> Now which one is that, Boy.
> Pitch perfect his father whistles the tune.
> It's Yeats', Father, or the answer is Twelve, or

perhaps it's O'Donovan's March – I don't know, Pop. This morning I feel confused.

> One, Two, Three.
> One, Two, Three.
> Again, Boy.
> (Gently)
> A Druid must know all these things.

Eileen Callahan

a torn shard of hair
a tear
a woman weeping, wailing
rail again
a woman weeping

       (in the heart is carried
        the half-moon appears / crescent
        by day
        at night
        turns,
        bowl-like
        filled with
        darkness
        light,
        mid-month mid-moon mid-tide
        pull /
              (mid-sea.

a woman weeping
wails
rails at the gate
of horn, of amber, of amethyst
the stone is locked in setting
the gate cannot be passed
this moon
this light
this life of decency / a long life
bitter and lovely
all at once.

December, 1976

The Shape Of The Body, Earth,
As Revealed By The Prophet Ezekiel

This is common enough, future

*

It reveals by increments which have more *danger*
than the common,
whole

*

As though the extra–ordinary
pertained

*

We are in the employ of gods
who have no ritual
                        (enactment

*

Children are the metaphor of promise:
Nothing is revealed.
We ask, only.

*

Attention must be paid.

*

Moon–dreams lead to madness;
Earth–roots are what sustain.

*

The romance is kindled by the voice in the dark;
nothing grows in that aire.

*

We have known this: It has been spoken.

> (the body, of loam
>   the clouds, surround

*

It is not easy
to walk the earth

Raymond T. Chandler

The Fairy King

Where the white owl guards the fir,
Where the woody silence falls,
Where the branches as they stir
Seem to lisp low madrigals,
There the fairy king is seen
On his throne of evergreen.

Where the brooklets coursing far
Musics choirless proclaim,
Tidings of a sylvan war,
Messages of rustic fame,
There the fairy king's commands
Travel to his loyal bands.

Where the hill-top greets the wind,
Rising from the sleep of earth,
And the hoary rock reclined
Dreams of buried tears and mirth,
There the fairy king goes up
With the queenly moon to sup.

Where the mossy cavern lies
Hidden in a nook of green,
And the jack-o'-lantern flies

Through the thicket lightly seen,
There the fairy king is laid
Sleeping in a dewy shade.

Where the foamy chargers stride
Out upon the windy deep,
Where the tempests in their pride
Spoils of mortal terror reap,
There he sails uncounted miles
To the far, enchanted isles.

Where the pale laburnums block
Sight unlawful from his porch,
And upon the quivering stalk
Climbs the glow-worm with his torch,
There he comes at night to hold
Levées of his chieftains bold.

Where the spectre-lights are lit
And the solemn caves of death,
And the misty mourners flit
Bearing many a cypress wreath,
There he lies in magic vault,
Casketed in ocean salt.

The Clay God

Clay God, what brood'st thou in the dust and mould
Of this dark temple and deserted fane?
What wither'd fantasies of power old?
What ancient tales of mystery and pain?
What secrets that shall nevermore be told?
What phantoms that shall never walk again?

What music of a ghostly dulcimer,
Or chanting of a cowled spectre-priest
Hear'st thou in this old shrine where many a tear
Fell to thee once, and left thee unappeas'd?
Thou art forsaken of all human fear,
And from thee yearning hath forever ceas'd.

Deep-sunken is thy once far-glaring eye,
Where the years a vengeance on thy cunning wreak.
Sad moonbeams banish'd from the living sky
Lie on the curve of thy once sacred cheek,
Like wraiths of beauty that, when love is by,
Fall in the dust no more to move or speak.

Old blacken'd lamp-chains hang about thy head
Stirr'd by the swaying of a mournful breeze
That gropeth in thy kingdom of the dead
Some memory of a fair, lost day to seize,
Until it too in ruin cold is laid
And roams no more at any storm's decrees.

Brood on, with silence for the pale reward
And pardon of thy misty centuries!
Brood on, no thundrous battle may retard
Thy dusty rule and thy uncourted ease!
Brood on, thou hast no comfort for the bard
As from the terror of the night he flees!

For thee all kings on golden thrones that sit
Are as wan vapours of the twilight lone.
For thee desire is a lamp unlit,
And ages like to distant waters run.
Silent thou read'st the page which thou hast writ
Needing no eyes and careless of the sun.

Chantecler

Los Que "Ya Pasan"

Los que hace tiempo habitamos
en esta orilla ex-mojada
del Bravo, constantemente
llevamos en las espaldas
la pena de aquel sujeto
que a dos pasos contemplaba

las claras linfas de un río,
en tanto que sus entrañas,
de la sed por los ardores
fieramente se quemaban,
sin que él pudiere llegarse
a beber el agua clara,
porque de firme cadena
su cuerpo sujeto estaba.

Tal nos hallamos nosotros:
nomás a unas cuantas brazas
de aquí, se halla nuestro México,
nuestra República amada;
pero nos está vedado
cruzar el Bravo y pisarla,
porque somos... lo que somos:
"los de la pelea pasada"
Y para aumentar las penas
de esta tan corta distancia
que a pesar de ser tan corta
nos resulta más que larga,
oímos continuamente
que a nuestro lado se exclama
por los hombres-gacetillas
que en ninguna parte faltan:
"¿No sabe usted, don Narciso,
que Petronilo "ya pasa"
porque le arregló su asunto
don Serapio de la Garza?"
¿No sabe usted que don Cleto
se marcha por las mañanas
"al otro lado", y el dia
tranquilamente se pasa
visitando "los cantones"
que le recuerdan su infancia?
Pues es la verdad: don Cleto
ya no se apura por nada;
tiene un lindo pasaporte,
un "sésamo ábrete", vaya,
con el que tres o más veces
a Nuevo Laredo pasa.

Y aquel otro, chaparrito,
que unas veces usa barba
y bigotes a la Kaiser,
que, cuando el huertismo, estaba
reclutando voluntarios
para enviarlos a las armas;
el mismo que hace dos meses
contra don Venus Carranza
si léxico "reaccionario"
con toda furia lanzaba;
que en favor de Félix Díaz
firmó la "beligerancia",
que era, en fin, más reaccionario
que Emeterio de la Garza;
este, ya olvidó sus penas
y sus rencillas pasadas,
y tiene su pasaporte,
y es, en fin, de los "que pasan"
    Y aquel otro, licenciado
de don Pancho de la Barra;
y el otro, que era en Coahuila
casi la "divina garza"
cuando estaba don Pragedis
moviendo la comalada;
todos al redil han vuelto,
todos por el puente pasan
"al otro lado", y "se mojan"
a su sabor... y no en agua.

                    *

    Y los pobres "pecadores"
a quienes la excelsa gracia
de la gente carrancista
ni queriendo les alcanza,
miran con ojos muy tristes
a los felices "que pasan",
a los que su pasaporte
con mucho cuidado guardan...
    Y yo los contemplo a todos,

y apunto a los que "se rajan"
sólo por cruzar el puente
por la noche y la mañana,
y exclamo: Si era lo lógico;
si aqui en su centro no estaban;
si deben estar con ellos...
con los hombres de Carranza!

El Heraldo de Mexico
Los Angeles, California
19 de novembre de 1919

Those Who Now "Cross Over"

Translated by M.B. Anderson

   We who for awhile now have lived
on this ex-wet(back) shore
of the Bravo[1]; constantly
carry on our shoulders
the pain of that fellow
who from a few steps away contemplated
the clear waters of a river,
at the same time his guts
were fiercely burning up
with the longings of thirst
without his being able to approach
the clear water
in order to take a drink
because of the solid chain
which held his body
under its control.
   Thus we find ourselves:
No more than a stone's throw
from here, our Mexico is located,
our beloved Republic;
but it is forbidden for us
to cross the Bravo and tread over there,

---

[1]River which divides México and the U.S.,
Known as the Rio Grande in the U.S.

because we are ... what we are is:
"those of the past struggle."
And in order to increase the hardships
of this very short distance,
that in spite of being so short
ends up for us longer than long,
we continuously hear right beside us,
the exclamations of the town gossips
who can be found everywhere:
"Don't you know, don Narcisco,
that Petronilo now "crosses over"
because don Serapio de la Garza
arranged his case for him?"
"Don't you know that don Cleto
goes over in the mornings
"to the other side," and spends the day
calmly visiting the spots
which remind him of his childhood?
Well, it's true: don Cleto
doesn't worry about anything anymore;
he has a fine passport,
an "open sesame,"
with which he's gone over
to Nuevo Laredo three or more times.
And that other one, Shorty,
who sometimes makes use of a beard
and mustache like the Kaiser,
who, when Huerta was in power, was
recruiting volunteers
to send them to rebel;
the same one who, two months ago
launched his "reactionary" vocabulary
with great fury
against don Venus Carranza
who signed the "belligerance"
in aid of Félix Días
who was, in fact, more reactionary
than Emeterio de la Garza;
this guy has already forgotten his troubles
and his past grudges

and has his passport,
and is, no less, one of those who "crosses over."
    And that other one, the lawyer
for don Pancho de la Barra;
and the other one, who was in Coahuila
almost the "divine heron"
when don Pragedis
was stirring up trouble.
They've all returned to the fold,
they all cross over the bridge
"to the other side," and "get themselves wet"
each to his own taste . . . and not in the water.
    And the poor "sinners"
who don't even care to be touched
by the sublime grace
of the Carrancista[2] people, watching with very sad eyes
the happy ones who "cross over,"
those who guard their passports very carefully . . .
    And I observe them all,
and I make note of those who back down
only to cross the bridge
at night or in the morning,
and I exclaim: "If only it were logical;
if they weren't here in the middle;
if they ought to be with them . . .
with Carranza's men!"

---

[2]followers of Carranza

Amanda M. Chase

Broken Rhythms
In a Mexican Labor Camp

"La Golondrina"
Thrummed
To a lame-stringed guitar.

Soft-eyed women
With plaited braids
At soggy tubs.
No gurgling dips
In flowing streams
To naiad laughter.

Metreless brown hands
Shaping limp *tortillas*
From grocery flour.
Lost the old tuned
Spat! Spat!
Of pestled corn.

Fierce gas flames
Scorching *frijoles*.
No long soft glows
Of charcoal, fanned
To long slow thoughts.

Behold that once-schoolmaster,
Slight-built and scholarly,
Nodding workworn
Over Spanish poems.

Note that carver of images
Whose dream-troubled eyes
Study with rue
His stiff track-mending hands.

Broken rhythms
All their craft and art.
Tune–lost their lives.
In exile.

America,
Can you give them
New Music?

Buriel Clay II

Memories #2

Yesterday we went kite flying
It felt so good
Enjoying the complexities of being a father
Like the great task of choosing the right
Color twine
Not that we had to match the color of the kite
Or any adult things like that
She just liked the way yellow twine looked

Yesterday we went kite flying
It felt so good
For the first time I was being given instructions
On the intricasies of maintaining a kite in flight
By this little fawn eyed four year old
You've got to tug on the twine periodically
Look, like this, otherwise it'll come crashing down
You've got to, Daddy, they said so on Sesame Street

Yesterday I went kite flying
It felt so good
But it hurt so bad
Realizing all the things about
Being a daddy I didn't know about

Consuelo Rosado Colton

Like Ocean Waves

If you should face the ocean
    And watch the break of day,
You'd see the waves dash on the shore
    And how they romp and play.
There are tiny ones and big ones too;
    And all are foamy white.
They chase each other to the beach,
    And on it spend their might.

'Way out you spy no ripples,
    But suddenly you see,
A great big wave come bouncing in,
    So happy to be free!
Then comes a wave unnoticed
    And spreads upon the sand,
And though it splashes lightly,
    It brings shells to land.

So with the playful breakers
    Our lives we shall compare.
Their splash—our happy moments,
    Our joys—the shells so rare.
And when life's waves leave sorrow
    And tears in their wake,
On life they've cast a shadow
    And hearts just seem to break.

Yet—like the mighty oceans,
    With waves so big and high,
We have our ups and downs—my dear,
    As time goes fleeting by.
And though our hopes sometimes are lost
    Upon a rocky shore,
Like ocean waves—we must not stop—
    But learn to hope some more.

Conyus

upon leaving the parole board hearing

deer feed on
the green slopes
in the
chestnut roam
of evening

spring again
faces me
beneath the bleeding
slash of redwood

trees in bloom
hollow bodies pendant
flowers in the moss

paths of sand
shafts of light
winding in & out
of shadows
to the summit

then descend
to the valley
like evening
ocean mist

clinging
to lost
horizons
i

Ina Coolbrith

Alone

The night comes on with a hint of tears,
    The in-borne fog with the in-borne tide;
And the last faint crimson disappears
    Where the sunset glory died.

And the wet blue hills in the mist are lost,
    The skies grow gray in the daylight-wane,
And the waning moon, like a wan, white ghost,
    Looks in at the window-pane;

A phantom light in the shifting wind,
    A wandering specter of the sky—
As one, of all the stars un-kinned,
    Apart and lone as I.

Haunted

The water, lapping, lapping in the reeds!
What stood beside it in the waning moon
And gave to it the sigh and sob of tears?
The sound of tears that nevermore is still—
The water lapping, lapping in the reeds.

    Was it a shadow there?
Or but the thin mist shifting in the wind
    Beneath the paling moon
    Of night's mid-noon?
Only the mist that like a thin white wraith,
    Seen and unseen—
    A white wan wraith
Beside the matted rushes of the pool
    That lies below the hill?
    Lies like a thing of ill,

Its slow dark waters lapping in the reeds,
    With sigh and sob of tears—
With sound of tears that never can be still,
The water lapping, lapping in the reeds.

Woman

What were this human
World without woman?
Think—just a minute!—
Without one in it—
A Man-Eden only,
Wretched and lonely.
True, there's a story
Scarce to her glory
Therewith connected,
But 'tis suspected
Man, after all,
Was quite ready to fall!
If fault, he condoned it—
And through the years since,
Eva has atoned it.

Woman! Be honor
Ever upon her,
Whether as maiden,
Shy, beauty-laden—
Daughter, wife, sister,
Who can resist her?
Or as that other
And greater, the Mother,
Her babe—blossoms moulding
To perfect unfolding—
The home-temple guarding
To richest rewarding.

Though none be purer,
Sweeter and surer,
Avenues wider

Now open beside her.
Each day some new way!
God send the true way
She may seek ever
With earnest endeavor.
Here to the dark, a light!
Here to the wrong, the right!
There the truth sifting!
A soul, here, uplifting!
Patient, prevailing,
With purpose unfailing,
Till at Life's portal
Through Love immortal,
Supremely she stands,
The *World* in her hands.

Woman! All honor
And blessing upon her!
Knowing her truly,
Knowing her fully,
All her completeness,
Tenderness, sweetness—
Though there be times, too,
Sweet hardly rhymes to,
All of the changes
Through which she ranges,
Moods, tenses, phases,
I sing her praises. ·

Antonio C. Correa

To An Ex-Soldier

You, who once were young and brave:
Where is that peace you fought to save?
What has become of every aim
Which once the joyous did acclaim?
You lie beneath the earth in rest:

You are the one who has been blest.
In quiet solitude you lie
While all the world goes thund'ring by.

A bitter smile rests on your face
As you lie watching from your place
You have a right now to proclaim:
"Have we who died all died in vain?"
What happens now you do not care;
For "peace" you fought—now you lie there.
You did your part as best you knew;
Are we, the living, failing you?

For Peddlers, Solicitors, And Agents

I warn you once;
I warn you twice, begone!
   I warn you thrice,
   In still a louder tone.
      But, if you feel
      You still must ring this bell,
         I hope you'll go
         Where you'll be sent—
            To, well....
            Just ring this bell.

Jayne Cortez

Rose Solitude

I am Essence of Rose Solitude
my cheeks are laced with cognac
my hips sealed with five satin nails
I carry dreams and romance of new fools and old flames
between the musk of fat
and the side pocket of my mink tongue

90

Listen to champagne bubble from this solo

Essence of Rose Solitude
veteran from texas tiger   from chicago   that's me
i cover the shrine of Duke
who like Satchmo   like Nat (King) Cole
will never die because love they say
never dies

I tell you from stair steps of these navy blue nights
these metallic snakes
these flashing fish skins
and the melodious cry of Shango
surrounded by sorrow
by purple velvet tears
by cockhounds limping from crosses
from turtle-skinned shoes
from diamond-shaped skulls and canes
made from dead gazelles
wearing a face of wilting potato plants
of grey and black scissors
of bee bee shots and fifty red boils
yes the whole world loved him

I tell you from suspenders of two timing dog odors
from inca frosted lips
nonchalant legs   i tell you from
howling chant of sister Erzulie
and the exaggerated hearts of a hundred pretty women
they loved him this world sliding from a single flower
into a caravan of heads made into ten thousand flowers

Ask me
Essence of Rose Solitude
chickadee from arkansas that's me
i sleep on cotton bone
cotton tails
and mellow myself in empty ballrooms
i'm no fly by night
look at my resume

i walk through the eyes of staring lizards
i throw my neck back to floorshow on bumping goat skins
in front of my stage fright
I cover the hands of Duke who like Satchmo like
Nat (King) Cole will never die because love they say
never dies

Anna Rozilla Crever

To Roland Hayes - Singing

In silken filaments
Your voice falls wide
Upon a blur of faces
Rapt and fair.
I am entangled—
Gossamer has tied;
I might escape,
But find the net too rare.

And now I am enchained
By ringing thirds,
Sweeping from lyric deeps
Where soul begins.
I'm taken captive
By your silver words:
O Necromancer,
Yours are lovely sins!

Weave not too fine a mesh
Out of your song;
Hide not too deep
With veiled tones my grief,
Lest in my ecstasy
I do life wrong,
And dream it always bud,
And always leaf!

A Woman's Tear

O what completeness in a woman's tear—
The whole of life is mirrored in its sphere.
I see an arch of promise shining there,
And broken shaft of crystalline despair.

There sparkles joy, there quivers keenest pain,
Clear jewel that so near the heart has lain,
Mined with the sharp edge of a poignant grief,
And rounded to perfection past belief!

Pearls of life's passion gathered fathoms down
Where joy with sorrow strives but does not drown—
'Tis from the soul's unrest comes beauty's ease,
And gems more lovely than from Indian seas!

Stanley Crouch

Lester

What I saw was so sweet
so high up in the air:
soft long tones
the colors of another home:
The soft: the blossoms of the air,
fragile, all things
but eternal, strong
          — also with that
dark entrancing
gentility of that black woman
or that beginner brown
talk also about a high yellow
don't leave her out:
Each one a tender stove.
And babies and beer,
put that in there too
Sue Sue Sue

Sweet Sue
or me leapin in,
a dancer,
a brown leaf in control of itself,
a part of the Tree of God
drunk or not, sleep or not
staggering if I want to.

But knowin I can dance
all the while.
Knowin *I* can dance.

Eusebio Howard y Cruz

Disenchanted

Like all boys, John cherished illusions.
Like most boys, John heard a call.
Like some boys, John heeded it.
So, he went to the other world—beyond Suez—
Where inhibition soon evaporates,
Where sun, and dampness, and dis-ease
Destroy the brain of intruders.

Like all men, John killed his illusions.
Like most men, John grew callous.
Like some men, John came back.
He returned from beyond, still heeding the call
Of his better self, ever intense,
Ever questing, ever pursuing,
Under the slag of indulgence.

Like all adults, John regretted the past.
Like most adults, John resented his folly.
Like some adults, John reformed.
Then he found hollowness, instead of solidity.
He foud hypocrisy, instead of truth,

He found fraud, instead of honesty,
And nausea from others' smugness.

And John went back to the spring blossoms of his iniquity,
To the truth of his abjection,
To the fact of nullity.
Illusions stayed lost.
The veil was rent.
But, John was content
Till his life was spent.

Victor Hernandez Cruz

Califomow

Winter in the sky and in the mind
Here we are in California
Researching the stars
California where the weather is
A fine balance broken by an
Overdose of rain around January
Sometimes February in and around
Those months it sneaks in
We are in winter and it gets cold
But to for what should it bother
I still remember the devil
Streets which looked as if a
avalanche of cocaine had come down
Upon them and the wind moving
Through them
Upsetting the snow
The snow frozen
Freezing you
Not in cool delicate califos
Where nature mas suave
Naturing naturolizando what
ever that thing that dances inside
Of us outside of us inside of us

Califonia bicycles y cosas
Deciphering codes
In doors in houses apartments
Which are outside along with the
Elementos
Facing the sky the top of this
very house is my head
Where el mundo resides recites
Messages that have clearly risen
On the horizon
As for one who remembers mountains
and streams on the streets of
The lower east side of Manhattan
It is easy now to smell the smoke
Seeing it take forms when my
Eyes are close inside gentle
Clear water creeks   on top of tar
Roof tops connecting with / con con
Roofs and tar and glass con roofs
Y fires escapos con estars more con
the mas of ConEdison who isn't my
Uncle nor do I have such desires
As for one who remembers mountains
before California or the Lower East
Side
    I contemplate contemplate
    Contumbao   Califonow
    Not forever winter
Not forever anything at all.

Esplendoriendote, Aun

A soft movement for your memory
Glistening legs   powder cinnamon
or white
Something shiny like wood rubbed
with cream
All softly united like the idea
of a danza a danzon not calvary

Music exciting a football
Softly and like a frog
Squeak if you wanna squeak
Scratch me gently
my forehead
inside like a Kodak color
projector
In tradition and out of it
is called the fountainhead
Where you receive evidence
Scratch it there to see yourself
while I eat your eyebrows
Don't frown or be crazy
Light a candle in the four corners
if you want
Slowly and clearly
sight arrested by your semi colon
          ;
Nothing can stop the curve
of me and you jumping
Making sense
Tonight
In California coconut trees
without coconuts
Fall and break sweetly
It's oil that I rub into your
question mark in English?
And in Spanish the question
comes upside down and is found
Entering the sentence and leaving
it at the end
¿ ?

El Camino Irreal

Spanish lesson number one:
S/ES
or backwards.

Artie Cuelho

Wheatville Trucking Blues

for brother Gene

Well, Gene came around
smoking his old cigar down;
one look in his eye—I knew
that Freightliner was gonna fly.

Hey get up on that Mack,
Pick up on all that slack,
I got the Wheatville trucking blues.

Well, Gene's got a tire to fix,
the Jimmy's losing oil bad in Conejo;
but the two-way said to wait on the leak,
that the digger's broke down at Cantua Creek.

Hey, gotta go, get that welding done
or we'll be at it from sun to sun,
I got the Wheatville trucking blues.

Well, Gene came back to the shop,
put his hand on a beet box;
T said Lord God I got some fishing to do,
Gene said hell I think your through.

Hey get after them loads of grain,
roll it like a long prairie train,
I got them Wheatville trucking blues.

San Joaquin Valley

Early May barley,
yellow mixed with green,
and tossed by the wind.

The tangled hair of grain
lying flat between the levies.

Another morning depot:
"Don't ask me where."
A plowed stubble field.
A barn. San Joaquin River.
Quail in an olive orchard.
A Mexican irrigator's stare.

Green grape vines,
row corn being irrigated,
pasture grass with dairy cows.
A fertilizer truck. Onions.
A valley town. Sugar beet dump.
Bamboo clumps. A tule canal.
Peach trees. A dove on the wing.
A tractor cultivating weeds.
A row of palm trees. Wild oats.
A headgate; a chicken hawk.
Downhome family cotton choppers.
99 business route. A walnut grove.

In an alfalfa patch,
a lone tree by a well,
symbol for my younger brother?

Beverly Dahlen

The Occupation

1

The interior colonies.
The flat landlocked sky.
One tree against it.
Horses.
The women and children surrounded.
The old men crippled on the road.

My father at home naming all the vegetables
growing in his garden. My brother camped
with his wife and child in the mountains.
The forests burning.
My father's voice on the telephone naming
*crookneck squash   zucchini squash   corn
tomatoes   cucumbers* . . .

I say the road has been closed for five days
on account of the fires. Several towns
have been evacuated. My mother says
it's because of the weather. I say
the weather has nothing to do with it.
She says maybe I need vitamin B.
I say I feel fine. I ask her
how is my grandmother. She says
she's home from the hospital.
She has cancer. She doesn't know.
No one has told her. No one says the word
dying.

My grandmother pushed to the sea.
All the way from Nebraska. Surrounded.
Refugee. Her back to the mountains.
Burning.

2

Black water in Oregon.
The Tualatin River
under a left-handed sky.
The crows in my father's garden
pick and gnaw. He talks.
The rat he shot in the backyard
beneath the willow tree. Wood chopped.
Axe-man. His traps in the old days
on Sauvies Island. Two-bits an otter skin.
The way we lived then.

My mother says daddy fix-it. Don't throw a thing
away. Oh yes. You bet your life. Your dad.
He knows.

There they are. In the country,
Cornstalks cut and plowed under
for the winter. Apples piled up
in the garage. Everything in order.
Eating and dying.

My gramma laid out the frown gone.
Her face still tan to the line
the scarf came. Dressed in a yellow suit
I'd never seen. Curled her thin hair.
How they talk. She passed away.
Gone in the rainy air.

And because she's gone
my sister and brother come flying
and I come overland
to see the country again. North
across the border in the middle of the night.
Medford   Grant's Pass   Roseburg   Eugene.
Pick-ups with gunracks. Going up
the hills for their bucks. Food.
How we talk.   Clams.   Fish.   Ducks.

My brother says K. Falls. Warm springs.
Going hunting. Shoot all the geese
in the world.

What a killing. How we talk.
All we ate. Everything
so good. You bet your life.

   3

Passed away. Back down the Willamette Valley
at sunset. Moon in the night.
Sleeping raggedly. Going south for the winter.
Black heart back there at the mouth
of the river. Can't breathe. Chains of bridges
at Portland. She's gone under out to sea.

A turning. In the mountains.
We've come a long way. The ends of the earth.

Thick fog in the valleys.
Here I carry you.
These dead animals.
These raw horns and heads.
The bloody hunchbacked rivers of Oregon.
The moon going down in the west.

Here I carry you alone sleeping
over the border to California
the bones of my crossed hands
in my lap and no words at all in my mouth

and come home in the morning
to my own house.

August—October, 1973

Betsy Davids

A Field Of Pumpkins Grown For Seed

What comes out this birthday weekend
like a sudden squash
is my shying harmony.

There was no speaking out
this garden summering, its unmouthed
solitary green balances & tabled calm.
It was a sweet unpeopling
& lambskin unlament, tended
not for myself but not
for others either:
for the blank balance of it.

Only now a mowing flute probes in,
lacing into the quiet halt
as blister wear.

102

How can I explain the white death of personality,
how ambulanced I was, & how
a loyal crocodile awaited me
in vegetable sleeps.
I know too well what tears mean
was my saying, so
I met my friends truly empty,
pleased & vacant, filled
with something not quite self,
pink & not a heart.

Old friends to whom I scarcely spoke, this weekend's gathering
now must be my stumble out of harmony.

I picked the teeth of solitude
to find the bite, a second navel,
marking 32nd birthday skin.

Pumpkin-plumped I am presented for the carving.

I will enter my 33rd year
carrying a plate of crocodile tears,
again to strain through teeth the shifting loyalties,
ready again to enter into
broken words.

4th November Rain Dance, With A Difference

a fall when all the myths i thought were mine
fell together in me
& it was another special person's season.

i felt it like a wedge of solid light
that forced an opening in me.

it was the rare familiar unfamiliar grace.
i felt it like itself, & then i felt it
like the other times, like
all the myths i thought were mine
coming around to call the season theirs

& the grave confusing rain began.

i face you off now, other moving faces of myself.
you can't have this one.
no repeat annunciation, repeat pieta,
no repeat romantic love & tragic love,
collective potencies pre-packaged.
you crowd now like blunt landlords come to claim
all common ground. this time you bring
an overstated case, this heavy anniversary,
your champagne strongbox. you have
your own consistency, not mine.
a wedge of sponge cake where
the wedge of light should be.

this time, may i refuse my old rain dances?
a face so new i couldn't memorize it
is dissolving into rainfall. this is not
the apt transfiguration.
this stamping on pre-plotted ground.
a face so streaked with newness
so unplotted
that i have to look again
through wetted lashes now to see
the special opening, the moving empty place
lit up by the world & radiant
where the season is its own mythographer.

this fall i have begun to be in sun.
"in sun" like "in love", with a difference.
the difference is the growing point.
all else is beside the point.

i face you now. i claim the difference.

Michael Davidson

Untitled

I am watching the vanguard move in,
it speaks from the everywhere it has left
and it takes everyone by surprise
even though they have waited for spring
for a thousand years; we need it
and its winds will raise the hair on our necks
before any leaf has begun to quiver;
already the melody is heard in the violins
and the swimming which precedes drowning
is entertained from the bridge;
"More room!" he cries to the empty covenants
where the lightning flashes over the plain,
a great grey front with hunched shoulders
sends all of the fathers scurrying like ants
from a flooded ant hole; the grammar
displaces families instantly upon contact; I am
not afraid of its words or the power of connection
by which the sky is mottled and the sea is grey;
I am waiting while the last red carnations
drag their heads, forgetting all they call
to mind in my grandmother's memory,
they are the last
and the fiction of their scent
has made her faint with joy
for the first and last time,
now she is speaking from Nova Scotia, from England,
from Ireland and where will she go next?

Untitled

Often he felt uncomfortable about the way it would come out.
When it came out in the wash he felt awful
but when she misinterpreted what he said
it began a lasting relationship.

They told him if it didn't come out
he should take something soothing
but when it came out without their telling him anything
he should take something solid.
When it came out solid she called him a good boy
and made him eat sweet potatoes which he hated.
When it came out in the news they didn't believe it
but after it was out for a while
it was just what they thought all along.
And when it came out that it was coming out of everyone
they began to run for their lives.
Soon it will come out in the waters and upon the rivers
and someone can dredge it and spread it all over the land
to bring out flowers and all manner of good things to eat.
If it comes out before it's called premature,
if it comes out after it is called patience which is a virtue,
if it comes out at all it's what was intended
and tends to refer back to the one speaking.
Coming out describes the way of coming into the world
and they are all waiting to find out what you will be
so that when you are out they will know how to call you
standing out in the rain with a friend.
At night the stars come out and the lights come on
but no one thinks of the blackness that comes out of the sunset
like a well with no cover
and the vipers and bats and lizards come out of nowhere
which is a word out of which other words come out.
When you grow up you grow out of puberty
but when it is too late you are growing out of your mind.
In the beginning was the word and when it was out
there was a space projected like a little star
out of which all the light we have ever seen came pouring
one word at a time.

Winifred Davidson

Irish

When I was born a wicked fay, for daft ends of his own,
Fetched this red land a changeling that he stole from blue Athlone.
Else why should laughter on my lips be crony to a tear?
Else why should my heart quake with joy when Irish words I hear?

There's Irish sorrow in my blood—I had an Irish nurse!
I know the exile's old lament; I know the renter's curse.
Though ne'er I saw an Irish child barefooted in the rain,
If I met up with one, I'd say, "There comes meself again!"

These eyes have never seen the skies that smile o'er Bantry Bay.
These ears have never heard the roar of surf along Galway,
These nostrils never knew the smell of Sligo's fresh-cut sods,
But I could sup with my heart's kin from Glengad Head to Cods.

For well I know an Irish heart is lifting in my breast,
Though I saw day far from moist Eire in the arid West.
There's Irish music haunting me—wild lilting strains unsung;
There's Irish in my dancing heels, brogue Irish on my tongue.

Diane di Prima

Revolutionary Letter #61

Take a good look
at history (the American myth)
check sell out
of revolution by the founding fathers
"Constitution written by a bunch of gangsters
to exploit a continent" is what
                    Charles Olson told me.
Check Shay's rebellion, Aaron Burr, Nathan Hale.
Who wrote the history books where *you*

                              went to school?
Check Civil War: maybe industrial north
needed cheap labor, South had it, how many
sincere "movement" people
                              writers & radicals played
                              into their hands?
Check Haymarket trial: it broke the back
of strong Wobblie movement: how many jailed, fined,
killed to stop that one? What's happening to us
has happened a few times before
                              let's change the script

What did it take to stop the Freedom Riders
What have we actually changed?
                              Month I was born
they were killing onion pickers in Ohio
Month that I write this, nearly 40 years later
they're killing UFW's in the state
I'm trying somehow to live in. LET'S REWRITE
the history books.
History repeats itself
only if we let it.

Ralph Dickey

Leaving Eden

Named and unnamed and renamed
armed and unarmed and disarmed
I have my convenant outside my womb
in the solitary confinement of my cells

The cries of my bones
like the cries of animals
followed me out of my mother
into exile

Slave Papers

At what point do the cars
on Highway 17
stop driving in this funeral?
I mean who's the celebrant.
Anyway?
As far as I can see
the Book of the Dead
is made of traffic tickets
desperado posters licenses
grocery lists receipts scotch
tape belts hangmen's nooses
piano wire kite string
and all the kites
that float out of Hell

Hester Dickinson

How Shall It Be?

How shall it be, when—some supernal morning,
    Longed for, and given of God's abiding grace—
Borne by a breath, and with no note of warning,
    On unknown paths, we two meet face to face.

So long it seems since you went sailing, sailing
    Far on a sea that, yet, I may not cross;
So long, since pitying breeze brought back your hailing:
    "Life is but love, and love is never loss."

And yet when dusks on all the hills are lying,
    And ships creep homeward through the Golden Gate,
I call to you and hear your low replying:
    "Sing and be glad, and still in patience wait."

Edward Dorn

California Landscape

Humming birds are close to junkies anyway
All that keeps them straight is the flower
And her control of plenitude in their cause
Curbing their overweening gluttony
And their insatiable singlemindedness
Yes, as the books say, they are pugnacious
But in them it is a quality absolutely without wit
So when they go for sugar in water with Red #2[a.]
They do get vicious as the supply gets low
And at this point harmonics drive these hoverers
Crazier still as it punctuates their slavery.[b.]
And there birdbrained anger spreads
through their frenzied holding patterns
Sugar, sugar.

A Variation On Vallejo's #III

The layers are still by water
The waterhens are killed in stills
And the entire general world fills
The night of this earthnight
Resting between glaciers, blocks,
Joints, the shoulder of the system
And the dead in the stillness in the ice
The lofty specimens trapped there.

We are the children of weather maps
Our only book is a canyon
In twelve volumes, a work
Widely available in a shorter version.

---

a.   Generic name: Acid Red 27
b.   An experiment conducted one bright hot day
     by Jeremy Prynne, using a #365 Marine Band Hohner.

Robert Duncan

Nel Mezzo Del Cammin Di Nostra Vita

at 42, Simon Rodilla, tile–setter,
   "to do something big for America" began
the Watts towers
(this year, 1959, the officials of which city
 having initiated condemnation hearings
 against which masterpiece)

         three spires
  rising 104 feet, bejewelld with glass,
shells, fragments of tile, scavenged
   from the city dump, from the sea-wrack,
taller than the Holy Roman Catholic church
   steeples, and, moreover,
inspired; built up from bits of beauty
   sorted out—thirty-three years of it—
the great mitred structure rising
   out of squalid suburbs where the
mind is beaten back to the traffic, ground
   down to the drugstore, the mean regular houses
straggling out of downtown sections
   of imagination defeated. "They're
taller than the Church," he told us
   proudly.

       Art, dedicated to itself!

The cathedral at Palma too
   soard above church doctrine,
with art-nouveau windows and baldachine by Gaudí
   gathered its children
under one roof of the imagination.

       The poem . . .

"The poet,"
Charles Olson writes,

"cannot afford to traffic in any other *sign* than his one"
"his self," he says, "the man
 or woman he is" Who? Rodia
 at 81 is through work.
Whatever man or woman he is,
 he is a tower, three towers,
a trinity upraised by himself
 "Otherwise God does rush in."
Finisht. "There are only his own
 composed forms, and each one
the issue of the time of the moment of its creation,
not any ultimate except what he in his heat
and that instant in its solidity yield";

like the Tower of Jewels at the San Francisco
 Panama-Pacific Exposition in 1915, this
"phantom kingdom to symbolize man's
 highest aims", glittering, but

an original, accretion of disregarded
 splendors
resurrected against the rules,
having in this its personal joke; its genius
 misfitting
the expected mediocre; an ecstasy
 of broken bottles
and colord dishes thrown up against whatever
 piety, city ordinance, plans,
risking height;

 a fairy citadel,
a fabulous construction out of
 Christianity where Morgan le Fay
carries the King to her enchanted Isle
 —all glass beads of many colors
and ricketty towers, concrete gardens,
 that imitate magnificence.

"Art," Burckhardt writes:
"the most arrogant traitor of all

112

putting eyes and ears . . . in place of
    profounder worship"
"substituting figures for feelings."

The rounds contain crowns.
The increases climb by bridges.

The whole
planned to occupy life and allow
    for death:

                a skeletal remain
as glory, a raised image, sceptre,
    spectral island, most arrogant,
"to do something big for America"

Rodia.

Jon Eckels

Jimi And Janis — Fall, 1970

Some people die
by too much noise,
others in too much
silence
but dying is best,
I guess
considering
most folks lose
their ears
in their pockets
or between
their legs.

Clayton Eshleman

For Milena Vodickova

What do you
mean by "happy"
Milena asked.
I punctured a hole
in Donald Duck, Pollock's
"The Deep" showed
the cenote
under Duckberg,
Donald and his nephews were
diving for Mayan treasure,
an Indian kid
reading a Disney comic
was slowly being absorbed,
the Ducks were swimming
through stagnant
mind, the kid looked
behind him, the comic closed—
he was on a nice sofa, yellow wall,
green grass outside, he wandered
down the barriada road dazed
by the Disney construction,
people were shouting, Indian
laborers were carrying signs,
"There's a thirsty looking group!"
Donald cried, "Hey, people,
throw down your banners and have
free lemonades!" coins spilled
from his glove, "A tall cool one,
merchants!" one demonstrator cried,
and another: "I'll have one here *and*
one for the road!" The Indian kid
was thirsty too, even though the air
seemed folded with water,
the stench from the barriada
pump where his mother washed;

114

Donald brought up a treasure-trove
and started to jabber to his nephews:
"These idols stand
for the Indian mind," Dorfman & Mattelart
translated, "once our adventure
is produced, and in some Indian
kid's hands, it
will be his wealth and we
his North American friends."
Milena's question
gets me, because
with Caryl not here, us
lacks the coherence of I love and
am loved, it includes
not only the South American I exploit
but Milena herself, the manikin
of a Russian soldier in the shop window
of her Czechoslovakian
breast, her heart
manikin-occupied,
a Russian dressmaker
at work with his palms—
in South America the soldiermaker
is soldered to hunger;
I must face my personal happiness
with that Indian
kid, I thought,
again the language
turned inside out,
my happiness is
faced with him like a building
faced with marble,
his energy
decorates me,
what I am is finished with his facade.

Frenstat, 10 July 1976—
Los Angeles, 6 November 1976.

William Everson

A Canticle To The Waterbirds
Written for the Feast of Saint Francis of Assisi, 1950

Clack your beaks you cormorants and kittiwakes,
North on those rock–croppings finger–jutted into the rough Pacific
    surge;
You migratory terns and pipers who leave but the temporal
    clawtrack written on sandbars there of your presence;
Grebes and pelicans; you comber-picking scoters and you shorelong
    gulls;
All you keepers of the coastline north of here to the Mendocino
    beaches;
All you beyond upon the cliff-face thwarting the surf at Hecate
    Head;
Hovering the under-surge where the cold Columbia grapples at the
    bar;
North yet to the Sound, whose islands float like a sown flurry of
    chips upon the sea;
Break wide your harsh and salt-encrusted beaks unmade for song
And say a praise up to the Lord.

And you freshwater egrets east in the flooded marshlands skirting
    the sea–level rivers, white one–legged watchers of shallows;
Broad–headed kingfishers minnow–hunting from willow stems on
    meandering valley sloughs;
You too, you herons, blue and supple-throated, stately, taking the
    air majestical in the sunflooded San Joaquin,
Grading down on your belted wings from the upper lights of sunset,
Mating over the willow clumps or where the flatwater rice fields
    shimmer;
You killdeer, high night-criers, far in the moon-suffusion sky;
Bitterns, sand–waders, all shore-walkers, all roost-keepers,
Populates of the 'dobe cliffs of the Sacramento:
Open your water-dartling beaks,
And make a praise up to the Lord.

For you hold the heart of His mighty fastnesses,
And shape the life of His indeterminate realms.

You are everywhere on the lonesome shores of His wide creation.
You keep seclusion where no man may go, giving Him praise;
Nor may a woman come to lift like your cleaving flight her clear
  contralto song
To honor the spindrift gifts of His soft abundance.
You sanctify His hermitage rocks where no holy priest may kneel to
  adore, nor holy nun assist;
And where his true communion-keepers are not enabled to enter.

And well may you say His praises, birds, for your ways
Are verbed with the secret skills of His inclinations,
And your habits plaited and rare with the subdued elaboration of his
  intricate craft;
Your days intent with the direct astuteness needful for His
  outworking,
And your nights alive with the dense repose of His infinite sleep.
You are His secretive charges and you serve His secretive ends,
In His clouded mist-conditioned stations, in His murk,
Obscure in your matted nestings, immured in His limitless ranges.
He makes you penetrate through dark interstitial joinings of His
  thicketed kingdoms,
And keep your concourse in the deeps of His shadowed world.

Your ways are wild but earnest, your manners grave,
Your customs carefully schooled to the note of His serious mien.
You hold the prime condition of His clean creating,
And the swift compliance with which you serve His minor means
Speaks of the constancy with which you hold Him.
For what is your high flight forever going home to your first
  beginnings,
But such a testament to your devotion?
You hold His outstretched world beneath your wings, and mount
  upon His storms,
And keep your sheer wind-lidded sight upon the vast perspectives of
  His mazy latitudes.

But mostly it is your way you bear existence wholly within the
  context of His utter will and are untroubled.
Day upon day you do not reckon, nor scrutinize tomorrow, nor
  multiply the nightfalls with a rash concern,
But rather assume each instant as warrant sufficient of His final seal.

Wholly in Providence you spring, and when you die you look on
  death in clarity unflinched,
Go down, a clutch of feather ragged upon the brush;
Or drop on water where you briefly lived, found food,
And now yourselves made food for His deep current–keeping fish,
  and then are gone:
Is left but the pinion–feather spinning a bit on the uproil
Where lately the dorsal cut clear air.
You leave a silence. And this for you suffices, who are not of the
  ceremonials of man,
And hence are not made sad to now forgo them.
Yours is of another order of being, and wholly it compels.
But may you, birds, utterly seized in God's supremacy,
Austerely living under His austere eye—
Yet may you teach a man a necessary thing to know,
Which has to do of the strict conformity that creaturehood entails,
And constitutes the prime commitment all things share.
For God has given you the imponderable grace to *be* His verification,
Outside the mulled incertitude of our forensic choices;
That you, our lessers in the rich hegemony of Being,
May serve as testament to what a creature is,
And what creation owes.

Curlews, stilts and scissortails, beachcomber gulls,
Wave-haunters, shore-keepers, rockhead-holders, all cape-top
  vigilantes,
Now give God praise.
Send up the strict articulation of your throats,
And say His name.

1951

Sarah Webster Fabio

Back Into The Garden

It's a hell

creeping back into
the garden, shedding

your badly worn skin,
starting anew;

worming into the
apple unrelent-
ingly until you
touch the hard core:

and always in mind
the thought and risk of
your being bitten
in two before

you've gotten far,
boring feverishly,
and all you've left
are split ends.

It's a hell!

But making it
the shiny seed's
your prize and
genesis.

Joan Falck

Pride For Hate

Could there be reason for hate
or is it all just a game.
    To find out the truth
then realize who's to blame.
    People slow down, stop and stare
but never really care.
    Tears, I can't seem to hide
these feelings have been shoved aside.
    Turning my back for a while

Trying to force a smile.
    No sense in being brought down
wiping off my frown.
    Taking the blows in my stride
I know I have nothing to hide.
All I have left, is my Pride.

A Forgotten Death

He lay there on the battlefield
not moving.
No one will come and weep.
He carried the weight so
proudly.

He was the brave of the two.
So strong.
But he had no choice to
live or die.
For nobody asks a horse.

Wisdom

Learning the ways of the Indian
Learning the ways of the Whiteman
Listen to my ancestors
Echo........
Listen to their cries.
White ignorance
Ancestral knowledge.
Faith in my forefathers,
for only good can
come of that.

Grant Fisher

July 4, 1976 / A Comment

In this carnage what massive flower unfolds?

Tire treads mark a pattern of petals
in fields that have worn thickets of bay laurel,
hosted hordes of deer whose curious & gentle eyes
have guided moon thru unreckond centuries,
on whom now rubber & chrome will mark
the fine edge of radio-tund bodies whose
spread life has become no more than
futurity's gambling, chips of miles per hour.

Meadow flowers glisten at the new curb,
irrepresible blossoms undaunted by
tire-whine, exhaust, crunching bag
of rabbit unburied on macadam face.

O Holidays! We roll out to the
floods of Las Vegas, trading the
boredom of our labor for the
aluminum gilt that spins upon
tables so green they might have been grass.
Our contagious patience like the cruel glee
of firecrackers & the approaching night
of blazing spectacular flowers.

The President seeks out the word
of jubilation & liberation
from parapets of wrong fort
wrong war   wrong harbor . . . to belt out,
perhaps, between the passing of bourbon
& the popping of champagne,
the very wrong song that has so well
maskt this country's futureless campaigns.

We leap in no direction & dance
to what is no more than the occasion

of a disturbance between merchants
& the establishment of an elected throne
that has no oxhide in its past, no
jade knife to its name.

Murdered eagles of the nation's pride—
bullet cringd & shatterd from helicopterd machine guns—
Wyoming   Vietnam   strip-
mine   oil tank   Alcatraz the most
beautiful,   imprisoned isle...
it is all the same. Bombs
blister the air. Ruddy blossoms...
Ruddy blossoms on this heart's
thatcht villages. The blackbirds
of my dreams frozen last spring....

Nevada thundercloud, most rare
of the summer—sky cotton
drenching health upon all that lies below!—
shatter fords & cadillacs!   send de soto
dodge oldsobile & chrysler abash
into dry tiles of winter's floodless canals!
Let the gamblers go on unopposd,
the mushroom's vapor races thru
cracks o' th' ground, soon to rise,
creeping thru soles of the unyielding.

Let the President drown out of season,
braving ice flows, again, on the wrong river
lauding the historic worth of his buttonhole
while en route to hysteric processions of blue
cotton   blue fingers   the black New Jersey sky.

And among these reeds where his body
will wash, Osirian, let flag take
root & blossom white upon the rustic
green of his flesh. Like pale ivory &
tapestries of earth's slow piling wealth,
let his bones spread thru the finite mud.
May my President's blood feed

the rivers as in the wild-bull-years before
these four scores of centuries which
upon an oak's branch have been waiting.

From his teeth, Thundercloud, out of their
powdering, make rise violet iris, wild among
the secrets of thick-forest Michigan's unguarded swamp.

Reymundo Gamboa

The Baby Chook

Gray hair
does not let
star-spangled eyes see
that the Baby Chook
de acá, de este lado
is liquid bronze
in and out of mainstreams.

His heart pumps traditions
through rainbow veins
while menstruating history
has shown bald statements
to have no reward:
his hands hold nothing.

Hope's still doing one-to-life
in statues.

In Indiamer
another architect's dream collapses
and his blood
made mole.

Güitado
he reads:
"West Side Rifa"

y le cachuchea a la huesuda
by not staying out
cause
to The Bonaparte of the Barrio
words often lose their meaning.

Guitar RS
make pimping puritan ears deaf
and Mexams do no echo for him.
Todos lo dejan abaniqueando

Neurotics sneak a peak
at this schizo's rejection
of a cosmeticized experience
while his antagonistic angel
gets him motorola
with du-pont glue and pacha.
When these additives are not enough
le quema los pies a Judas.

This trinity parades
through the veins in his brains;
ya solimán
this valiente gets so high
he admits
that thought grass is a gas
he must some day be below it.
Doesn't matter.

This Frito Bandido
will paint, write, scratch on walls
til they tell his rehearsed vision
of being taken off the cross
and delivered to an unrented grave
for revolutionaries that do more
than liberate farts wearing tennis shoes.

The Baby Chook must act:
maybe paint, maybe write,

maybe scratch on walls
til they talk.

Virginia Garcia

Pompeii

There was a city like the rest
Of cities, and the heavens blessed
Its portals. Quiet winds were sent
At eventide, and shadows blent
With sunshine where the grapes were pressed.

There roses bloomed their loveliest.
And there were fountains manifest;
No prophesy of sad portent;
"It died too young."

In eves where birds were wont to nest
Were found the birds. The passing guest
Had seen a city of content.
With life and singing redolent,
Where now he sees in dust confessed:
"It died too young."

Barry Gifford

Bohemian Cigar Store, San Francisco

Last week
I was 28

Rumpled-pants Pete
plays pinball

Sicilian cardsharps
in hats

One Sunday
when Domenico

and Rosa
owned the place

old men
wrinkled eyes

blazing like
Corsican suns

handed my
daughter around

the bar
mumbling 'bella, bella'

Glauco

¿ . . . . . . ?

Translated by M.B. Anderson

Luego no digas que yo,
que tú, que fué, que no fué,
Que aquello, que lo otro, y que
Fritó fué y mal se guisó.

Que vino, que se tornó;
Que por aqui, por allí,
Que así no fué, que fué así,
Que aquello, que lo otro, que esto;
Que al fin vengas por supuesto
A echarme la culpa a mí!

La Gaceta de los Estados Unidos
Los Angeles
24 de agosto de 1918

Later on don't say that I,
that you, that it was, that it wasn't,

126

That that, that the other, and that
It was fried and poorly prepared.

That it came, that it was returned;
That by here, by over there,
That it wasn't like that, that it was like this,
That that, that the other, that this;
That at last you will of course come
To put the blame on me!

Lawrence Gracia

The Sabre's Song

Heard you that shivering song
Piercing the stillness of night,
Sung by a sabre that swung
Flat on men's heads, left and right...?

Heard you those quivering notes
Ringing in icicle strain,
Nights, like whispering ghosts
Mingling with curses of pain...?

Heard you its splintering twang
Ending in thin muffled hum,
Hum of its long-toothed fang
Thrumming skulls for a drum...?

Heard you its shivering song
Rising in crescendo scales,
Ending in splintering twang
Preluding men's dying wails...?

Joanna Griffin

Song

it lies

      to Orpheus   as   server   to   Apollo   and   Dionysius

                        and the balancing

      why should the sweet singer lose his love

      how did he look on her   before she sank to earth

              how did you look on your bride

Orpheus

              and Eurydice   taken by earth

              her own,   the serpent's tongue

              what did it tell her

that Orpheus did not sing

      what kind of wedding is it the bride dies

      in the   grass ,   flowers   ,   and how

      do you look on her now   Orpheus   Orpheus

      whose song died in the wind

Gnosis: Interstice

Traveling over the city

    (the great holy light beast

    where the lights   rise

    where the lights   shine   shimmer

        in the waters

          (the dancing beast

traveling over the city prowling for holy precinct

where is

new   Jerusalem?

The city of my heart stands just as white
as you stand in this dawn
but the gold touches
all day
the tips and spires edge
our eyes
the slight glow
all day
secret secret gold
all the day
secret secret heart
all night
the light kept in
some place where

weeping rises
just hear it
in the night
wind from the sea

Jessica Tarahata Hagedorn

Smokey Robinson

hey nellie
how long you been here
did you come with your daddy
in 1959   on a second-class boat
cryin' all the while
cuz you didn't wanna leave the barrio
the girls back there
who wore their hair loose
lots of orange lipstick
movies on sundays
quiapo market in the morning
your grandma chewin' red tobacco
roast pig
yeah . . . and it tasted good

hey nellie
did you have to live in stockton
with your daddy
& talk to old farmers
who immigrated in 1941
did your daddy promise you
to a fifty-eight year old bachelor
who stank of cigars
and did you run away to san francisco
go to poly high
rat your hair
hang around woolworth's

chinatown at three in the morning
go to the cow palace
& catch smokey robinson
cry & scream at his gold jacket
go steady with ruben
(your daddy can't stand it
cuz he's a spik)

& the sailors you dreamed of
in manila   with yellow hair
did they take you to the beach'
to ride the ferris wheel
life's never been so fine . . .

you & carmen harmonize
"be my baby" by the ronettes
& 1965 you get laid at a party
carmen's house
& ruben marries you
& you give up harmonizing

nellie
you sleep without dreams
& remember the barrios & how
it's all the same
manila the mission chinatown
east l.a. harlem fillmore street
& you're getting kinda fat
& smokey robinson's getting old
but your son has learned to dance
o yes, he has . . .

"i don't want to / but i need you
seems that / i'm always / thinkin / of you
though you do me wrong now / my love is strong now
you really / got a hold / on me . . ."

Steve Halpern

Our word
fall is when winter falls,
like night falls;
but the season falls right
off the trees.
Figs, apples,
pears and limes are rolling loose.
The berries are gone,
the walnuts green.

Friday night
and everyone is busy.
The best thing to me
is the night, and
my bike: a
madman's sails catch
the white wind
of the moon.

Green
moss under leaves
on naked rocks   and stumps
on living trees   in
all its places
implies water (the
banks of invisible streams.)
Moist
fertile
immense in being,
stealing my sleep
by night.

I remember how sand feels
against my feet. Press
and it takes my shape.

I remember that the real smell
doesn't carry far –
when I've been inland I
wait and wait, until
it startles me, just a
few hundred yards away.

Last May – no, a year
before that –
some waves unrolled
themselves for me.
The tireless sound of
that beach
snapped into focus;
when I saw the waves fall
I heard them and
when they were white water I
heard them. The
sound came closer
with the shrinking wave,
touched the beach
and left with it. I
could separate the voices
of blue-green counterpoint.

At home, on
a hill it's
a memory. But
with time my
body turns bent, like
a bow; a
stiff half-circle holding
something in.

The ocean's held; half-circled
by the horizon, working itself

by sending waves,
trying to drive them through the beach.

In time I come down. Apprehensively
I come down. Walking
the rock and pasture on my way. Carefully
I butt the small half-circle
against the huge one, and
hope it makes a strong
container for the waves.

Jana Harris

Tastes Like Chicken

I have driven the deserts,
I said.
I have driven them alone,
across the Cascades
across Lake Chelan
into the dry heat
into the Desert, the East.
That wild asparagus by the roadside
and the rattlesnakes
I wanted for dinner;
"Tastes like chicken,"
everybody said.
"Tastes like chicken
and if y'r careful
could be twice's cheap."
I meant to run one down
on the road back to Omak
on the road across the reservation
to Big Goose Lake.
A snake with seven rattles
        —I chased her from beneath
the hot tires of the truck.
Chased her across the graveled road

back to the dry grass
back to the magpies
and the dust.
Snake.
You high ass, high cunt
thin legged
high stepping
Snake.
You taste like chicken!
You and your long back bones
your blond-bellied tease;
com'on, Miz Snake,
Bite.
Teach me the sting.
I know that energy
the rage,
slipping beneath the tar weed;
the S ribbon in the dust
of your swan-necked retreat.
I know it all,
all except
for the sweet sure bite
and the skill.

William J. Harris

Hey Fella Would You Mind Holding This Piano A Moment

for Reg & Susie

As you are walking
down the street
this guy asks you
to hold his violin.
It's a Stradivarius.
Soon as it falls
into your hands

you start playing like crazy.
The violin
almost plays itself.
Your powerful hands
nearly break the instrument
but the music is gentle and sweet.
You sweep your long artistic hair
out of your face.
Everybody in the room
in the bull ring, in the
audience, in the Coliseum
starts clapping
and shouting "Encore & Wow."
Everybody whoever
thot you were
dumb & untalented
goes apeshit
over your hidden genius.
"Gee, I never knew you   .
played," says your astonished high school
principal.

A Daddy Poem

My father is a hand-
some guy.

Looks like
a cross between
Clark Gable & Ernest Hemingway.
If you don't believe me,
I got proof:
Once a white woman
(at one of those
        parties)
said to my father,
"You're good looking
for a colored man."

Bret Harte

Further Language From Truthful James

(Nye's Ford, Stanislaus, 1870.)

Do I sleep? do I dream?
Do I wonder and doubt?
Are things what they seem?
Or is visions about?
Is our civilisation a failure?
Or is the Caucasian played out?

Which expressions are strong:
Yet would feebly imply
Some account of a wrong—
Not to call it a lie—
As was worked off on William, my pardner,
And the same being W. Nye.

He came down to the Ford
On the very same day
Of that lottery drawed
By those sharps at the Bay;
And he says to me, "Truthful, how goes it?"
I replied, "It is far, far from gay;

"For the camp has gone wild
On this lottery game,
And has even beguiled
'Injin Dick' by the same."
Then said Nye to me, "Injins is pizen:
But what is his number, eh? James?"

I replied, "7, 2,
9, 8, 4, is his hand;"
When he started, and drew
Out a list, which he scanned;
Then he softly went for his revolver
With language I cannot command.

Then I said, "William Nye!"
But he turned upon me,
And the look in his eye
Was quite painful to see;
And he says, "You mistake; this poor Injin
I protects from such sharps as *you* be!"

I was shocked and withdrew;
But I grieve to relate,
When he next met my view
Injin Dick was his mate;
And the two around town was a-lying
In a frightfully dissolute state.

Which the war dance they had
Round a tree at the Bend
Was a sight that was sad;
And it seemed that the end
Would not justify the proceedings,
As I quiet remarked to a friend

For that Injin he fled
The next day to his band;
And we found William spread
Very loose on the strand,
With a peaceful-like smile on his features
And a dollar greenback in his hand;

Which the same, when rolled out,
We observed, with surprise,
Was what he, no doubt,
Thought the number and prize—
Them figures in red in the corner,
Which the number of notes specifies.

Was it guile, or a dream?
Is it Nye that I doubt?
Are things was they seem?
Or is visions about?
Is our civilisation a failure?
Or is the Caucasian played out?

Sadakichi Hartmann

Tanka I

Winter? Spring! Who knows!
  White buds from the plumtrees wing
And mingle with the snows.
  No blue skies these flowers bring,
Yet their fragrance augurs Spring.

Tanka IV

Like mist on the lees,
    Fall gently, oh rain of Spring
On the orange trees
    That to Ume's casement cling—
Perchance she'll hear the lovebird sing.

Tanka VI

Tell what name beseems
    These vain and wandering days!
Like the bark of dreams
    That from the soul at daybreak strays
They are lost on trackless ways.

Haikai I

White petals afloat
    On a winding woodland stream—
What else is life's dream?

Haikai III

At new moon we met!
    Two weeks I've waited in vain.
To-night! Don't forget!

Haikai IV

Oh, red maple leaves,
   There seem more of you these eves
Than ever grew on trees.

Bobbie Louise Hawkins

I

A wet day long ago
lost to all but memory
that lights it now

A shadow show

A green day wet with rain
Odors rose from the ground
pine needles and shadowed air

It is the clarity
of that loss
is the light
brings it back before my eyes

puts the sound of thunder in
today's sunshine

IX

Branches and leaves and
a breeze that blows
words
through my head at night

"Aren't you *tired* of romance?"

A breeze blows the skin
on the water
of the lagoon
into ripples
in the daytime

"Aren't you *tired* of romance?"

God-damn glamor that will insist
a little perfection
never hurt anybody

A perfect
A perfect
blue sky over the lagoon

Lyn Hejinian

Beginning With The Local Boys

The local boys hunt everything out
of season — deer, bear, fish, pheasant.
You hear the sound of rifle shots long
after hunting season is over.
    During the months when the salmon,
and, later, the steelhead, are spawning,
they fish at night with pitchforks,
hiking down to the creeks rather than
leave a car parked along the road to
betray their presence to the Fish and
Game Warden.
    I know little about their relationship
with girls, though in town one sees
them together in groups of six or ten,
eating french fries and sticks of jerky,
chewing gum, smoking, preening awkwardly
under the light of their teasing and

jostling. There is nothing else for them
to do, of course.

Awhile back two men from San Francisco
bought the movie theater and showed
pornographic movies for seven dollars
and fifty cents a couple. None of the
young people were allowed in the theater,
but in spite of that the theater owners
did a good business. After two months,
however, a group of local citizens burned
it down.

At the grammar school, on parents' night
or at the Christmas Fair, where one sees
 the married couples, it seems like nothing
so much as that they've mated and lost
interest. The children are there, as sole
evidence of a previous relationship. The
connection now is ritualized and emotionless.

That it has been repeated makes it
no less worthy. One could speak as well,
and as oft, of the moon.

Song

for the Dance, Inland and Out

Imagine that you could run close to the foam
farm. We had fast horses
and a pair of heavy draft horses
plunging against the rocks.
The hens were molting, three pin feathers
back and forth. My feet have been burned,
stung, and chilled
in mud heavy with manure and straw.
The barns were warmed by the cows
as if within a shell, damp and gray
picking tomatoes and corn. Snitch,
ketch, rake
the fog. We stepped on sharp barnacles
and slipped on the kelp,

the hay harvest, the full moon,
the old apple orchard,
and the sand.

David Henderson

Felix Of The Silent Forest

*to Felix the Cat / Noveltytoons, USA
& Ed Krasnow*

Felix   you horizon dance
Who are these people who say
they have known you for a long time?
who are those friends
who attack you by the same handle?

In this age of debarkment
            epoch of mass inter-regimentation
    no longer have we cause to stay away
for not diving in
            it is the age of epaulet & picket line
            vertigo and alliance

Felix walks here and there
Felix walks the City
sometimes fast sometimes slow
like a dying man wanting everything he sees
not wanting to desist   to leave
never to allow Fate Palance
to have his way

Felix stops & then goes on

Often
Felix walks the City hungry in every sense
of every gastric salivating phenomenon
thighs   to eyes   to mouth

He is wooed by Tad's $1.19 steaks
as well as 2 for 25c Hamburgers on forty-second street
                              the Crossroads —

He has bent in supplication
over 25c potato & gravy meals
in Pole Town Avenue "A"
as often as fried chicken fantasies
down Avenue "D" — the downtown Harlem
        On upper Seventh Avenue
he watches his plate being piled high
with fish & fried potatoes
the oil soaks and drips down
Felix thinks of cholesterol   chest pains   heart spasms
                yet   he passes fish
        to watered–down hot sauce   to mouth with gladness
    plus joy to the plastic-blotter bread
which picks up the grease

Felix
sits in Martin's Bar   Smiths   Blarney Stones
Bowery deformed men's bars   the Silver Rail Harlem
Shalomar-by-Randolph's   Regan's on Staten Island
the Jerome Avenue Spa or Sylvia's Blue Morocco Bronx NY
        Felix sits in any bar 3 or 4 for a dollar
wondering if
anyone he loves
wonders where he is

Juan Felipe Herrera

in the cannery the porpoise soul

in the cannery the porpoise soul
& the shadow fins of spirit boats lie awake
the hundred hooks & flying reels
one harpoon
& the silver fleshing in the nets

the mayor is waiting / counting scales
dreaming new quotas & tuna coasts
(under the table blood & payrolls
swim to the shores on a crucifix of oil).

in the cannery the porpoise soul
steals a dagger for the engines throat
tuna fins etch an X
on the green stone of the ships floor

there are documents with worker sweat
files & rolled sleeve salt
a spear of sails & anchor years
(lost)
inside the shoulders & against the ropes
(somehow)
a policy gunned the waves back
before the porpoise sea was born

mar 3

cuantos vientres
van flotando en las olas
cuantas sangres
y campanas de madera
una cruz de san juan apostol
una rueda de gaviotas en la brisa
quiero quemar el mar
con las minas toscas de un beso
quiero romper las nubes
con una espada de arena y aretes de fuego

at the moon cafe

chow mein & a memory of playing chess
(over a turquoise table top)
some rice & a few pawns to caress

                pawns dining with their papers
                a castle of ink
                a knight of despair

africa
was taken by the king
(he didnt have to move)

mexico
was taken by the pope
(on his way to eat)
he didn't have to pray

gallery of time /

Yesterday the gallery hung
the mustache of zapata
& the look of blood
over walls painted antique white
the compassion of van gogh
sold for a bone of sheep
a coat of smiles
and a brasserie of wine / yesterday
murrieta's head was weighed
& given away with a cocktail
of maraschino red & visceral blue
texas was brought under glass
in a tube of words
(bought aesthetically by a ship of wolves)
a memory now
over cognac & apertifs of spurs / yesterday
the rhythm of jesus steps
the texture of buddha's eyes
the harmony of tlaloc's heart
the oil of vishnu's fire
the balance of moses' serpent staff
auctioned & taken down
& traded
for the opal of herod's dreams

for the throne of mars
for the arms of islands tightly roped
in the cellars of america

(where they smell of flesh & burning love)

let me talk of the years / 500 (L.A. 1969)

let me talk of the years
years
strung like sweat over nails & bones
years
rung like ancient hooks in the throat of spring
years
torn like oranges over a sidewalk in space
100
blue eyes and white ferns were cast
blue dreams and white centuries were burned
blue flesh was made where once there was only white
blue nails on white coffins were thrown
white
people were chained to swallow blue spears
& white was space turning into red
blood.
200
blue brothers were forgotten
blue deserts were left alone
white flowers meant white jets
& blue rivers never meant white snow
300
let me talk of the years
years pressed like wood
years driven like trains
years
lonely on sidewalks blue with rain
400
i remember caroline
just like i remember juan
i remember broken amber shoulders

& venice drowning in burgundy
I remember endless piers rusting in her golden arms
& the long sea full of doors
& the frozen sky without windows
the burning bones of chrysanthemums
& the hurling flags inside the fence
500   .
blue eyes & white ferns were forgotten
yet the river smiled
the eagle spoke
blue thunder & black mountains kissed

Jack Hirschman

And

Much that was counted
poor, when there was
   no daybreak when the sun rose,
     although there
        the sun rose
   and could be felt,
still poor for want of light,
and still
      this way the way
the day was counted and the night
numbered,
and all was as before
      there was a shining.

Forms would come and go,
    would pass
      and in the narrow
  places where stakes had been
       set
eyes would be there, waiting
to be grown in with

the aroundness of
          time,
to take shape from the depth
of the groundless,
          the supple abyss
made from the memory of chains,
of cages.
I went through the wind of it all,
in another
          life. But are
     there other lives,
is more a question I ask
what's left of class
in the schools
                penetrated by song
through and through to
the wet
          hum of the ocean.
"People are boats, although
                    on land,"
Mayakovsky wrote
beginning the poem of Lenin.

The floating, the floating!
And in
          what's scuttled, wrecked
at times, the jettison
the floating
          poems. Woodbine
I come to smell, as if a pipe stood
at the end of the long
     haul longshoremen
                somewhere
stuff into the hull
of their hope.
Of wood. Of tree. The paper on
which we write
          the element
               of our faces.
Know the grains

by shaping them from
    what we have sailed
or touched
        is the bark
of our own
        dogged forest of heart,
its clench
like fist
        or teeth, its pounding
like the ocean
against rock,
its minarets always
        glowing
with distances
immediately attained.

        What keeps
    in all these
            seconds

    time?

Mine is of what has none,
is the poem,
that is its own

            holding

no thing so firmly
fragile only   this break
in it, this
        climb, this
limit, is
illimitable   land,
as it arrives

150

in its being arisen within,
        and from all angle   of meridian,
the sound of
its

        inner voice, earth
invisible

transformed by this ground
breaking –

        ceremony of

the quiet quake, look
the gutter is
opening to

        the center
        of the,

and the letters

are fire, the sun, is,

and the alphabets, all,

and the moon –

how can that be that can be –

at the same time,
        given,
                reflecting
the tides of the flames of the poem
upon the faces
as unburnable ether,
        a binding glow,

the verb for *to be*
understood.

                        San Francisco
                        1975

Patrick Holland

Horses In November

It is because there is a mountain
and mountains have horses,
horses in November,
eastern Nevada.
In the high hills
horses drift.

On the mountain
the gravel is brittle
the horsehooves are yellow
and further south
are donkeys
and deep
hand-dug wells.
They have let a rope down
to tickle the dark water,
albino fish grin at it
then swim away.

On the mountain
the horses spread out,
they are drifting leeward
in a grey wind.

Red Dakota

In the wheat of Red Dakota
there is nothing,
but the great rock turning
at the mill grinds down
rolls the miller's daughter
in her sleep, thighs wrapt
'round a red horse.

In the wheat of Red Dakota
in the dust,
great red combines
in a paler red sun,
red as the hair of my head was
you couldn't mistake me.
I stood out with an uncle
who came to teach Indians
to farm
someplace along the Missouri,
a soddy
and wildfires burning
on the plain.

Teaching the world to farm!
Irishwinter—legislature,
bourbon and matches down
the governor's well,
my father moves up;
the grandfather, a tailor
dreaming of perpetual motion
in a barn
Near the Bad River which
buckles and thunders the
icerunning spring,
I start out
up a low red hill;
at Fort Pierre
a rock marks the north continent's
Center.

Lawson Fusao Inada

At The Stronghold

For Miles and Toti

Miles is so sufficient
he makes me

breakfast with a flick of his wrist—
                              little cakes
                              of oceans and islands.

Toti is into
                  stirring,
mostly,
but if I ask him
                  he picks the burrs
                  off the tops of my socks.

Then they demonstrate
the adaptability
                              of scissors and cardboard,
                              making up games
                              that rule about life.

I give them
                  many-bladed knives,
little men in blue diving suits

and remember me.

                  There's a cool
                              Tlingit wind
                  blowing over
                  water all the way from Japan
                  blurring the surface
                  of my eyes,
                              the deeps
                  pulling me
                              down and in.

                  *

                  Up over Greensprings,
                  the pass, crash
                  of wheeled
                              cataracts

154

screaming logjams
into and out of
switchbacks

with a flick of fins.
Eyes. Brown
eyes of bottles,
                        squirrels
that never learn.

*

Count your
            self
lucky
to find a deer
            by Pinehurst. Bless

you.
      She
is the soul
            of women among huckleberries,

soft, fine eyes

            before the invasion,
            the cry.

            *

            Lately, in the drought,
            I am obsessed

            by clouds, their
            forming, knowing

            them only as
            dispersal flowing

over me
lately

in the drought.

       *

K. Falls ain't
got nothing
for me.
      Unless I had a need
      for gutters, for

official termination,

         my brown eyes
         welling over at the rim

         brown spit
         bottoms of bottles,

         my brown spirit
         slumped in some stirrups

at the terminal.

       *

Hell, I'm not trying to do
nothing for nobody
but me,

my own cause,
my destiny

come round
to me.

I need my own
sense
shaped into place

in a strong body with
whole bones
                with no

disease in the marrow,
the smolder of shrapnel.

Not even the need
for legend,
                something

monumental to build on,
                        something
grand, just
my self,
my own scope and destiny,

so when my
time comes, I can go

                off and die

                like a man.

                *

        Captain Jack,
        I come to you

        in respect,
        out of a need

        for communion.

        I will not dance and sing
        in your sacred cinders

        where even today
        the trail
        is difficult to walk upon.

We, too,
walked upon this ground,
and though our
stronghold
was made for us,
to hold us in,

we, too,
heard the geese in the wind,
the wind in the tules

and dreamed
in our brown bodies

of peace and the good land,

of home.

*

And so I come to you,
Captain.

And if you were to meet me
on the difficult terrain
of a parking lot

you would extend your hand to mine.

*

There is a mystery
how you survived

this desperate place
of edges and wind.

The commissioners were many.
They bled in the heat.

There were so few of you.
What did you eat?

There is no mystery.
Fat white ladies with small dogs
and weak husbands
are still on the track.

The lava bed
is a place to sleep.
Heat, rain, cracked
sweet cinders, the red
tule rope of resistance—

this is how we sing and survive—

the entire
one of us
gorged with the knowledge

of paved genocide
trying to find its way here.

*

        Here, in this stronghold
        I have hid my heart,

        a battlement
        strong at the marrow,
        stored here

        for when the time allows,

        fists in the throat,
        a volley
        of words and rocks
        in strong boxes

        back of the heart
        behind mazed
        trails spiraling

        to my music,
        where no one is allowed.

Here, in this stronghold,
I hide
myself
to myself,

deaf with my pulse
running through the walls

where my life is carved,

ancient signs
where the hurts happened,
the loves, the births,

all in calligraphy
that nothing but the blood

deciphers,
or cares

to be allowed

to this stronghold

where I show my heart.

*

"Question 27: Are you willing to serve in the armed forces of the United States, in combat duty, wherever ordered?"

No.

"Question 28: Will you swear unqualified allegiance to the United States of America and faithfully defend the United States from any and all attack by foreign or domestic forces, and foreswear any form of allegiance to the Japanese emperor, or any other foreign government, power, or organization?"

No.

160

Hirohito?
Him people
like you na me.
Me no go
Chinchinahtee
Me go
Tule Lake.
Me stay
Carifonia.
Home.

*

All I wanted
was a place to live,

how we had always known,

women among huckleberries,
tules that teach
children of junipers, geese, and sky.

All I wanted
was to fight to live,
to be left alone.

All I wanted
was a concession to dignity,
our own reservation.

All I wanted
was our own
defeat.

All I wanted
was to die.

*

Looking into the eyes
                of my children,
                the gifted young

who wished me in women's clothes,
who silently called me
                white and compromiser,

I see the *why*

        I am
        the renegade
        I am,
        the revolutionary
        I will always be.

                What land we had
                we must have back again.
                This is the stronghold,
                the heart, the spirit
                the land, the heart.

                This termination, this
                extermination, this
                compromise to survive.

                The fenced-in barracks
                still stand
                beyond the ancient carvings
                of Prisoner Rock.

                The signs are right.
                The spirit. The land.
                We must have back again.

                Those of us still alive
                singing assimilation
                with the flick of wrists,
                thrive on the sick
                blood of subjugation

here on this very land
where we died.

Captain Jack
will be hanged
tomorrow. "Instruction
to all persons
of Japanese ancestry ... "

This is the stronghold,
the heart, the molten
flow solidified
blood of ancestors.

The blood of us
is the red tule rope.

What are you worth
in the eyes
of your sons?

The blood of us
is the red tule rope.

*

As our stay increases—
                summer into fall—

the wounds and pain
            fall from our feet

as we begin to know
            the paths
            of the stronghold
            the scars of battle
            smooth places
            to stand upon

            as our stay

increases
to the span
of our life

as we begin to see
buttes and geese,
juniper and sky

as all clouds
form at Shasta
and return there.

Captain Jack,
father,

you teach us

to stand
to plant
our feet in the ground

you teach us

to stand
to raise
our eyes from the ground.

*

My sons,
you are beside me now.

No.
You will not be leaving
for Oklahoma.

No.
No one will take your photo
in front of the barracks.

Yes.
We are willing to serve.

Yes.
We swear allegiance.

> And if my old time is allowed,
>
> I will go off into the hills
>
> with the flute of my father
>
> and sing the song
>
> of geese in the wind
>
> of wind among tules
>
> of the red tule rope
>
> of blood that always flows
>
> of clouds around Shasta
>
> and listen, and grow
>
> silent and still
>
> in my own, in my own
>
> wisdom and dignity
>
>
> as a man.

from *Our Album*

I. *"Before the War"*

"Before the war"
means Fresno, a hedged-in house,
two dogs in the family.

Blackie, the small one, mine,
lapped at his insides
on the floorboard, on the way to the doctor.

Jimmy, my father's shepherd,
wouldn't eat after the evacuation.
He wouldn't live with another master

and pined away, skin and bone.

With feelings more than pride,
we call him our one-man dog.

II. *Mud*

Mud in the barracks—
a muddy room, a chamber pot.

Mud in the moats
around each barracks group.

Mud on the shoes
trudging to the mess hall.

Mud in the swamp
where the men chopped wood.

Mud on the guts
under a loaded wagon—

crushed in the mud by the wheel.

III. *Desert Songs*

1. ALL THAT WE GATHERED

Because there was little else to do,
they led us to the artillery range
for shells, all that we gathered,
and let us dig among dunes
for slugs, when they were through.

Because there was little else to do,
one of them chased a stray
with his tail between his legs
and shot him through the head.

2. SHELLS

A desert tortoise—
something mute and hard—

something to decorate
a desert Japanese garden:

gnarled wood, smooth
artillery shells for a border.

When a guard
smashes one, the shell

cracks open and the muscles ooze.

3. IT IS ONLY NATURAL

The pheasant is an Oriental creature,
so it is only natural
that one should fly into camp

and, famished by rations and cans,
break out in secret, native dance
over a fire, on a black coal stove.

4. SONG OF THE 442ND

Caged creatures
have curious moods.

Some of them choose
to be turned

loose in a group,
to take their chances

in the open.

5. STEERS

Because a dentist
logically drives a butcher truck,

I rode with my father
to the slaughterhouse on an afternoon.

Not hammers, not bullets,
could make him close his eyes.

6. HE TEACHES

He jerks the eyes
from birds, feet
from lizards,

and punishes
ants with the gaze
of a glass.

And with his sly
gaze, his child's face,
he teaches

what has its place,
and must be
passed on to others.

IV. *Song of Chicago*

When the threat lessened,
when we became tame,
my father and friends
took a train to Chicago

for factory work,
for packaging bolts.
One grew a mustache
and called himself Carlos.

And they all made a home
with those of their own—

rats, bedbugs, blacks.

Kenneth Irby

Homage to Coleman Hawkins
for John Moritz

—still hearing the Hawk in his region
following his season

across the Northeast shorelines, heart
                                    strike

of the horn, dive
bomber of the home

front porches

that there have to be porches
in the heat of

—he raised his horn
across the Missouri fault

as sure as the rise and now the fall of sap

the rubber plant
and geranium of affection

from Washburn from St Joe
following the tornado

jazz hounds direction

yoke of going somewhere else
to find out home

—so fall the leaves
in Massachusetts

settling home, a longing
for all Northeast corners everywhere

the pressure upon the body
of the Pacific mental

of the Atlantic visual
of the Canadian

anterior elemental

—so falls the warm November
Medford rain

as fine as winter
California

pooling the brain

having no known direction, even
. . . only the open road

the eyes closed, leaning forward into
the only riches

the great souls
solo

Henry Jackson

Cicero

Cicero always came out on top.
He was Harlem's authentic hero
Ever since his mother cried for joy
By herself

She brought up her bright and pretty boy.
She had groomed him to win
Not to be like his daddy
Who pimped her into poverty
Before the local police took him
For some other nigger, then pulled the trigger.
Cicero was told what he was spozed to do
And smart enough to know
Life was too short
To waste one second
Being a child.
Cicero at twelve
The age Jesus started to preach
Went out into the streets
Big for his age everywhere.
He learned to offer himself to old ladies
The very moment they let their loneliness slip:
Being nice, he gave them consolation at a price.
Now and then he hopped a ride downtown
Where he caught the eyes of well-dressed young men
On Madison Avenue.
He never allowed himself to forget
What he had to do to get what he wanted
And he was not going to lose
Not to the midnight callers
Who closed the deal
When they pulled off his bargain underwear
Without seeing who he was
Or how much they had to pay
To get what they wanted.
Cicero always came out on top.

Cicero was first kid on the block
To discover the mountain of snow
Where tenement women and men
Got their first taste for free
But paid the rest of their lives
To the white lady
With permanent strings on all her things.
And Cicero saw he couldn't help but win

If he made the lady
Work for him.

So at sixteen he started to deal
In corners of catacombs
Junkies entered at their own expense
To slit open their veins
In the night to holler
And moan
Sometimes all night long
Waiting
For Cicero
Who received their possessions
Their stolen dollar bills
Their quick-money lives
That he supplied with the white lady's snow.
They had nowhere else to go
Cause Cicero took over the block
After learning all the lessons
From Big Willie the neighborhood teacher
Who thought he had taught Cicero everything
Till they met on payday behind a hallway door
When Cicero
At eighteen
Knowing life was too short
Aimed Big Willie straight in the head.
It was Big Willie's time to go
Cause Cicero knew one lesson more
Than his teacher.
Cicero always came out on top.

And Cicero was determined to stay on top.
He had nothing to fear
After looking death in the face
So many times
He became a hero
And legend too
On 116th Street and Seventh Avenue.
His mother moved out the neighborhood for good
To a brand new house on the Island:

172

Cicero even bought some acres in Las Vegas
Guaranteeing himself on a rainy day
A place to stay and lay.
He was not going to end up like his daddy;
He was a new breed
Determined to get every thing he could
Every day he could.
Nobody ever schooled him to get the Nobel Prize.
Life was too short
And it wasn't his fault
People are weak as they are
He was born poor as he was
There was no way out of his skin
(Wasn't everybody locked in?)

Somebody had to lose
But not him
Always determined to win.
So Cicero kept the traffic going
From the back seat of his red and green limousine.
He stayed on his job.
That's why he heard the police sirens
But didn't hear the men in the mob
The night they surrounded his car
And rammed its headlights into Cicero's face.
He was nearly blind
When the blood gushed through his brain,
The night the sirens stopped
Cicero, authentic hero, always on top.

Elsie Janis

California

I left the hills of emerald green,
And entered a land of tan,
Where all I saw was a grazing herd,
And sometimes a lonely man.

And all the time through that land of waste,
I was living again in my mind
My life in that bungalow, covered with flowers,
In the land I had left behind.

Though the sky is blue, it's a paler blue,
And the sun has a lemon ray,
While the orange sun that I love so well
Is two thousand miles away.

And now I'm a thousand miles farther on,
And snow lies over the land;
From habit I reach out to gather a rose,
Then gaze on an empty hand.

Oh, California, magic spot,
Where the sky and the sea are blue,
Some lovely day when my work is done,
I'm coming back to you.

Robinson Jeffers

Phenomena

Great-enough both accepts and subdues; the great frame takes all
    creatures;
From the greatness of their element they all take beauty.
Gulls; and the dingy freightship lurching south in the eye of a
    rain-wind;
The airplane dipping over the hill; hawks hovering
The white grass of the headland; cormorants roosting upon the
    guano-
Whitened skerries; pelicans awind; sea-slime
Shining at night in the wave-stir like drowned men's lanterns;
    smugglers signaling
A cargo to land; or the old Point Pinos lighthouse

Lawfully winking over dark water; the flight of the twilight herons
Lonely wings and a cry; or with motor-vibrations
That hum in the rock like a new storm-tone of the ocean's to turn
   eyes westward
The navy's new-bought Zeppelin going by in the twilight,
Far out seaward; relative only to the evening star and the ocean
It slides into a cloud over Point Lobos.

Ronald Johnson

Letter Picture

Out from this floor of words
the whole

is threshold:

The World is Coming

through wide corridors.

Hundreds of doors hinge under us,
in a page

one, inside another

inside another.
THE WORLD IS COMING

high and wide, in the vacant air . . .

straight through the four white walls of the real

until it no longer appears

different
from what the eye sees.

Obelisk

Two ways I see
in simultaneous noon—

eye to eye
the great round sun rises

on both horizons.

I see an outer

inner moon.

Jeanetta Jones

Christmas 1976

sun
shrunk in circumference
sheds all day
crisp
golden light
of morning
atmosphere scourged
clean
wind out of northwest

chill
verge of frost
cats fat with fur and
fat
coffee
aroma travels slowly
huddled
molecules
nippy air

a few leaves
fallen
ferns down
Monterey pine brazen green
five o'clock stream
of headlights
sweater
weather

California winter

Duck Hunting in North Beach

sun
shadow of wooden stairs to the flat above me
he takes her pretty head in his mouth
lets her live

le berger

Unicorn Street
Varennes
Green
upper Grant
long hill down to the slough
reeds reflected in dark windows
drakes
carry knives
pools of light
quiet
rustle of wings heavy with flight
too tired to sleep

tension
sharp sweet smell in the air
humorous
humiliating
poignant

men in small boats
enter floodwater
of their own volition

birds and men
impelled
topography of strange forces
serious country

a strong hand closes on my upper arm

iridescent feathers
emerald green
rosy
illumination
light or blood on my eyes
hand on my neck
stroking
the caress expands
his hand
tightens
another minute passes I am short of breath
astonished
stars
too large for life
fall
hard
voices
harsh breath close to my ear
map the crazy road he flies down
seeking rest

men who turn wildness inside out
for a sign
post
old coin
luck
particular labor

all roads
lead to Tombstone

the old west
(as Rome)
roads built to make our way easy
make our way
endless

Bunichi Kagawa

Hollow Summer

Along the hard ground no longer creeps
The dew to tell of the year's invisible trust,
Pure as the thin cry in a dream;
    And as in dim concentration,
The sun, far above the rootless hour
Weaves the slow change of earth;
I, hiding the strength of days,
With brain gradual as the cluttering sleep
Of leaves, hiding a sunken path that curves towards memory,
Invade my history defined by the hasty blur
Of passion to this hollow summer.

O the stubborn poverty locked in brain!
What love, what quick rain
That comes upon what summer's desolation
Shall know my door? The quiet of ruin,
That cannot be crushed even with sleep,
Supports me with its wide labour of stillness,
As I, heavy as the slow-crumbling pillar of light,
Stand away alone from the snare of dream.

Silent Intimacy

The lovely ease of flowering
And fruiting of the trees,
Dreams through the old years,
That we may read therein
The civility of Nature's career.

Though in Nature there is no pity,
No answer and no memory,
One imperial afternoon is enough
To hold the remembered light
Of one years, now lost and dim.

Hidden Flame

A portion of decayed smile magnified
Upon the mirror . . .
Or perhaps other belief or quietness
Nourished of its own leaves and ends
Now withers gradually within me
Like the noiseless death of light.

Life seen through the hollow caves
Of my eyes dotted with this or that
Of doubts or somehow or a belief
Crumbles like the wall of wind spent;
I touch it and the beyond with careful
Totality of my hand, the dense structure
Of a feel complete and mute.

And gradually, the dark flame of will
Lurking behind the hands that touch,
Hands that grasp, and hands that feel,
Eats into my body left mostly alone
Like the ceaseless pillar of waterfall.

Lenore Kandel

Woman Chant

were I a wise woman in the hill tribes
rough Jewels hung in my grease slick hair
and dreams spewing out of my mouth
as I chanted by the dawn fire

raising my arms with the flight of the wild birds
                    sky trumpet   knife wing
                    that lifts the light
Scatter, night children!
run to your holes and dens
creep to the roots of grandfather oak
the daywind is blowing out the stars
Scatter, spirits that walk between the worlds
rejoin your yesterdays once more
Thus and thus I would sing   I would chant
I would squat in the thin cold dust and stare to the fire
gleaning revelations from ember and flame and the tracing of sparks

were I a wise woman of the hill tribes
I would have a skin bag with a certain feather
fever come here and fever go
I would have a skin bag filled with everyday magic
rare stones and bones and herbs that grow
where the clouds hide the mountain

this I would do that the people grow stronger
that the young grow wise and the wise be loving
that the earth bear us lightly
that the night give us shelter
that the day give us laughter
that we share with each other
with the eagle   with the salmon
with the bear   with the otter
with the planet   with the stars
                    may it be

Dead Billy

you're a long way gone from here, Billy
body becoming earth and the rest of you farther than star light
messages across the green glaciers of interstellar drift
death alters the reference points
when I think of you I look beyond Orion
maybe   I see a tarot deck spinning through a magician's hands

181

or your smile rising in the Bat nebula
somewhere beyond the bend of space
the tenderest memory I have of you is you completely nodded out
clasping your baby in the total security of unfeigned love
you were a green flame of unacceptable truth
and you ring like a zen bell
spiraling through infinity like you always knew the way home

Iwao Kawakami

The Room

(the years have closed a door
   open it and find a room)
this, for you and your brother
   mind you now, keep it clean
A room with swinging window panes
the wind is a hand pushing against your face
you unlistening boy, standing and shivering
   wasn't influenza bad enough?
(a world shimmers before your eyes—dew on unkempt yard
   grasses, paper bubbling on rusting cans)
that useless alarm clock
   you awful, you kids—lazy, lazy
The sun is the flash of a new knife
my brother sleeps in profound dark
(dream of Minnesota—the freezing wind, the white winter)
hang up your clothes
   the mothballs drop, do not step
Here is my black cap
I hate my green velvet suit
(child, was it tragic? Child, you could not retreat with your
back against the grammar school fence)
remember the Saturday
   the mop, the broom—dustpan, water
On this my shelf—books, magazines, folders
I know my brother's—tops, pliers, wrenches

182

(a truck roars over the Nevada desert—you are a dusty rider
    against a singing blue sky)
stop fighting, stop you two
    rolling all over the floor
Your bloody nose—you laugh
the helplessness of my twisted wrist
(by Lake Michigan you lit a pipe—the room is gone and
        there is
    nothing between us but a continent of smothered years)

Bob Kaufman

Waiting

SOMEWHERE THERE WAITS, WAITING
A BOOK IS WAITING, WAITING,
TO BE WRITTEN.
COLD COLD PAGES, WAITING,
TO BE WRITTEN,
MAN SEEKS GOD,
IN A BOOK

SOMEWHERE THERE WAITS, WAITING
A PICTURE WAITS, WAITING,
WAITING TO BE PAINTED
COLD COLD CANVAS, CANVAS.
WAITING TO BE PAINTED.
MAN SEEKS GOD IN A PICTURE.

SOMEWHERE THERE WAITS, WAITING
A WOMAN WAITING, WAITING,
TO BE LOVED, WAITING,
COLD COLD WOMAN,
WAITING TO BE LOVED,
MAN SEEKS GOD
IN A WOMAN.

SOMEWHERE THERE WAITS, WAITING
A MAN IS WAITING, WAITING,
COLD COLD MAN, WAITING,
TO BE WANTED, WAITING.
MAN SEEKS GOD
IN MAN.

SOMEWHERE THERE WAITS, WAITING
A BABY IS WAITING, WAITING.
WAITING, WAITING TO BE BORN,
COLD COLD BABY, WAITING,
TO BE BORN, BLOOD OF EARTH,
WAITING TO BE.
MAN SEEKS GOD,
IN A BABY.

WIND, SEA,
SKY, STARS,
SURROUND
US.

Come

Come let us journey to
       the sky,
I promised the Moon.

All that I come from
All that I have been,
All that I am
All that I come to
All that I touch,
Blossoms from
       a thorn,
AROSEAROSE

Love is the condition
of Human Beings
Being Humans.

184

To be beloved
Is all I need
And whom I love
Is loved indeed,
There never was a Night that
Ended, or began,
Forms breaking
Structures imaged,
Come love,
Love come.

Andrea Kelsey

Medicine Journey

Since the beginning, it was said,
    Mina'who loll teh
Your dream will tell you of your death, coming.

One came into being under the mountain in northworld,
    Who did not know his dreams, meanings.
Entered into the southeastern world in a dark cloud.

After a time, that one slept, who did not used to sleep.
    Who did not know his dreams, meanings.
He went, in his dream, to east ocean, death place.

        Feather piece said,
        Sing, sing, sing this song.
        And you will live again,
        Hai yac a quan ney, this way
           Only, hay yac a quan ney.

Mina'who loll teh
His dream will tell him of his death, coming.

      I go away, my heart to be a shadow
      I will turn into a ghost. I will visit east ocean.

There will be crying around the fire.
There will be crying around the fire.

> Sing this song and you will
> Live again,
> Hai yac a quan ney, this
> Way only, hay yac a quan ney.

They danced him up at east ocean.
They danced him up at east ocean.

Perhaps It Is That Way Always With You

Nin nes sawn new one, chillee will loh.
If you work against the world, the world will work
> Against you.

Des con weh tah un'.
I guess just today
Perhaps it is that way always with you.

> If you don't do right,
> > You are not in harmony
> You have left something undone,
> Perhaps it is that way always with you.
> Des con weh tah un.

California History

There was a terrible drought all over this land,
And giant serpent-like animals came out of the
> Salt-slime where water used to be, and
> Slithered across the foothills that
> Surround us now.

The world was holding its breath.
And there was no wind, and when

The wind went away the clouds couldn't
Come, and the rain couldn't come, because
The world was holding its breath.

And the people went out looking for clean, cool water
And found only salt-slime, and where they
    Looked for water they left
    Their bones, buried...pink, yellow, blue,
    Reddish bones. Because the world was
    Holding its breath, and the wind
    Went away.

They left their bones, and now upon the mountain
    Trails, across the valleys and foothills,
    You can hear them, talking about the time
    The rain went away, when there was no water,
    And about the serpent-like creatures and
        About how they left their bones,
    When the wind went away, and the world
    Held its breath.

Power Does Not Know Time

Power does not know time.
Power does not know space.
Power is like the wind, the south of a woman's wail.
Power is all encompassing.
Power makes things happen.
Power changes things.
Power is within each living thing.
Power is within each thing.

There is no limit to power.
    There is no distance. I can fly.

Before the time of order, the word was
    Watery.
Before the word getters devised a way to
    Scoop up the world,

Powers ran rampant across the watery mist.
Watery mist rising, where the rivers were to be.
   Powers ran rampant across the water mist, like
   Wind, coming like the sound of a woman crying,
      Weaving mysterious things, that have no names,
To put the world in order.

It is time for the people.
It is time for the people.

Out of the belly of the mountain, out of the
Center of the earth, the people came.
They came out, that time, from the center of the
   Earth. To see that the world was in order.
   To hear the song of the earth, to know the power
   Surrounding them.
The stars rolled across the sky like sea waves.
And coyote danced with the stars.

It is time for the people.
It is time for the people.

These are the songs that you will sing, people.
These are the dances that you will dance, people.
This is where you will fish.
This is where the acorns are.
Listen to your dreams, they will tell you things of
   Powers. They will make things happen. They will
   Change things.

There is no limit to power.
   There is no distance. I can fly.

It is time for the people.
It is time for the people.

I am from the earth.
I am from the center of the earth.

The power of a prayer is real.
The power of a song is real.

Edward C. Kemble

Blowing Up The Wind

"Ever blowing, colder growing, sweeping madly through the town,
Never ceasing, ever teasing, never pleasing, never down;
      Day or night, dark or light,
Sand a-flying, clapboards sighing,
Groaning, moaning, whistling shrill,
      Shrieking wild and never still.

In September, in November, or December, ever so,
even in August, will the raw gust, flying fine dust, roughly blow.
      Doors are slamming, gates a-banging,
Shingles shivering, casements quivering,
Roaring, pouring, madly yelling,
      Tales of storm and shipwreck telling.

In our bay, too, vessels lay to, but find
No shelter from the blast,
Whitecaps clashing, bright spray splashing,
      Light foam flashing, dashing past.
Yards are creaking, blocks a squeaking,
Rudder rattling, ropes all clattering,
Lugging, tugging at the anchor,
      Groaning spars and restless spanker.

Now the sun gleams, bright the day seems,
      Hark! he comes is heard the roar;
Haste to dwelling, dread impelling, heap the fire,
      Close the door.
Onward coming, humming, drumming,
Groaning, moaning, sighing, crying,
Shrieking, squeaking, (reader, 'tis so).
Thus bloweth the wind at 'Frisco."

Ed Kissam

Riding The Thermals

Riding the thermals
the glider pilot
feels them move
like forest mammals

rustling, invisible,
riding the thermals
the one you always
can find is Albuquerque

powerplant–buzzard–eye
view of the city (huge

stationary mushroom
of churned up air.)

Powerplant windspout
heat rising out of
Jurassic coal, from
skeleton of ferns

while in this infinitesimal
present we trample it all
underfoot

building the mushroom,
sending the mycorhizzal
filaments outward

Kaiparowitz, San Juan coal
turned dazzling light
on Sunset Strip,

megawatts steaming off of the coal
to city, to reef
our soft polyp bodies

leaving behind the shell
earth ocean breaks on.

History is replaced
with current
through tubes of neon

pink, blue, green
to announce the Age of the Cocktail Lounge.
The guy who stokes the furnace
that stokes the lights

he gets to recycle his anguish
and beat up the shiftless
hippie or indian

or fuck that particular
sloppy broad,
third from the end of the bar,

motel room w / color TV
perhaps very faintly
nightwind outside
the drawn curtains

he will brush it aside
a minor distraction
as equally

when he comes that comes
as a minor distraction
to wind or buzzards
or brush in the moonlight.

But he is the spore
of the mushroom,
merely the underground
phase of an alternating generation

tiny but multitudes
when it comes to the transactions

of energy
and capital,

merely a footnote
in the annals
of geologic time

his thoughts, loves
birth and death etched
very faintly

in the updraft of heat
up off the city

as the weight of it
presses him into the silt

brother, sister
to the fern

carried on thin skeleton of words.

Moving On

Presumably, all the yellow truck needs
is kingpins
at which point, in exactly one month
I can be picking cherries in the Dalles
with technical assistance from Juan
stuffing the pails with both hands
and 60 bucks a day.

At home base, the whatever they are
do show Mendelian variations, not
surprising me, given a population so
huge that California is still jewelled

every spring the millenium.

Steve Kowit

Xochicalco

This morning, up at those ruins gleaming
like tombstones in the sun, the three of us
sat in the shade of a crumbling temple
& considered the seasons.
We modelled out the ecliptic with stones
fumbling like gradeschool kids with equations
we only half-understood
& giggled over our ignorance
there where a thousand years ago
Toltec astronomers calculated the revolutions
of Venus & perfected the calendar.
Xochi-calco: beflowered city. Rolando
called it a geophysical center
where priests engaged in a study of time itself
& Topiltzin, the prince, revealed himself
as the feathered serpent. Gold,
blood & cerulean flowers
flourished among the wild grass.
Up there you could see the whole countryside:
the road unwinding into the valley
under a sky of pure ceremonial blue.
It was our last day here before heading south.
In the afternoon we wandered among temples,
strolled thru the ball court,
offered the last of our bread
to a couple of scrawny dogs
who trailed us around the ruins,
& tried our hand at some rubbings
that ended up like those scribbles
people make in rapture, under acid,
imagining they've caught some unspeakable essence.
Too bad. I would have wished to have taken with me
a print of that signature
Mary discovered in midafternoon,
half buried among the priests & glyphs

on the temple of Quetzalcoatl:
an exquisite hand pulling a block
of worked stone by a braided rope:
one of those fragments the rains
of a thousand years had not yet laid waste.
I was shaken by it,
it was so tender & deftly
wrought & spoke with such grace
of the artist's life
that I lie here, a millenium later,
awakened by it to a flood of feelings,
reminded of all these people I won't see again,
& of my own life,
the greater part of which is already spent,
& of my own work.
Tomorrow we leave.
Our backpacks lie by the open window.
Out over the canyon
Venus–Xolotl gleams in the night sky.
The clock ticks like a restive heart.
With love & sorrow
I have carved these figures out of the language
that you may remember:
Julia . . . Rolando . . . Miguel . . .
called forth,
your faces drift thru the dark like spirits.

Geraldine Kudaka

Paranoia

Paranoid people are bad lovers
but make good bodyguards

they float like plastic bags
snakelike
            slittering
across the room

they get you in their grasp
they eat you alive

you try to take a bath
but the mask does not wash off...
then you finally realize
paranoia is contagious

you walk down market street
and get confused
thinking all the wigs once belonged
to an eskimo
who was scalped for pelts

you pull out a mango
the phone rings
your ex-husband calls up and wants to know
if you've thrown away his baby

a 200 lb. man carefully balanced
on an undersized seat
rides thru on a motor scooter—
and you know
a man of forty should stop
playing games

your shallow lady friends
surround you
and pretend to be interesting people
while they talk of this man
and that man

in the background, the operator says:
this is a recording
        the number you have called
is disconnected—
Please hang up and try again...

by the time you get home
you lock the door with a note
to all your bad lovers
saying: "Go To AUCKland!!"

you take the phone off the hook
and warn your kitchen stove
not to hand out scraps to strangers,
elfs, ex-husbands, stray husbands, stray cats,
strange cats, and paranoid people

Joanne Kyger

September

> The grasses are light brown
> and ocean comes in
> long shimmering lines
> under the fleet from last night
> which dozes now in the early morning

Here and there horses graze
> on somebody's acreage

> > Strangely, it was not my desire

that bade me speak in church to be released
> but memory of the way it used to be in
> careless and exotic play

> > when characters were promises
> then recognitions. The world of transformation
is real and not real but trusting.

> > > Enough of these lessons? I mean
didactic phrases to take you in and out of
love's mysterious bonds?

> > Well I myself am not myself

> > and which power of survival I speak
for is not made of houses

It is inner luxury, of golden figures
that breathe like mountains do
          and whose skin is made dusky by stars.

from *Trip out and Fall Back*

In this endless dream of parties, Gordon Baldwin
drives a tractor across the field. I am watching
John Thorpe and his drinking buddy, Angelica Clark,
standing by the pool table at the side of the field.
How can you be monastic and drunk at the same time,
she says, and advocates a return to Protestantism
as the Middle Way.

Philip Lamantia

Untitled

The mermaids have come to the desert
They are setting up a boudoir next to the camel
who lies at their feet of roses

A wall of alabaster is drawn over their heads
By four rainbow men
Whose naked figures give off a light
That slowly wriggles upon the sands

I am touched by the marvelous
As the mermaids' nimble fingers go through my hair
That has come down forever from my head
To cover my body:
A savage fruit of lunacy

Behold, the boudoir is flying away
And I am holding onto the leg of the lovely one
Called beneath the sea
BIANCA
She is turning
With the charm of a bird
Into two giant lips
As I drink from the goblet of suicide

She is the angelic doll turned black
She is the child of broken elevators
She is the curtain of holes you never want to throw away
She is the first woman and the first man
And I am lost to have her

I am looking for the region
where the smoke of your hair is thick
Where you are again climbing over the white wall
Where your eardrums play music
To the cat that crawls in my eyes
I am recalling memories of you BIANCA

I am looking beyond the hour and the day
To find you BIANCA

o

r   v

g   e

a   h

t   e

n   i   l

I   w   I   e

B   O   C   c   t

o   V   E   t   h

d   o   r   g

o   m   i   i

w   i   c   n

n   n   y

g   b   b

i

r

d

s

I

put

my   ner

ves   over

my   eyes   my

veins   over   my

skin   and   think

HA!   I   decipher

the   talk   of   the   gods!

Beryle LaRose

Rolling Thunder

Thunder rolls in the distance,
   lightning dances across the tree tops.
As the thunder grows nearer,
   raindrops fall lightly on our Mother Earth.
The thunder reaches a deafening pitch,
    the rain falls heavier as mother nature
      protests the obscenities brought down upon her.
As she bathes, in the beautiful soft rain water,
   seemingly, the land is once more washed clean.
Like a new born baby,
   the sun glistens on the wetness of her blanket.

Untitled

   Walk with me
   through the leaves of trees.
I am the wind,
   whistling down the canyon,
   whispering to the sweet grass,
   impregnating the seed of life,
caressing all.
I am a tree,
   come stand by my side,
   let my branches embrace you,
stand tall, stand straight,
   ageless beauty bathed in truth.
I am the flower,
   that adorns our mother,
   hold me in your hands,
   smell my sweet natural fragrance,
let me be free.
I am the rain,
   that quenches thirst,
   softly cleansing everything,

    stand under me with uplifted face,
and bathe in nature's kisses.
I am the mountain,
    climb over my body,
    waste not my blanket,
    for I will provide,
    food for our children,
    take no more than necessary,
so that there remains a balance.
    I am all around you.
    I walk by your side,
    protect you, hurt you, love you,
I am life.

Resident Artifact

cold marble is my home
deteriorating buckskin, my clothes
white eyes staring unfeeling
foreign voices ringing
fingers pointing
laughter, snickers
"oohs and ahhs"
"she is a young girl,
how could she dress that way?"
"no class"
words, empty words,
echo apathy, curiosity, mimicry.
amateur anthropologists,
with their accumulation of academic assumption
judging, on sight alone
my way of life.
making fun of my religion
questioning my status of princess
daughter of a chief
degrading my pride,
because it does not fit in their world
their world of narrow minds

minds that can only see black or white
release me!! give me back to my mother!
For you only hold my body
in this house called a museum!

Spirit Mountain

Memories of my childhood
gives me a warm feeling.
Seeing a mountain
at a distance in springtime
made one feel drawn
to her majestic body.
Searching for the unknown
experiencing the birth of nature,
therefore experiencing and relating
thoughts of nature to human life.
First a seed
then birth into bloom,
as precious to me
as the rare lady slipper
on Spirit Mountain in the spring.

Alan Chong Lau

"Sun Yat Sen Comes To Lodi"

1

SUN YAT SEN COMES TO LODI
grandfather in pinstripes
mouth sporting a toothpick
tells friends, "no sin, no sin,
no sir, no sin to get excited"

mr. yee's four year old beaming in a pink meenop
hair's done up in pinktails

sam wo has closed his laundry
only day of the year he would do this
excepting new year's

the good doctor smiles
from a sedan's back seat
cheers resound
delta dust flies

there is the speech
"china will be china again"
this brings tears

not losing a minute
to sip
he tells us all that money buys arms
money drives out manchus

most people understand, there is little hesitation
the new york yankees have not yet won the pennant
it is too early to predict weather or the lucky number
but money is dug from pockets
pulled from cloth bags

when the time comes
he says thank you
a cry of genuine sadness
a rush to take seats for a last picture

photographer tong yee
fumbles underneath a black shroud like a soul leaving body
poses change   legs shift position
nobody seems to mind too much
only local banker wong hesitates
meeting the public often, he declines
offering a bigger contribution instead

grandfather sits by the doctor's side
pausing only to doff his hat
remove a coin from the ear
and drop a wet toothpick in a spittoon

2

he is proud of that picture
brown and bent in one corner
the only photo left in the family album
since big sister's marriage

there is also a newspaper clipping
with the headline,
"S U N   Y A T   S E N   C O M E S   T O   L O D I"
spread out all in characters
that could be relatives telling a story
or scales of a black bass dripping evidence of water

never having learnt the language
i just have to go by hearsay

my ship does not need a helmsman

> "a ship depends upon
> its helmsman for direction
> the great ship china
> is guided by mao tse tung"
—As seen on the entrance to one of the floors of the people's republic of china
department store in kowloon-hong kong

1

here i lie in chinatown
coughing into my mattress
soaked with the odours
of salted fish
dark years old

home is not
never was
this graygreased
smokefilled room

the walls
smell the same
as the rotting wood crates
from china
that lie piled
with my memories
buried under old papers
of sun yat sen
scented with mothballs

i go outside
and spit
throwing up specks of blood
half cooked soystained rice
for the insistent pigeons

i am a sick dog
and though my tongue
lies continually out
my tail remains standing

2

the young ones
born here
or f.o.b. (fresh off the boat)
snot dripping from the nose
asses strutting
under the streetlamps
simply regard me
as old man
which means docile dog

i know it
don't think i don't know it
but my heart
is not in the fight
of children

it lies in the bones
and ashes of my wife

who died waiting
in the home of my province
feeding the ducks
staining her apron

the young barbarians
urge me to protest
in a western style
this gray life

they thrust red books in my face
but i see nothing
except the pigeons
leaving droppings
on my bench

they do not realize
i would rather
withdraw from what
i have never belonged to
than to embrace it

3

here i lie in chinatown
may the rain soak
my ashes

may the muddy rivers
carry them home
to my province

a ship does not need
a helmsman
only a woman
who strokes my brow
and laughs
at the moon
when it is full

2 Stops On The Way Home

for jeff chan and the tofu store in marysville

BEANCURD

1

once
maybe two times a year
when returning home
stop in marysville

past orchards, fruit stands
sweet musk of rotting peaches
collide with death smells of skunks
in the valley's heat

dust
hurting up eyelids
fruitpickers sun brown
a speck of red bandana
their only shout

this japanese
with a store of woodplanks
lined with fishing poles
immigrant groceries
wading boots slumped over the counter

coca cola vies with kimchee
scallions and mudstained fish
spotted tails still flop
over in a tin
bucket

i cry for nehi
momma rushes into a toilet
lined with newspapers
she can only half-read

but in a backroom
the lardcan
sliced in half
tucked between round
baskets of beansprouts

cubes of white tundra
in clear icy water

WILD POTATOES

   2

jump a stone fence
ancestors built
years before

muddy currents oozing silt
water skipper characters
on a glimmer

take off the shoes
dig dig deep
deep underneath rushes
you smell
whenever they burn the delta
out

even without light
grandma can still pick out
the tenderest green shoots

water just soaks cuffs
alone in darkness
we move to the hum of mosquitoes

the occasional moan of a train
in the distance

Joaquin Legaspi

Needle—

Earnestly, one has need It be said— cruel
In every tongue of all races to dwell
On shortcomings, like pointed steel must pierce
The grieving nerves from its growing live fears
Suffer the chills and fevers— off and on.
A malady as one's sole companion
In pains and joys strung as beads— mad schemes
That tingles in farcical harmony;
Remnants of some lost dismembered dreams
To be sensed in its dire ignominy—
Not a cacophony— but clacking din
Made by vultures at a carcass seen.
Hungrily your heart needs some surcease
Record not the hurt from fate— dismiss
And let the sane desires be not a curse.
Branded in tell-tale punctures' ugly scars.
The monkey grips your back without slack.
Your mind is numb and as your aching body
Cry for 'It'— the only hope as counter attack
Completing the sound rest of destiny . . . . .

*   *   *

From the primitive land of China—
There was, the acupuncture first waged.
Remedial to ailments through its media—
Recover one's normal health, thus evade
Aches and pains from its unwanted feature
Probing with the pins of acupuncture.
As pills, spirits or grass encompass
Fictional joy temporarily it does.
From "Iron curtain"— "Bamboo curtain"
To "Bull-shit curtain" there sustain.

Lulu Delma de Leon

Fearless

I walked through yesterday
With slow and careful pace.
I lived it, calm, away
With no steps to retrace.

Today is easier still.
I find it needs no striding.
Today I do my will.
For today I'm riding.

Tomorrow I don't fear,
For there is no denying—
Though tomorrow isn't here,
Tomorrow I shall be flying.

George Leong

TW Dance

Come on people
dance—
Third World People
no matter where you are
your eyes tend to be
brown—and hair
black and brown—
dance
the rhythm motion
of our bodies dance
our lives
   sing the song
   of our bleeding hearts
           and

our happiness it can't be beat.
From the tropics of Afrika
to Brazil to philipines
   the deserts of
   Sahara   Gobi   Mojave
The rice fields of the world
the drums of war / peace
the feet of the children
        the old
swingin' the same ancestrial
hips–sing the song
    that of the bleeding heart
    and happiness that can't be
    beat
dance to our strength
  how we exorcise the devil
with our united fist–how'we earn and pay so dearly
to recover and protect freedom
When diablos blancos
"the man" comes to confiscate
and destroy—
          dance

          dance
Dance with me fine Afrikan Queen
  black as your soil that
  bears fruit so sweet
Dance with me fine Asian Queen
  brown like grain
  that nurture our strength
Raza y Indio y Caribé y
Musica Latina—
  dance
  dance
with guns
  dance
with love
  dance
we are fearles
  dance

with all our love
    dance
we are fearless

Philip Levine

Saturdays In Heaven

When the woman next door
came home from work, I heard
her pass my door cursing her
own life and the dark.
She fumbled at the lock,
and inside the dog howled
from his ancient well
of sadness. The building
went back to its rest,
I was neither awake or asleep,
then or now, that March day
in heaven. Far off I heard
the noon sirens born
of each cell's need to cry out.
This was what we waited for,
"The Revenge of Asia" we stood
in line on Saturdays to see.

*

The rose drew in its breath
and dreamed a thousand years,
the lettuce walked the aisles of heaven in love with dirt.
From the burning almond tree
the winds spoke to us.
That solitary messenger,
the magpie, closed his wings
and waited. Your face,
that held the flush of dawn
in the strong bones under

the eyes and the flat forehead,
darkened. Now the moon
could close and touch you
all it wanted. Its light
streams in and fills the caverns
and again for a moment
you hear the winter stars.

*

Take your hand and place it
so on the crown of my head
and call me by my one name,
and I'll answer in the voices
of wonder, I'll kneel
beside the blood as a child
kneels, praying to waken
in one world. My life
falls out of my pockets—
keys, coins, matches, a knife,
hankie, wadded notes
from the farthest stars,
little words that crossed
the night and came up bad roads
to my hands, flakes of pain
and sweat, seeds the wind blew
onto my skin for safekeeping.

*

A man born in Michigan
can laugh at anything. He
can kneel, in his underwear
before God. The woman
next door can sing in unison
with an old dog. I could
spend my life talking
to the earth, but it turns
to ashes. The gray fox
who must have dreamed

these leafless woods, he
is the king. Each night we
rise in our eaten gowns
belling our skulls, drumming
our breathless chests,
and dance before the fires
of the flesh. At dawn
beside the breaking river,
an old man and his woman,
whose child was wrapped
in newspaper, come home
to their damp clothes, eat
in the cold, and move on.

Making It New

All morning
rain slowly filled
my hair, misted
my glasses as I broke
the old curbing of US 24,
and Cal, grunting behind,
loaded the pieces
into the wheel barrow.
"Go slow, man!" but I
was into it. Now, at noon,
we sit under a tree
sharing my lunch. Cal
looks tired, his light
brown skin almost gray.
His father, he tells me,
caught him last night
with white boys in his room.
"I told him, 'Don't look
and you won't see.'" The rain
comes down harder, a wind
picks up, swirling

the few leaves crushed
under the trees. My damp arms
shiver in the sudden chill
of autumn. We are the dignified
by dirt, digging our way
down US 24 to Monroe,
Michigan, where the waters
of Raisin Creek foam
with the milk poured
from the mill, and the great
slow barges from Ninevah
drift in the current,
loaded with yellow spices,
rubies like headlights,
and the whores of the East.
Cal lies back and closes
his eyes. I smoke and let
him sleep. An hour passes
and not one car. At first
his blanket of newspaper
rises in the breeze, a giant
butterfly mottled with slaps
of rain. Cal sleeps on,
his face as open and soft
as a child's, his feet
crossed at the ankles,
the black leather cap
fallen back on the grass.
"Cal," he said the first day,
staring into my eyes,
"is short for Calla, the lily,"
the yellow furled one
his mother so loved. Far off
a car hisses down the road;
it's Teddy, the Captain, come
to tell us it's raining
and we can fly home
or go back to work
or get lost. I leave
Cal, the dark wet bride

of the wind, and go
out into the rain
to get the word—we aren't
ever gonna make Monroe.

Jack London

The Worker And The Tramp

Villanelle

Heaven bless you, my friend—
You, the man who won't sweat;
Here's a quarter to spend.

Your course I commend,
Nor regard with regret;
Heaven bless you, my friend.

On you I depend
For my work, don't forget;
Here's a quarter to spend.

Ah! you comprehend
That I owe you a debt;
Here's a quarter to spend,
Heaven bless you, my friend.

Walter Raleigh Lovell

Whut De Folks At Home Hab Done

(Written during the Third Liberty Loan Drive)

Dah ain't no use en worryin' 'bout der Hindeb'g line,
'Ner wond'rin why de Yanks ain't crossin' o'er de R'ine;
'Kase der me'sure ob de battle, an de killin' ob de Hun,
Dat depen's upon de doin's whut de folks at home hab done.

Dah ain't no use in talkin' 'bout de winnin' ob de wah,
An' a-spinnin' ob yo' the'ries tell yo' tires de lowah jaw;
Talkin' is a cheap thing; takes Bon's to fight de Hun,
And de outcome mos'ly 'pends on whut de folks at home hab done.

So yo' buy dem Wah Stamps, honey, an' a Liberty Bon', or two,
Den help erlong de Red Cross, like de odder fellows do;
Den sabin' food, an' coal, an' gas, only orter be jes' fun,
When yo' know de boys are countin' whut de folks at home hab
   done.

De Dixie boys am comin' an' dey's singin' as dey tramp:
Dey'll kill der deblish Hun, an' hang dat K'iser scamp;
But how soon de job am finished, an' dey sta't home on de run,
Dat depends erpon de doin's whut de folks at home hab done.

An' when de wah am ober, an' de trouble all is pas',
When de dobe of peace am sailin' o'er de land and sea at las',
When de boys bring home de bacon, —tells de story eb'ry one,
Dey'll tell how much es'pended on whut de folks at home hab done.

Daddy's Baby

She's a darling little maiden,
   She's the finest kind of girl;
She's a pretty, brown-eyed lassie,
   With a dainty little curl.
My! to look at such a picture
   Makes your head commence to whirl.

But what makes her such a beauty
   Are her charming little ways;
And her voice is just like music,
   As she kind of shyly says,
"I was once my Daddy's baby,
   But I'm grown up nowadays.

"Now he's got another baby,
   And she's very sweet, you know;
If she weren't then I'd be jealous,

'Cause my Daddy loves her so.
And I love my baby sister,"—
    But she whispers sweet and low.

"I've got the sweetest secret
    That a girlie ever knew—
Will you promise not to tell it—
    Promise faithful, good and true?
Since Daddy has another baby,
    I've another Daddy, too.

"My other Daddy's awful nice,
    And loves me lots. You see
He has no other baby girl,
    He loves just only me.
He tells me when I'm full grown-up,
    His little wife I'll be.

"I love my realest Daddy lots,
    I'll love him all my life,
But he's my mother's husband, dear,
    So I can't be his wife:
For if I'd marry Daddy, too
    'Twould cause just lots of strife."

Curtis Lyle

Mortuary Science Mandala

We are rising from the sea
We are embracing dolphins
We are bent and augmented to the form of desire
We are impulse-pulse potentially planets

Spirit at work in the electronic sunset
Atone-tone-tune-tolls invisibly

A festival of flower tremor of joy tremolo

The cycles of collective communions
The startling substance of light in the consecrated city
reaching up to the whole wide existence of human awareness

Bridge across a deep motion gorge
The legacy of the man-made canyon chasm grave opening
to release the link process of substance up
across the capa–city
These are the days of collective skill and conquest

Five-fold the features of the mind separate and identify
the devotion of harvest and work to the divine with pleasure
The sacred technicians flood the form with energy
and rebuild the body of stark intuition

The float flower of lotus laughing on top of the lake
delivers the sermon of the service root mud bottom song
The petalled balconies driving the gondola of the integral

If I cut you I must realize that I will bleed
Spirits is not a star
sequence is not a symbol
mental is not the mind
blood and water flow directly and actively into the love-call-real
Incandescent carnival

Interchange and commingling first
then inspiration from the depth of strength
from the seed of concentrated inner need
from the harvest of the thing sown
from the creation of clone from the seventy series
comes the engine rising in the back of the mind of man

Blessed is the song bestowed
Blessed is the spirit filled full
Blessed is field sustained the work done
Blessed is the soul released into twice one beatitude

The broken sleep achieved memory entwined to value
The struggle is founded upon its finish

Courage must be muffled against the cold
Character must be thrown against the universal crisis and molded
Man must dare to charge the storm
Attack lightning crush silk the straw hat of ambition burned
at the entrance to the new level

Illumination is a canyon a narrow path an arrow seeking
the heart of a stone deep root elder brother dry bone
wilted marrow drove zen junctions 96 to 105 walk on

Love is the one
Love is the beginning
Love is the bearer of light and motion
Cupped heart far from the furnace of value
Explode the erotic God of the depths
Let the dream ride the real!

The sufferer sits alone isolated from himself
in air-conditioned darkness the guards drop candy bars
every three hours for his personal illumination
on thursdays the chaplin brings him the blood
of another recent dead friend and pours it in his eyes
This is for him the mystic company of perfected beings
This is for him the ordeal of liberation exalted

The last stage has now become the first
The slaves are masters of themselves
The intuitions are new the flesh fresh the theory
of organic rebirth now fact the tensions broken
The children of the tender virgins filled with tenderness

Revelation psychic sunboat structure the sea is wonderful
but I am unconscious and cannot breathe
I need the open window the glass-bottomed wine of my reality
The underside inside the depths of my mind
is now translucent
if I can swim and breathe at the same time
I'll be alright and eagerly real

The flag turned into an eagle
The eagle turned into the eye of a man

Searching for his shadow
his eye went out
and he then became the ear
of the planetary rhythm
It told him to look ahead and plan

Mountain stream
clear up the day like you did the night
I want to be the star in my nature
I want to be poppy source not drug or transference
but source I want to be poppy source
I want to be mountain rock celestial canyon pure alpha
delta soil seeking the level of water
chill morning dharma imbibed
I want to be seven dreams flowing irresistably

I want to be eagle dream
The straw on the floor of the stable of the new age
I am bold enough to ask for a little help
the power to rise with purpose
the power to fly high the power to live in the focus of the sun
the power to be one of your heralds the power to crow
with the crowning chanticleer the power to drink resin and resonate
the coming of new days
If you'll just announce me I'll be there

I want to be eagle dream streaming consciousness
Mud floor dog day looking only up
Pierce my shadow the seance of the meadow calmed by rain
The disappeared pain turned to ecstacy and Saturn joy claim
the future of the planet and I'll stake it out for you
The tender care of dawn cradled
If you're able to announce me I'll be there

Lewis MacAdams

Charleston's Evening Bells

The acrobat's the baddest mammal. He's
aloof and trembling in the coliseum shadows
because tonight's the night
and he's cool, and smoking and
she turns to greet her acrobat.
Snow is closing down the acrobat's eyes
and lighting in her hair and I'm
tumbling down into a kind of reassessment—
thirty years a banker, quietly withdrawn,
blow out the candle. Acts are ruthless,
comrades, brilliant snowy lesions.
Whiskey sour? Push it then,
away from you, and smoke and pills also; and lift
your head up off the carpet,
wrap her shoulders in her mother's racoon fur,
kiss her one last time, and walk her to the door.

Nathaniel Mackey

Poem For Don Cherry

"mu" first part

The day before the
         year begins woke to a
glimpse of her
            scratchy legs
Lotusheaded, squatted
      by the side of the bed
Sat upside a Hill to
      wait for rain or

```
        watch the sun set
                        See
        how far the way we'd
                            come
        went back
```

"mu" second part

The mouth she wore,
who although she wore jeans I
could see she grew hair
on her legs,

her bald feet.
And at the Stream,
who in her cupped hands held it, thirst,
or some worship,
                    whichever.
All the mud, alive
with eggs, with likenesses.
                            Noises
came out of it.
                Calls.

teo-teo-can

The coarse
cloth of
Moorish cante

The fluted
bone of our lady's
blown upon thigh

The enormous
bell of some trumpet's
inturned eye,
some endangered
isle, some

insistent Mu

become the
root of whatever
song

Geraldine Seelemire Mac Leod

Night Mountain

And still must I think of Shelley, standing here
With stars below me, yet with earth's assurance
Hard against my feet.—Sheer
Like a bird toward sky-dark have I come,
Thoughtless of heart's endurance.
. . . Heart has stepped bravely with the feet . . .
My thought it is that's numb.

Star-seeded world at my feet!
Could Night's black hand that flung
Those yellow grains so carelessly
Have let fall one in this still brain,
How would my voice have risen fearlessly!
How would my song have splintered pain!
How would I have sung!

But no—my soul is numb!
My throat can only cry
Out of this mountain-silence to the sky:
Shelley!—forever singing—yet forever lost—Oh, come!
Gather this moment—break it into song!
Here within touch of me it waits too long.
I cannot sing! I am forever dumb—
I will be flesh forever—never song!

Out of the dark, like leaves broken and brown
That cover a dead wind—or like the slow return
Of ash after the blowing flames have ceased to burn—
Where rose my cry, the silence settles down . . .

Native

Mine was a mountain-morning.
I am the child who stood at the foot of the mountains.
Birth was for me like the birth of the birds; or the borning
Of cubs to the coyote. The mountains
Stood over my mother and gave of their peace and their storming.
The valley that swung like a nest and clung like a cave...
Like a nest between peaks; like a cave in the side of the mountains,
Gapes in my thought like a wound in the side, like a grave
Hollowed out of the rock.
                There a glacier anciently gouged out its grave like
                a warning!
A warning?—A promise! The bones of the birds and the coyotes
Are native as stones in these mountains!

Alvin Manook

Hal

When the sunshine lures Society's dregs
Down to MacArthur Park,
Hal comes to sing for them.

His creaky wails stab the air
With thirty years of pain;
While the lonely faces identify,
And aged fingers clap for more.

Hal bought a coat of indifference
from Society's store;
No family ties
No alibis
He is.

He's a welder by trade,
Courtesy, B.I.A.
Money trips from his fingertips

Nearly every payday,
to impress nobodies.

The blue cruisers know him well,
They've slammed the grill on him,
Three and twenty times.

When he was ten,
Hal was orphaned,
Then betrothed to
The American Society of Street People.

Untitled

I see again in print
Someone denying their part
In the event at Golgotha
And I take this to heart

Truth will light the way
I was there by scheme
On that day of disrepute
When the gentle Nazarene
Realized our ancient dreams

Whether I played dice
or,
Mesmerized by the blood and gore
I put compassion on ice
With eyes of lead
I stood there
As perspiration told
His silent war

Maybe I pounded the spikes
(Just doing my Job)
While I steeled my psyche
To his mother's cry

Pity is always in good store
When guilt rules the conscience
For I withheld my comfort
When the Victim dramatized
Calvary.

Untitled

When cities bury Indian custom
In shrouds of progress
I come alone—to the ocean.

The waves bring secrets to the shore
Bids me unlock the past
Where deposits of golden mysteries
Bear the message of new hope
And I must gather wisdom
From the ancient one.

Paul Mariah

Let me call this pine

Let me call this pine
Careless Fire.
The heighth is sixty feet
but there are no branches
until the last few feet.
The black charcoaled trunk
extends up
where the stars burn
in Calaveras County
next to the "No Trespassing" sign
on Forest River near West Point.

Was there violation in trespassing?
Or in the fire burning the pine?

There were charred stumps
all around. Stubs of trees.

Charred the air around us.
Stunted, the growth this world
fights against.

Edwin Markham

Outwitted

He drew a circle that shut me out—
Heretic, rebel, a thing to flout,
But Love and I had the wit to win:
We drew a circle that took him in!

Jim Marks

Where Jazz Goes

Yes, I added a little jazz
   To my distance.
Jazz blew through the thin trees
   Of the expensive forest.

I ran to tell the world
   As this music drove deep wedges
Into my flesh.
   Sounds screaming over the blue horizon
Where birds go.

Where birds go, music goes,
   Motion and flesh, where texture is born.
Blues and butterfingers,
   Birds and peacocks.

The streetlamps burn dim
   Over the rented earth.

Sunday morning after the gigs,
   The town is quiet.
Music and morning blues,
   Come back, jazz. Add more
Distance to my world.
   Stay in my bleeding space.

Walter Martinez

Golden Land

Golden land sunk
Into your bones
Roasted contours
And blue beach
The relationship
Of foams and sands

Flocks of feline fogs
Enter the crevices
Of your deepest bays

Lights sway and dim
Sweat again is air
Heads begin to spin
A milky way swing

Moving to rhythms
From the earth
The grass is high
The moon is bright
Crystal crimson wine
Plus so much night
Reveal the princess
Nude...

Destiny

(fragment)

Ah, once again, I am here before you
like a vague, yet everpresent memory,
to present, as in a court of law,
the honey–dew, the flower–song, my
hummingbird, my bluefound–jade nest.

And, as in a court of law-ley-loi, lies
the spotlight gaze of some brutal judge
who will immediately dismiss the case
as a defect of a useless and obnoxious
artifact...

Ah, somewhere between the bridges
where East meets West (L.A. that is),
where the smoggy and starless skies
wed the concrete and fishless streams
in an orgy of cables and train tracks.

Here, somewhere, I will sit down
and, illegal or not, contemplate
the scene; and to the surprise
of some, I'll have a thought or two
about life, love and no place to go.

Beulah May

Voodoo Song

Never any path, never any track,
Who goes here will never come back.
Hid among the grass, hid among the trees
A fire that snaps and crackles in the breeze...

Old drum quiver like a murdered heart,
Voodoo, voodoo, dance your part.

Wake little serpent coiled upon my knee,
Lift up your sullen eyes and stare at me.

Stretch your jaw till the venom drips,
Dart your forky tongue and lick my lips,
Weave a charm with your hammer-head,
Dark man, dark man, soon be dead.

Out in the coulee all alone
The turkey buzzard will hear him groan.
Never any path, never any track,
Dark man's bones will never come back.

Francisca Carrillo Vallejo McGettigan

A Ballad Of California

(Conchita Arguello)

The fog hung low across the Gate;
The hour preceeded dawn;
A ship, with cargo ladened deep,
Loomed dark that fateful morn.

Upon her deck with brooding frown,
Impatient of delay,
Rezanof stood, and cursed the mist
That blurred his charted way.

For here, at last, within his reach,
If Fortune played him true,
Were corn and beef and precious greens
To feed his starving crew.

For weary days through icy sleet,
Through driving rain and spray,
His sturdy ship had labored on
To gain Saint Francis' Bay.

And look! By seeming force of will
By strength of mind imposed,
Uplifted by a changing wind,
The thinning mist disclosed

Unto the Russian's searching eye,
A vista all undreamed—
A beauteous Bay that stretched away
To where the sunrise gleamed!

Now from the grey adobe fort
That, like a puny child
Stood guard, there came a cannon shot;
The Russian paused, and smiled!

The Juno dipped her flag and made
Reply when questioned; "Who?"
"From whence?"—"For what?"—"From Sitka Port,
Good friends would speak with you!"

Then to the beach in boyish haste
A youthful Spaniard strode,
And from the ship with measured dip
Rezanof's seamen rowed.

He told their plight, credentials showed,
The young Don held his peace:
"The Comandante is not here...
I am his son, Luis."

With courtly air Rezanof bowed,
As Luis proffered rest
Until his father should return
To greet this honored guest.

"My time, my humble roof is yours,
And waits your will, señor;
I beg you, come; my servants wait
To open wide my door!"

At dusk the Russian came ashore

On friendliness intent,
And standing by her mother's side
The fair Concepcion bent.

Was it to be? Had fate so planned?
For as their glances met,
Each knew that soon within each heart
Would friendship love beget!

* * *

The days sped by; the weeks took wing—
He charmed both old and young;
The Padres, too, succumbed and grew
More friendly, one by one.

In all good time, gruff Don José
Returned. He liked it ill;
This guest, a heathen, foreign-born...
Conchita, radiant! Still—

The luxuries his women craved,
Shawls, laces, silks and wool...
This stranger had! Of goods *he* sought
The Mission stores were full.

Could Christian soldier see them starve?
Would Spain his act condemn?
Arguello mused.. He'd *not* refuse
To feed these starving men!

So, while the Juno's hold was stripped
Of Oriental yields,
Her decks were heaped with food-stuffs reaped
From California fields.

Beneath the softly shining moon
Each night, Rezanof came;
Conchita listened as he told
His dreams of wealth and fame.

He pictured vast, palatial halls
Where snow-peaks towered above;
Rich, gay resorts and gracious courts,
And then...he spoke of love!

At her demur, he vowed he'd go
To Don José for leave
To press his suit. "None shall impute
My good intent, nor thieve

"The rose-tint from my darling's cheek,
The semblance of a sigh...
Or single tear dim eyes so dear,
Far sooner would I die!"

Then, hand in hand to Don José
They went for counsel sage;
But ire befogged the father's sight,
His mood quick flamed to rage.

"Your Excellency has presumed!
My daughter knows full well
The laws of Christian Church and State
Regarding marriage! Tell

"Your love to other ears, señor;
And you, my damsel proud,
Seek out your room, no pagan groom
Our honored name shall cloud!"

With bursting heart Conchita sped
For consolation sure
To weep upon her mother's breast,
A refuge fond, secure.

Rezanof said no further word,
But frowning, turned away;
Then off he strode to quickly load
His ship to sail next day.

*　　*　　*

Good Doña Ysabella went—
No moment did she pause—
But straight away to Don José
To plea the lovers' cause.

With tact, she soon convinced her spouse
Their child would pine away,
If plans were not arranged at once
To set the wedding day.

So Don José and Padres four
In council long and staid,
Decided that the Russian seek
The Spanish monarch's aid.

The Holy Father, too, must bless
With dispensation rare
The marriage vow, and so allow
The union of this pair.

Rezanof bowed to circumstance
And told of his resolve
To sail away without delay
This problem deep to solve.

A grand fiesta was declared;
The pueblo rang with song;
The night made gay with dance and play
To speed the hours along.

Then, came The Day! With solemn mien
The last farewells were said.
Conchita's smile was bright the while..
But soon, composure fled!

A prayer rose, trembling, to her lips,
"Dear God! It's time to part!"
He kissed her. "Adios," she sobbed,
As tears relieved her heart.

Swift he was gone! With anchor weighed

The brave ship set her sails,
To catch the breeze from western seas
Where zephyrs grow to gales.

The sunset flamed beyond the Gate,
The sky glowed crimson bright;
The ship with precious cargo full
Sailed forth to meet the night.

*   *   *

Years came; years went; and day by day
The maiden, patiently
Her *Aves* said and hopeful pled,
"God keep him safe for me!"

She served the poor; she tended them
From swaddling cloth to shroud,
But ne'er again Rezanof came
To claim the love she'd vowed.

His fate was learned from stranger lips
Her heart well may have quailed,
But not a tremor shook her voice;
No doubt her faith assailed.

Unending days of storm and sleet
Had brought him fever, pain;
Death stalked him on Siberian wastes,
Death won! Love fought in vain!

*   *   *

Her years were lived in charity,
Devoted, unafraid;
Her sole acclaim, the cherished name,
"Conchita, valiant maid!"

David Meltzer

Untitled

Grandmother Sarah
re-married at 90 & went back to Europe on her honeymoon.
No more hotel rooms
with milk & sweet butter on the windowledge.
No more Workman's Circle
monthly ghost-quest socials
for Grandfather Benjamin,
who came to America to become a tailor
& died on my bed in Brooklyn,
cancer spreading terrible wings within his body.
Grandmother Sarah
always a good touch for music & money
playing mandolin with thick fingers
as sun set over Broadway parkbenches 13 floors below.

Minor-key schmaltz trembling Yiddish grief,
pain & pride of time & tribe
in a lacey white blouse clicking her tongue
making music for her grandson, a wolf
in the room's only chair
listening to Russia, hearing Jews in Paradise.

When the music left her hands
Grandmother Sarah told me stories
of the village she was born in,
a river ran thru
its green & golden fields.
Young men intrigued by her dark beauty
called her The Gypsy.
But now, she'd say,
the village is no more,
its young men all dead,
bombed off the map by Germans
during the last war.

*

It was music, music
you could not make,
music barely heard,
the rabbi pacing back & forth
between our desks at *shul*.

            *

      What do I know of journey, they
who came before me
no longer here to tell of it
except baggage of old papers
bound-up & found in library stacks.
The crying of history makes it all vague.
Was it myth we all came here to be?

      What do I know of journey, I
who never crossed the seas into the alchemy of USA
no longer anyone's dream of home.
Their great great grandchildren jump state's ship,
drown in void *Torah* is too late to warn of.
Here *tohu* is *bohu* & form void & America
another pogrom, another concentration camp
more subtle & final
than all Hitler's chemists could imagine.
Home, *ha-makom*, no longer hope. It holds
light reaching back from eyes
watching Asians & Blacks die on TV.
We restore the shore & our dream is gone.
It mixes into shadows growing tall behind us.

      What do I know of journey,
they who came before me
kept what they left but now they are gone.
Invisible shells cast off
& in flaming hair arise
orphans of collapsed Shekinah
caught between earth's end & heaven's end
& what do I know of journey,
I a child when children were murdered
waiting on lines with their mothers & fathers,

238

gone in gas or the flash of atomic *ain-sof*
squinted at in movie-theatres.
Ancients sit on stoops too tired to mourn,
turn inward to blood rivers mourning lost *shtetls*.
They can not take me with them
& I can not bring them back
& what do I know of journey, I
who never spoke their language.
The old ones are dead or dying
& what is left desires less & less
& what is less is what is left
& children run off screaming
Elohim Elohim!
into freeways filled with the starlight of cars.

Anna Blake Mezquida

Chinatown

A bit of East within a Chinese wall
Of magic, color, smell and sound,—
Enclosed, and yet forever bound
Unto the West; an alien, bartering all
Its Asian mysteries in coin of trade;
Sharp, yet hidden as a sheathèd blade.

A town of fantasy, pagoda hung;
Of flowered balconies with lanterns strung,
And slant eyes beckoning from balustrades.
A young town wrapped in dreams of dead decades:
A weaver making garment of the woof
Of commerce, wound with vision of Lao Tzu
The mystic; and the sad songs of Tu Fu;
And love of great Ming Huang, with soul aloof.
A town of sleeping homes, when day is through;
The Occident alone wakes up anew,
To eat and dance upon the Shanghai's roof.
Stamping its maudlin mirth with cloven hoof.

Here's teak from forests older than the T'ang.
Silks, sandalwood and ivories displayed
Behind plate glass. Brass, cloisonné, cool jade.
A bell that once in Manchu temple rang.

The Dragon and Republic in parade.
Firecrackers popping in toy cannonade.
Chop suey. Ginger. Nuts. One, Doctor Chang,
Compounding wizard's brew of herb and fang.

The day's news on red paper on brick walls.
Shark's fins and octopus within a monger's stalls.
And, lone as Ishmael, upon a stone-paved street
A prisoned wildcat screaming in his cage
At greedy buyers, who would rend his meat
And grow to strength transmuted from his rage.

A withered man, with dimming eyes grown old,
But fingers delicate as any girl's,
Sits fashioning strange marvels from raw gold,
And jewels them with rubies and with pearls.

In houses of the Joss the sweet punks burn
To Buddha. At carved altars Ancients say
The Taoist prayers in poesy of fire;
While at Confucius' feet the sages learn;
And in a mission church some young boys pray
To Him whose cross gleams whitely from the spire;—
The incense rises, drifting higher, higher;
All earthy passions die, and tired hearts sing,
And hope is like the peach tree in the spring.
Small, silk swathed children, robin breasted, bright
And pert as sparrows, yet as strangely shy
As mountain quail in sudden flurried flight,
Flash out of alleys, cross curb, ever nigh
To death beneath some grinding juggernaut;
Then tiring of life's fan-tan, so dear bought,
Turn into other games, serene, alone,
Till dragged within doors by some gibbering crone.

Here, the Six Companies hold solemn meet;
There, reedy music and the oboe calls
Unto the playhouse down the little street;
While ghosts of slain men stalk within the halls
And gape across the tables of the Tong;
The Piper pipes, and Death strikes his dull gong.

Some twenty posters ask for charity
For white man's need; the yellow will respond:
Of time, of gold, of self, equally free,
His spoken word good as a witnessed bond.

Within its Chinese wall, East goes its way;
And at the edge, upon each slippered day
The West crowds hard, lustful as sin,—
Yet never wholly enters in.

Fog

You are all things to me—
All mystery!
A silver harem veil
That hides dark eyes
And smiles and glad surprise;
You are a mist of tears—
The welling up of sorrow in the heart;
You are a dull, gray cloak for fears;
And you are mother-wings
That cover all small frightened things
And guard them in a world apart;
You are white, yearning, gentle hands
That soothing touch my aching breast
And bring me rest;
You are the cool, sweet breath of Night
Whispering all dream-delight
To tired lands;
You are the wild, brave, free
Salt-spume of the restless sea;—
All things! All mystery!

Shadows

The night comes down and shadows creep;
   They climb with me the oaken stair;
Across the moon the gray bats sweep,
   And foul the air.

I hide in bed and close my eyes;—
   I feel the shadows stir and crawl;
Within my room a blind bat flies
   Against the wall.

And yet a strange voice whispers low:
   Had I but walked with lifted head,
Had I but turned and faced the foe,
   They would have fled.

Harlequin

I gave to *you* laughter—though I knew tears;
   "Ah, never," you said, "was there man more gay!"
I danced to your piping, my little dears,
   And you did not see that my world was gray.

Jack Micheline

It is not Here on Earth I am Seeking

I don't know what I am seeking
in the cool night
Rivers and birds
a sensuous lip
a rainbow of dreams
past waterfalls
the ruins of cities appear and fade in front of me
awkward man
he dresses and clowns
seeking love and shelter in criminal ways

I want to rip off the mask of the sniverling lip
from a want that runs from an abstract pose
from a lie

This reality lies deep in the ground
or high in the sky
it is not here on earth what I am seeking
it is not in speechs or books
or in the heat of bedrooms or palaces or parties
it is not the dried heart or dead conscience of our age
it is somewhere that a child knows and is forgotten
it is an eye of a dog ravaged in streets
or in a open smile of a baker or shoemaker
it is by the fireside of rivers where men share bread and song
it is not here in the cities that drown me
that take my heart
and leave me limp and wobbly
drunk on eyes and feet and faces of the multitudes
I must travel to some far off place
where rivers flow
and stars dance
where children bring garlands of love
and emeralds to the soft breeze of heaven
where prisons are not known

it is not here on earth what I am seeking
scavenged and torn bleeding from wars
and greed and shameless murders
let me just weep for the beauty I see and walk alone
to whatever dream and heaven I seek
then I will die with swans in the river
and send my love to strangers and friends
this poetry I breathe which is life and my heart
and to you who seek the unknown
I send you love and the rivers

October 24, 1964
London, England

Joaquin Miller

An Answer

Well! who shall lay hand on my harp but me,
Or shall chide my song from the sounding trees,
The passionate sun and the resolute sea,
These were my masters, and only these.

These were my masters, and only these,
And these from the first I obey'd, and they
Shall command me now, and I shall obey
As a dutiful child that is proud to please.

There never were measures as true as the sun,
The sea hath a song that is passingly sweet,
And yet they repeat, and repeat, and repeat,
The same old runes through the new years run.

By unnamed rivers of the Oregon north,
That roll dark-heaved into turbulent hills,
I have made my home.... The wild heart thrills
With memories fierce, and a world storms forth.

On eminent peaks that are dark with pine,
And mantled in shadows and voiced in storms,
I have made my camps: majestic gray forms
Of the thunder-clouds, they were companions of mine;

And face set to face, like to lords austere,
Have we talk'd, red-tongues, of the mysteries
Of the circling sun, of the oracled seas,
While ye who judged me had mantled in fear.

Some fragment of thought in the unfinish'd words;
A cry of fierce freedom, and I claim no more.
What more would you have from the tender of herds
And of horse on an ultimate Oregon shore?

From men unto God go forth, as alone,

Where the dark pines talk in their tones of the sea
To the unseen God in a harmony
Of the under seas, and know the unknown.

Cuba Libre

Comes a cry from Cuban water—
From the warm, dusk Antilles—
From the lost Atlanta's daughter,
Drowned in blood as drowned in seas;
Comes a cry of purpled anguish—
Sees her struggles, hear her cries!
Shall she live, or shall she languish?
Shall she sink, or shall she rise?

She shall rise, by all that's holy!
She shall live and she shall last;
Rise as we, when crushed and lowly
From the blackness of the past.
Bid her strike! Lo, it is written
Blood for blood and life for life.
Bid her smite, as she is smitten;
Stars and stripes were born of strife.

Once we flashed her lights of freedom,
Lights that dazzled her dark eyes
Till she could but yearning heed them,
Reach her hands and try to rise.
Then they stabbed her, choked her, drowned her,
Till we scarce could hear a note.
Ah! these rusting chains that bound her!
Oh! these robbers at her throat!

And the kind who forged these fetters?
Ask five hundred years for news.
Stake and thumbscrew for their betters?
Inquisitions! Banished Jews!
Chains and slavery! What reminder

Of one red man in that land?
Why, these very chains that bind her
Bound Columbus, foot and hand!

She shall rise as rose Columbus,
From his chains, from shame and wrong—
Rise as Morning, matchless, wondrous—
Rise as some rich morning song—
Rise a ringing song and story,
Valor, Love personified.
Stars and stripes espouse her glory,
Love and Liberty allied.

The Millionaire

> *Gold, gold! thou'rt a curse—yet a blessing with treasures untold.*
> *Old! cold! but waking the furious flames of desire!*
> *Leaving in ashes each heart that tastes of thy liquid fire,*
> *Dream of the youth and the sage, oh, beautiful, syren gold!*
> —*Mary Lambert*

> *Abu-Hâriri—world renowned—*
> *Tells how a starving Arab found*
> *A diamond, lying on the ground.*
> *"Oh, if this shining stone, instead,*
> *Were but a single date," he said*
> *"A cruse of oil, a crust of bread!"*
> —*Lucius Harwood Foote*

The gold that with the sunlight lies
    In bursting heaps at dawn,
The silver spilling from the skies
    At night to walk upon,
The diamonds gleaming with the dew
He never saw, he never knew.

He got some gold, dug from the mud,
    Some silver, crushed from stones.
The gold was red with dead men's blood,

The silver black with groans.
And when he died he moaned aloud,
"God! but they've put no pocket in my shroud!"

A Nubian Face On The Nile

One night we touched the lily shore,
And then passed on, in night indeed,
Against the far white waterfall.
I saw no more, shall know no more
Of her for aye. And you who read
This broken bit of dream will smile,
Half vexed that I saw aught at all.

The waves struck strophes on the shore
And all the sad song of the oar
That long, long night against the Nile,
Was: Nevermore and nevermore
This side that shadowy shore that lies
Below the leafy Paradise.

La Exposicion

New Orleans.

The banners! The bells! The red banners!
The rainbows of banners! The chimes!
The music of stars! The sweet manners
Of peace in old pastoral times!

The coming of nations! Kings bringing
Rich gifts to Republics! The trees
Of paradise, and birds singing
By the bank of De Soto's swift seas!

Lincoln Park

Unwalled it lies, and open as the sun
When God swings wide the dark doors of the East.
Oh, keep this one spot, still keep this one,
Where tramp or banker, laymen or high priest,
May equal meet before the face of God :
Yea, equals stand upon that common sod
Where they shall one day equals be
beneath, for aye, and all eternity.

Custer

Oh, it were better dying there
On glory, front, with trumpet's blare,
And battle's shout blent wild about—
The sense of sacrifice, the roar
Of war! The soul might well leap out—
The brave, white soul leap boldly out
The door of wounds, and up the stair
Of heaven to God's open door,
While yet the knees were bent in prayer.

Edward Montez

Day Dreams

Daydreams of riding across a green hued plain on a painted pony in
pursuit of a great buffalo and feeling the earth tremble beneath me.

And leaping from a precipice of a sacred mountain and transforming
into an eagle, freeing my soul and entering into an unending
universe.

Daydreams of walking among brown skinned people free of foreign
diseases, hypocrisy and needless butchery—unassimilated.

Day dreams of walking with the elders and listening to their wisdom, and being in awe of the medicine man's power.

And walking across a land that is unscarred and unpolluted, and being in harmony with all the living things.

Drinking the sweet waters from the rivers and streams and breathing the clean air, feeling the presence of the great spirit.

Daydreams of those who respected the great spirit, those who were slaughtered in the name of god by so called civilized christians.

I Died Before

Drab memories flood the black and red terrain of my mind as death angels hover nearby, hoping I'll die.

But I died before, in brownstone alleyways after crawling through the excrement of a dog who didn't care.

I died in lonely railyards of Chicago while thinking of Florida and California huddled in a frozen boxcar.

I drowned in my own green slime puke in the gutters of America and was eulogized by empty tokay bottles with no more remorse.

I screamed for the mercy of anyone's god as I was kicked and beaten to death in the drunk tank of Sacramento.

I starved to death in a dusty cardboard shack while my children cried for food and warmth from the freezing wind.

I drank in every stinking bar and fornicated with every whore of every skidrow and died in every vacant lot.

I was stabbed to death over a bottle of wine and three cents in change, and my salvation army shoes were stolen too.

I died in total junk oblivion and dried blood at the bus depot before I could catch the next bus to nowhere.

I committed suicide amid the dying dreams of my dying mind and coyotes howled a mournful wail on silent mesas.

I died in a slum hotel fire in San Francisco, and along Mission Street in all the vermin infested flop houses.

I watched my body slowly disintegrate from cirrhosis and cancer and wondered if my people still remembered me.

I died from a broken spirit on every filthy and lonely street of every city, and every dusty road of every dusty reservation.

I watch death angels hover nearby, hoping I'll die, but I died before——and I'll probably die again.

I Remember

I remember the scent of acorn soup cooking and deer meat frying in quiet evenings of summer.

And shivering under thin blankets in winter and watching the wall paper dance to the force of the winter winds outside.

I remember the cry of an owl in the night and I knew it was an ominous warning, a cry of death.

I remember running in the dust behind the medicine truck when it came to the reservation, lifesavers was a free treat.

And grandpa sitting in his favorite resting chair under his favorite shade tree with his dog "Oly" by his side.

I remember running naked and screaming with my aunt in hot pursuit, a stick in her hand, she always caught me.

And every summer we would swim in the river and let the sun bake us until we were a shade less than purple, basking on the riverbank, undisturbed, at peace.

And I remember grandma toiling in the beanfields while I played with my army truck on the fender of a "49" Plymouth.

I remember going to the movies in town on Saturday nights with fifty cents in my pocket, thirty five cents for the ticket and the rest was mine.

Eating popcorn and drinking water from a discarded coke cup and rooting for the Indians to win, and they never did, but that was yesterday.

Fort Bragg, California

Just riding around in the rain one night with some friends, cruising down the main drag of Fort Bragg in a fifty-nine chevy, digging the sounds of the Stones, smoking dope, drinking beer and sipping ripple.

And getting busted in a most dramatic way in the glare of headlights, spotlights, and flashlights, surrounded by a dozen redneck law enforcement officials with pistols and shotguns pointed at our hearts, poised for the kill.

After all, Fort Bragg is just down the coast from a place where other rednecks killed a whole tribe of Indians with axes, knives, and clubs not too long ago, and for a while it looked like we were the candidates for another massacre.

With hands on tops of squad cars and feet spread apart we were frisked from head to toe and pockets emptied also, the only evidence found was a half full gallon of ripple which was very funny and we laughed about it in the rain.

But the redneck law enforcement officials didn't laugh and they hauled us off to jail and took our fingerprints and pictures too, but we still thought it was funny and we laughed and sang all night and peed on the mattresses.

And when the sun arose the next day after a long night in jail and the rain had stopped we all realized where we were and somebody said, "Those bastards might have killed us last night," it wasn't funny anymore, Fort Bragg ain't a fun place.

José Montoya

Gabby Took The 99

Gabby took the 99
The 99 highway
El highway 99
EL JAIGÜEY
The ninety nine
Donde se requió el troque
Con aquel jentío
The HIGHWAY
Down the 99
Up the 99
Ah, por todo el 99

El noventa y nueve
As you leave the 99

WHO LEAVES????

.. who ever leaves the
cold
    ugly
        dry
            hot
                slippery
                    bloody

Dirty
    foggy
        sleek
            powerful
Ninety nine?

NOT RAZA, Okies, Arkies,
Chapos, Armenians—not even
THE MOHIGGENBOTHOMS!

That impersonal 99. And

Not even crosses for the
Dead alongside this road
Of the timeless vanishing
Point.

And in that infinity
You dared to dream, Gabby.

The riches that passed
As you turned trays, loco,
Y el 99 te iba a llevar
Pa ya, Gabby . . .

El Gabby took the 99—
La salvación!!
. . . and he died in Viet Nam
Of an overdose, pa
Cabala de chingar!

And Visa laughs
And Dina laughs
And Goshen and Cutler
Y el 99 laughs
And all do the
Tecato tattoo taps.

From '67 To '71

Flowers are growing where
We planted bayonets

Hopelessness provides a respite
And reckless impulses subside

I no longer wait for the rains
Only cold winter evenings

I wince at revolutionary talk-talk
And a tear and a smile confuse
My prodigies

...I don't want to recall
When I became ineffective
But I do!

Alejandro Murguía

Text of the Lizard

—in the moon of cold winds

Ants march by
single file
moving their dead
Close to the ground
scratches my silver belly...
through the thick grass
into the peaceful valley /

A single owl called in the trees.

Mr. Blue Jay, the jackrabbit, the deer
and brother lizards
welcome me–
They do not ask why
I don't talk–
Why my lips are stitched–

They Know

I carry the message for the brujo
sealed in my mouth...
My visions don't let me sleep /
At night
my head goes swimming through the universe

Por los caminos de Cuachtemoc

A crescent moon lights the highway to Chiapas. Night stretches
on before the headlights of the bus. In the hillside dogs are barking

254

. . . there must be footsteps on the road tonite.

In 1529 the bearded ones took Cuachtemoc to Guatemala, after burning his feet because he refused to tell them where the gold was. They walked him down this same road, chained to a yoke, feet bleeding, bits of skin left dangling on the cactus—thru the Isthmus of Tehuantepec, in seasonal storms, asphalt highways shimmering in their oily rainbow. Third class bus sadly waiting in the station of Tuxla-Gutiérrez. A fading yellow sign above the ticket counter that read

TORTURED ONES ONLY

They hung Cuachtemoc from a ceiba tree in Chiapas, beneath the moon shedding silver tears, next to the highway like a prince of thiefs. Tomorrow the tree will be photographed by tourist trying to capture spirits on celluloid.

The dogs keep barking in the passing countryside, the passengers stay awake and restless while the headlights of the bus continue to cut the night and throw shadows on the highway.

Renaissance: Roses Of Fire

(in memory of los angeles)

flowers for the masses
that march in the procession
they will march forever
rivers of fire in their veins
police sirens in the streets.
the national guard
along the cobbled roads
carry the soul of a man
they have beat him again and again
and still he has not broken or yielded /
the last martyr
wanting to be and not wanting to be
roses of fire and death.

golondrinas fly around the tower
cooing amongst themselves
seraphins of spanish origin /
oranges rotten in the fields

lemons that will grow no more
slim fingers of the rich
stunted fingers of the poor
golondrinas watch from the tower
and coo the afternoon into submission.

a senorita in the plaza arranges her rebozo
fixes her mantilla and beats the summer with her fan.
her long gone lover dances between her muscles
her lips are red
her nails are polished
O los angeles that will never grow again
she eats olives with her fingers
O los angeles that lives so easily
and dies so quickly.
statues of green iron in the park
lemons of yellow wax in the shade
clouds of blue onyx in the sky
roses of red death in the throat.

Harold Norse

I Attend A Poetry Meeting

I attend a poetry meeting.
they eat canapés, gossip,
drop some Big Names, drink a little.
they are not young. the host looks bitter,
wags his short white beard,
calls on them, one
by one. in a circle
round the comfortable room
they read their little poems,
their voices subdued,
barely breaking the silence.
comments are murmured. they
seem afraid of something
or someone. maybe they know

this is not poetry. this
un-happening. what
can shake them into life?
a gray Angora cat strolls in, makes a
pathetic sound. it's too soft. my turn.
I produce a manuscript. I am new here.
I read, in a hoarse croaking voice, with a
head cold, a long
apocalyptic prose poem.
I take risks.
turn violent phrases.
kick a few sacred cows.
lick no asses.
all hell breaks loose. I am attacked.
the poem's banal, pretentious, disgusting.
one calls it crap (he's a dried-up poet).
indecent. immoral. cliché. show-offy.
cries of Rape! I have RAPED poetry!
the host looks unhappy.
"in all the years we've met, *this*
is the first time," he bleats,
"the very *first* time we have—uh—STOOPED
to—ugh!—anger—" he looks daggers
at me. I sit almost smiling, taking
it all in. why are they so incensed?
have I ripped them off?
exposed ugly secrets?
the rain of labels keeps falling:
rules I've broken,
taboos violated.
then, quietly, I tell them:
I wrote the poem 20 years ago,
young, hungry, lonely.
had to purge myself
of rage & powerlessness.
of academic restrictions.
if I have offended you
by handling big themes
with the inadequate craft of a
groping bungler who puts feeling first

(to you a romantic myth)
well, tough shit.
your myths are not mine.

I made them feel again.

for the first time
they snarled at each other.

William Oandasan

Round Valley Songs

> *"first there is the word*
> *the word is the song"*

song gives birth to
the story and the dance
as the dance steps
the story speaks

*

the woman with white hair
only whispered   Tatu
but through my ears
30,000 years drum

*

in dynamic color and strength
two Filipino gaming cocks
appear from across the water
in the yard pullets cluck excitedly

*

swimming up the Eel
a spirit sings   corn

ground in the old way
draws the milk of Earth

*

free as the bear
and tall as redwoods
throbs my red drum
as spirits ride high

*

long ago brown bears
sang round our lodge fires
tonight they dance
alive through our dreams

*

in the chipped and tattered
weaving of a willow basket
the voice of an ancient age
sleeps dreaming of breath

*

the cold mountain water
that quenches the deep thirst
drums my magic fire
drums my medicine pouch

*

above manzanitas near the cemetery
from fresh currents of night air
the voice of ancient ones
burns in our blood again

George Oppen

'And Their Winter And Night In Disguise'

> "So with artists. How pleasurable
> to imagine that, if only they gave
> up their art, the children would be
> healed,   would live.
> —*Irving Younger in* The Nation

The sea and a crescent strip of beach
Show between the service station and a deserted shack

A creek drains thru the beach
Forming a ditch
There is a discarded super-market cart in the ditch
That beach is the edge of a nation

There is something like shouting along the highway
A California shouting
On the long fast highway over the California mountains

Point Pedro
Its distant life

It is impossible the world should be either good or bad
If its colors are beautiful or if they are not beautiful
If parts of it taste good or if no parts of it taste good
It is as remarkable in one case as the other
                                        As against this

We have suffered fear, we know something of fear
And of humiliation mounting to horror

The world above the edge of the foxhole belongs to the
        flying bullets, leaden superbeings
For the men grovelling in the foxhole danger, danger in
        being drawn to them

These little dumps
The poem is about them

Our hearts are twisted
In dead men's pride

Dead men crowd us
Lean over us

In the emplacements

The skull spins
Empty of subject

The hollow ego

Flinching from the war's huge air

Tho we are delivery boys and bartenders

We will choke on each other

Minds may crack

But not for what is discovered

Unless that everyone knew
And kept silent

Our minds are split
To seek the danger out

From among the miserable soldiers

Simon Ortiz

They Come Around, The Wolves—
And Coyote and Crow, Too

I told you about those Wolves.
You must talk with them,
meeting them someplace,

mountain trail, desert,
at your campfire,
and call them Uncle or Brother
but never Cousin or In-law.

"I am happy that you recognized us
and called us by the proper term,"
the Uncle said.
He was sitting there
with his hands held together,
met my eyes and then, being humble,
dropped his gaze to his hands.

"We come around
but we have a bad reputation,"
the Uncle said.
"I'm glad you came," I said.
He smiled but his eyes were sad.

"I was so pretty
and everyone liked me.
My voice especially.
Everyone would stop to listen,"
said Crow.

Coyote was silent.

"I would sing and sing.
Mocking Bird and even Parrot
were jealous of me.

My feathers would shine and shine,"
said Crow.

Coyote was silent.

Thinking Coyote wasn't listening,
Crow asked, "Are you sleeping?"

"No," Coyote said.

262

"Did you hear what I just said?"
asked Crow.

"Yes," said Coyote.

And Crow waited for Coyote's comment.
When it didn't come, he decided to sing.

"Cawr, cawr, cawr," Crow sang.

"Stop," said Coyote.

Crow waited for the favorable comment
He closed his eyes and made ready to bow.

Coyote silently crept away.

"Are you my friend?" asked Coyote.
"One can't be too choosey," said Crow.

That Time

Agnes' aunt killed the goat.
I held it down, sitting on its belly.
I could feel its whole vibrating life,
the red blood, thinly spurting
in a low arc, and then just flowing.

Brian stood by, his childhands clutched.

Agnes' aunt is a gaunt, thin Navajo woman,
never married, takes care of Chee,
her dead sister's husband.

We skinned the goat, cleaned the guts,
and cut up the meat,
and saved the best parts for Chee.

We put the goat's head in the coals to cook
but the dogs stole it,
and it was half eaten before we found out.

We took the goat meat to a Squaw Dance.
Chee carried it under his arm in a sack,
and he wore his flatbrim hat and a new shirt.

That was that time.

Ernesto Padilla

S.S.

Walter H. J. Rauff
I live within you.
We share the earth
We both dream desires within the same night, but
Walter! You have destroyed my dignity.

There is not one sin that you
have committed that I could not have prevented
Just as you have always shooed me,
submissively, back into my blue volkswagon bus.

Last night I dreamed the nightmare of my sister again.
She lay crouched, burnt crisp
black wire wound
tightly
round her neck
her wedding finger and
thumbs
missing

I vow to you Walter I shall not have children
before I am no more

Second Coming of Reality

My poem withdraws backward
into itself
by the law of introversion

dictated by landscapes of subjectivity.
    The astrological signs
    might as well kill dogs.

For my self
I will follow
my poem into
the cave

I have utterly become
the other
who speculates about his poem
as it dances slow motion to
a degree zero stop:
a disembodied shadow,

no longer
suggesting
referents.

He can finally admit only
to an unnamed desire

which is worthless of me
who am left over.

Praxis

My poem asks me
    under what conditions
    am I to be forgiven?

None

You are
our sin
our project

It would be point less
to retrace old symbols

which would clutter
our future worlds
reincarnation was a back
door

and I deny the way of
all poems

and one of you
could make me
scoot over

and fall out of myself
into praxis

There are no Truths, There is Only Taking Of Sides

I research my old comic books
        Daffy Duck
        Little Lulu
        Sluggo
for the old answers.

I wake-up myself.
Scrutinize my dreams.
        Do I hunt rabbit?
        Do I pick tomatoes?
        And for how long now have I believed you?

I overturn my dreams,
        stalk reality,
name all things by
feelings,
        wade through the mathematical
labyrinth of codes
        tracing aftershadows of synapse,
        a trail of failures.

There is only one scientific conclusion.
        when our sun burns out

I shall crawl backwards through
los callejones de la vida
to the center of warmth
to see if the lies develop again
in the same old ways but with
new
masks.

If I could only ban the letter
reality
from our coloring books

Michael Palmer

The Library Is Burning
(*Eighth Symmetrical Poem*)

The library is burning floor by floor
delivering pictures from liquid to sleep

as we roll over thinking to run
A mistaken anticipation has led us here

to calculate the duration of a year
in units of aloe and wood

But there will be no more dust in corners
and no more dogs appearing through dust

to question themselves uncertainly
Should it finally be made clear

that there's no cloud inside no body
no streetlamps, no unfoldings at five o'clock

along the edge of a curved path
Masters of the present tense

greet morning from their cautious beds
while the greater masters of regret

change water into colored glass
The stirrings are the same and different

The stirrings are the same and different
and secretly the same

The fear of winter is the fear of fire
disassembling winter

and that time the message was confused
it felt the most precise

Without Music

"Les lettres qui formaient des mots artificiels"
            —Reverdy

Small sun against the lower edge licking us
She showed me her tongue coated with thorns

A careful life of stars in a redwood box

times labor's loss not mine
based upon the loss itself, 'not mine'

. . . formed such words imperfectly bodied

as empty sleep weighed against dream
bodies and parts of bodies distributed

according to given laws
                        across a field
Who could help but love the equations

night's music hung from each line
the headless man looks at the quarter moon

and the moon watches the man
resting invisible beneath a tree

luminous city   sounds that pour
from the center of a courtyard

where we watch ourselves talk
This poem is called Rebuilding the House

Kenneth Patchen

The Shapes and Intensities of This Man, This Confucius

However that principle of reason
Which we receive from the sky . . .
That unalterable target,
And in us tranquil
The harmony of result—Who brightens
Your perfection? What produces
The rooted order of the good action?
Is man evil, or the world?
Do I write in my system?
Does any other direct me?
Have I followed my own footsteps
In a land which I do not know?
Should I do the life I seem to have,
Or does it hold holes in my real fabric?

If the truth is inside,
And the form outside,
What is the truth of sleep?

What is the truth in the flame
Which eats at your rejoicing forms?

A Matchstick-Viewed-without-Regard-to-Its-Outer-Surface

Was enabled to ride.
>First on a "wafer."
>But it set up a roar and presently fled.
Remember that even the gorilla will feel lost without his roller skates
if he has become accustomed to them long enough.

Then on a sort of tile. Which was very like being flopped about in the
wee small hours of the night. However, that is not another story;
and the children are going back along the unlighted way into the
forest now. Perhaps this time will be the last time for any of us to see
joy and innocent pride on a human face again.

Then on a blind turtle away out ahead but running the wrong way.
>On a plate shaped as a shield.
>on a shawl slung across a pit.
>On the castaway wheel of a Ferris.

What Is the Beautiful?

The narrowing line.
Walking on the burning ground.
The ledges of stone.
Owlfish wading near the horizon.
Unrest in the outer districts.

Pause.

And begin again.
Needles through the eye.
Bodies cracked open like nuts.
Must have a place.
Dog has a place.

Pause.

And begin again.
Tents in the sultry weather.
Rifles hate holds.

Who is right?
Was Christ?
Is it wrong to love all men?

Pause.

And begin again.
Contagion of murder.
But the small whip hits back.
This is my life, Caesar.
I think it is good to live.

Pause.

And begin again.
Perhaps the shapes will open.
Will flying fly?
Will singing have a song?
Will the shapes of evil fall?
Will the lives of men grow clean?
Will the power be for good?
Will the power of man find its sun?
Will the power of man flame as a sun?
Will the power of man turn against death?
Who is right?
Is war?

Pause.

And begin again.
A narrow line.
Walking on the beautiful ground.
A ledge of fire.
It would take little to be free.
That no man hate another man,
Because he is black,
Because he is yellow;
Because he is white;
Or because he is English;
Or German;
Or rich;

Or poor;
Because we are everyman.

Pause.

And begin again.
It would take little to be free.
That no man live at the expense of another.
Because no man can own what belongs to all.
Because no man can kill what all must use.
Because no man can lie when all are betrayed.
Because no man can hate when all are hated.

And begin again.
I know that the shapes will open.
Flying will fly, and singing will sing.
Because the only power of man is in good.
And all evil shall fail.
Because evil does not work,
Because the white man and the black man,
the Englishman and the German,
Are not real things.
They are only pictures of things.
Their shapes, like the shapes of the tree
And the flower, have no lives in names or signs;
They are their lives, and the real is in them.
And what is real shall have life always.

Pause.

I believe in the truth.
I believe that every good thought I have,
All men shall have.
I believe that what is best in me,
Shall be found in every man.
I believe that only the beautiful
Shall survive on the earth.

I believe that the perfect shape of everything
Has been prepared;
And, that we do not fit our own

Is of little consequence.
Man beckons to man on this terrible road.
I believe that we are going into the darkness now;
Hundreds of years will pass before the light
Shines over the world of all men...
And I am blinded by its splendor.

Pause.

And begin again.

Oscar Penerando

Beau-Rhet

There was this
        ragged iron bar
that by accident crushed my
toe
when I with leathered gloves
        worked with steel
in Alaska with
that restless part
        (they had their reasons)
of my people—young as 16
old as 84—
        filipinos I

had been away
        6 months you see
working
        in canneries in
fishing boats on waterfronts
in Bristol Bay in Anchorage
served time in
Kodiak
stowed away too (then
changed my mind) and now

am sitting
in the living room of my
basement apt.
in the Mission district of
San Francisco

unlacing my boots
the boy's left
elbow crook'd
around my right
knee his fat fingerettes (right hand)
doodling too with the
laces when he
saw it

     Daddy!
your toe.
it's black! looking up at
me and adding

Did it hurt?

(that got me)

Didn't even ask
why the blackness the horror
how it happened or cared to
I imagine

He just
wanted to know
with rounded eyes
how his father
took

the pain

October 72, Kodiak

274

Rhetoric

I feel
a pimple
growing out of my
forehead,
Bayani said.
(we've been gambling, you see.)

Konting nana
konting puyat
tigyawat,
I said.

But how
(pounding the table)
do you make it
relevant, though
said Lou.

All power to the pimple
I said.

Tom Raworth

9:00 PM. May 1st 1970

for Ed Dorn

mounting a stag's skull remains
the province of a tiny man
who standing on a bolt peers
across eye socket rim at antlers
(the magnetic north) that are not his
heads   east again
upon a giant brown and white
saint bernard   which leads me
to today   obsessed by thoughts

of drowning in hot water in the dark
the hound's bark drifts
through trees in the night spring air
venus is out

Entry

major turnpike connections in eastern united states
audubon, witchcraft, akbar
all for san francisco

ordinary people
i have killed poetry
yes   and i had to tell you
books are dead
refer others to your own
experience perhaps
identical thoughts flicker
through each head at the same time
intelligence was the invader from space
and won   defend your planet

now that sounds intelligent

Eugene Redmond

Lone Song

First fears, first tears on autumn window pains,
Left over hurt from summer   / dregs of Illinois madness /

California song is subtle sting;
California chill is quiet, coy — cat / walk —
Not noisy and nervous like midwestern winters.

My mood, then, often comes — is drumhummed — by mail;
My fury, my flame, my fidget caught postcard–quick,

Caught and cornered,
/ bulletinboarded / shored upon saltfilled tomorrows /

Brother Sister Nephew Niece:
Vital vibes on wire, on lyre - kincords /
Bloodcords of sounds or strings: spontaneous
COMBUSTION of blood inside *trees,* inside *seeds* and *shells* —
Inside xylophones, telephones and saxophones.

Señor Pepe's Promenade

Food frets / promenades at *Señor Pepe's*
Refried beans /
A golden hostess in breastsmiles
Wearing restraining wall of knit
/ sweatered señorita /
Swelling up / out horizontal mountains
/ miniatured /
Burritos /
Enchiladas tucked in tortillas /
Mexicali beer
/ the sun liquified & bottled /
and *sheGlows*
SheGlows, strung like flamenco melody
Rolling over the shores
/ slamming the beaches /
Of my ears;
From sunfractured frames / walls /
Mute as history and motionless as murals,
/ girldancers; sombrero'd señor stare /
Guarding this tradition
/ this hummingheat toil /
This knifeForkPlate chatter and clatter,
this feast and fiesta:
ChaCha-spiced lips
Snacking, wacking away at Mexican scrumptiousness;
"Wa-atch eet seen-yore, thee plate eeze hot"
The waiter wises
/ from a blue vestjacket snaps /

Lowers baked dish to tablecloth
/ blue /
Straddling carpet
/ blue /
Whose designs / topo–rhymes scurry / wigglehurry like tributaries
/ blue /   sky
And the room hatdances /
Drowning in Flamenco melody
Buttered in beangrease
/ and *sheGlows in Mexicali Beer* /

Ishmael Reed

Jacket Notes

Being a colored poet
Is like going over
Niagara Falls in a
Barrel

An 8 year old can do what
You do unaided

The barrel maker doesn't
Think you can cut it

The gawkers on the bridge
Hope you fall on your
Face

The tourist bus full of
Paying customers broke–down
Just out of Buffalo

Some would rather dig
The postcards than
Catch your act

A mile from the brink
It begins to storm

But what really hurts is
You're bigger than the
Barrel

The Author Reflects On His 35th Birthday

35? I have been looking forward
To you for many years now
So much so that
I feel you and I are old
Friends and so on this day, 35
I propose a toast to
Me and You
35? From this day on
I swear before the bountiful
Osiris that
If I ever
If I EVER
Try to bring out the
Best in folks again I
Want somebody to take me
Outside and kick me up and
Down the sidewalk or
Sit me in a corner with a
Funnel on my head

Make me hard as a rock
35, like the fellow in
The story about the
Big one that got away
Let me laugh my head off
With Moby Dick as we reminisce
About them suckers who went
Down with the *Pequod*
35? I ain't been mean enough
Make me real real mean

Mean as old Marie rolling her eyes
Mean as the town Bessie sings about
"Where all the birds sing bass"

35? Make me Tennessee mean
Cobra mean
Cuckoo mean
Injun mean
Dracula mean
Beethovian-browns mean
Miles Davis mean
Don't-offer-assistance-when
Quicksand-is-tugging-some-poor
Dope-under-mean
Pawnbroker mean
Pharoah mean
That's it, 35
Make me Pharaoh mean
Mean as can be
Mean as the dickens
Meaner than mean

When I walk down the street
I want them to whisper
There goes Mr. Mean
"He's double mean
He even turned the skeletons
In his closet out into
The cold"

And 35?
Don't let me trust anybody
Over Reed but
Just in case
Put a tail on that
Negro too

February 22, 1973

Sixth Street Corporate War

Not all rats live in sewers
Some of them dwell in 100,000 dollar
rat's nests on the Alameda
and drive to work in a Mercedes
laboratory rat white
You wouldn't even know they were
rats
on the mailbox it says Mr. Rodent

As big as a coffee table book
(The only book in the house)
he spends his time nibbling ratboy
in a rathouse with its
cheesy rat kitchen or scampering
on a rat sofa or in a bed of
rats
Or you might find him at the Ratskeller
wetting his rat whiskers on
rat soup
"my favorite drink" said
This shareholder rat there he
go old bureaucratic rat investor
in rattraps where people live
like rats

As years went by he gained more
status until he became the esteemed
Doctor Rattus
Crashed a tomcat convention and
demanded to be put on the
banquet

This even woke up Scrounger
or Mr. All Claws,
the toastmaster tomcat
catnapping on the dais
after a night of pre-
convention howling

"whaddya say, boys"
said the thrice decorated
rat scrapper
"rat cocktail
rat of the day
rat a la carte
or rat mousse"?

The other cats being
democrats cast their
votes by secret ballot
gulp!

Foolology

Shaken by his bad press, the wolf
presses north, leaving caribou to
the fox,
Raven, the snow player gets his
before buzzards with bright red
collars move in to dine near the
bottom of a long scavenger line

This poem is about a skunk, no
rather about a man, who though
not of the skunk family uses
his round-eye the way skunks do

After he eats, his friends eat
He is a fool and his friends are
fools but sometimes it's hard to
tell who is the biggest fool this
fool or his fool friends

By the time they catch us
we're not there
We crows
Nobody's ever seen a dead crow
on the highway

First moral: Don't do business
with people for whom April first
is an important date
they will use your bank balance to
buy eight thousand pies, tunics,
ballet slippers with bells and
a mail order lake in the middle of
a desert for splash parties

Second moral: Before you can spot
fools in others you must rid yourself
of the fool in you
You can tell a fool by his big mouth

Untitled

Today I feel bearish
I've just climbed out of
A stream with a jerking
Trout in my paw

Anyone who messes with
Me today will be hugged
And dispatched

William Nauns Ricks

Night In California

When the sun is sinking slow
  Behind the mountains blue and white,
And the mist upon the town is falling low;
When the mocker's sleepy note
Seems to stifle in his throat —
  Then to us in California, it is night.

When the Mission's chapel bell
    Is ringing out calm and clear and light;
And the padre's gentle Ave seems to swell,
Till the nightingale's sweet song
Seems the beauty to prolong —
    Then to us in California, it is night.

When the 'cacia's scented flower
    And the orange blossom white
Seem to lend a subtle fragrance to the hour.
When the palm tree's gentle sigh
Breathes a tale of days gone by —
    Then to us in California, it is night.

November, 1902

To The Oak Of Oakland
(The tree in the city hall plaza is dead.)

With heavy hearts they come to me
    To write your epitaph, old tree;
But how can I, a new-found friend,
    To you a greater honor lend?
What grandeur eulogies devise
    Than these old friends with tear-dimmed eyes?

What tales they tell of youthful days,
    Of bold adventures and of plays;
Of trystings, and of lovers' vows
    Which you have known beneath your boughs.
The loss of these, it may be broke,
    The ancient heart of you, old oak.

A thousand years you stood they say,
    While nations came and passed away.
The first red children of the soil,
    You saw a stronger race despoil,
Then saw these men-in-mail give way
    To sandaled priests of finer clay.

These goodly men, whose dream was great
    Of brotherhood, succumbed to fate.
Close where they dreamed beneath your shade,
    A concrete road have moderns made.
This newer race, whose swift feet run,
    Unheeding; to the setting sun.

This younger race, seems not to see
    The service of your life, old tree.
Your shelter to mankind forgot,
    But few remain to mean your lot.
Your passing is the common end,
    "From dust ye came, to dust descend."

This is the law for mundane things,
    But from the dust on spirit wings
The coul, which knows no bounds of time
    Flies phoenix-like to that fair clime,
Where trees, or man (of fleeter breath)
    Shall no more feel the pain of death.

Oakland, California
May 23, 1916

Today Is All We Have

If yesterday held joy or pain,
    We know it will not come again.
Of countless centuries a part;
    No more the past may reach my heart.

Tomorrow — Angels may not know
    The winding way life's streams may flow;
We can but hope its path may be
    The right one to eternity.

Since yesterday is gone and dead;
    Tomorrow still a pace ahead;
Our only hope lies in today,
    Our love to give, our debts to pay.

Then let today our pulses thrill,
    To do whatever good we will;
Mayhap tomorrow's sun will bring
    Our highest hopes before the king.

Today lived well with hope and cheer
    Will gild the past and coming year;
Will spread sweet flowers in our way;
    Our past and future is today.

Al Robles

i-hotel

International Hotel, Kearny St., San Francisco

let the mabalian tread around
the i-hotel rice fields
and pregnant nuns

manong, the clearings on the mountain
slope is ready, and the cogan grass
is thick around your body

swallow seven stars
it's time now for me to cut the grass
round your body
trap wild pigs
lay down your bolo in a basket of rice

squat on the floor
balance your mind on heels
listen to the tinkling of bells
and of brass amulets, and the beating
of gongs

pour coconut oil over your hair
rub down the body hard

pin-stripe macintosh suits
cling to hot savage bodies

rise up on heels and toes
bend the knees
twist the body encircling the gongs
dance around the small rooms

manong, the rice harvest is ready
come out of your room
let the ifugao women cook bangkodo
over little fires, balancing pots
sunk in a bed of tribal ashes

Floyd Salas

Steve Nash
Homosexual Transient
Executed San Quentin Gas Chamber
August 21st 1959
For Killing Eleven Men
And A Little Boy

This is about the killer who gets away
This is it from the viewpoint of the murderer

Dedicated to Tony Curtis and the Boston Strangler
and to Johnny Wiesmuller
and Jane
with thanks to Jack Micheline

"There are much worse things to be
than a swinger of birches." Robert Frost

I am a big cat
six-four

long stringy body
with sloping shoulders and big hands
hands that hang down like small paddles
like balls of weight with big knuckles
big hands I can spread around a basketball
knobby hands
from having to work all my life
in canneries
and on construction jobs
out on the farm picking grapes
or prunes
bussing dishes

I think I'd like to kill me a few guys
guys who think they're tougher than me
because I take it like a girl
guys who live down where I do
in skidrow rooms with hotplates
in poolhalls
in the cafeterias late at night
guys who wear clothes they buy
from the Jew at the army-navy store
guys who don't take too many baths either
and smell like the rooms I live in
faint reek of sweat
and wrinkled shirts

Sometimes I pick me up a kid down at a park
or in the front row of some shoot-me-up show
downtown
but mostly guys
it's okay unless they make fun of me
and if they do
I bust um
and sometimes croak um
I get em alone and kill um
I choke um after I hit um
When I hit um with my big fists
swinging like sledgehammers
down at the end of my long arms

I knock em dizzy
I knock um cold
Then I choke um to death
if I don't already kill um with my big fists
for making fun of me

I'm an Okie
That's what people think
But I'm really from Texas
Gauky kind of guy
bony face
high cheekbones
not goodlookin
country kind of rube down on the streets
That's what I look like
Black hair and dark-skinned
from a stain of indian blood
back there

These sailors pick me up and then laugh at me
mock me
So I slug the guy in the back seat with me
right in the nose
knock him cold
Then I grab the yoyo in the passenger seat
up front
and strangle him
I break his neck while his buddy tries to keep from crashing
rolling off the end of the pier
jams on his brakes and throws open the door and tries to run
But I catch him with a smash to the side of the head
knock him out
throw him back in the car
and push it off the end of the pier
with all three yoyos in it
push it down into the black water with a muffled splash
down down below in the oily water
deep down in the oily water
out of sight in the black night
so that nobody will see it until daylight

at best
deep deep down
in the oily water

Then they are after me
Then I have to run
run from hotel room to hotel room
run everywhere I go
run from the guys in the gray clothes in the greyhound bus station
with grim faces
run when they chase me
run down a back alley
disappear into the darkness
stay close to the walls of the buildings
until I get to my room
a buck-fifty a night
run because I can't hitchhike out
not even in the night time
with the black and white cop cars cruising around
run to the railroad yards and hop a freight
but it's a passenger train
and they're still looking for me
They know I did it and they're out to get me
I'll do anything
I'll stay in the back
I'll pay when the conductor comes
I'll do anything

But a guy comes in
and he has a grim gray face and gray clothes
and he sits down next to me in the club car
I stand up where I can get the jump on him
bust him down with one punch
or crack his neck

He looks up at me
and I see his white collar and black coat
when he asks who I am

"Who I am?" I say. "You're no priest!"
"Yes I am," he says. "Look!"

and I turn to look and see
all three sailors looking at me
but younger
rosy-cheeked and blooming
They do not speak
They are as perfect and still
as in a coffin
but standing up
They are standing up
They are after me

"Confess!" the priest says.
"Confess?" I say. "This is a trap!"
And I grab the priest by the collar
and smash him in the face
throw him out the backdoor
over the rail of the last car
and see him bounce off the tracks
and tumble down the embankment
then I turn and smash into all three sailors
punch them around like bags
so fast they don't even move
knock them all down
then jump off the back of the train
and sail feet first down the embankment

It gives as I fall
gives under me
and I fall slowly
ride the edge down
like a wave crashing slowly on the sand

Then I run down some streets
and hop up onto a house
jump from rooftop to rooftop
as teams of cops
crisscross the streets under me
like commandos in a war movie
shooting up at me
I hear the bullets whine

They whine because they can't get me
They whine but I get away
I see the cops crawling over the rooftops
behind me
gaining on me
They are gaining on me

I watch myself escape now
I am Floyd standing down below in the streets
along the sidewalk
with all the others
watch as the six-four killer finally gets treed
treed in a tree four stories high
five six maybe

He climbs to the very top of the tree
bullets whizzing around him
calling his name
sound dying out with a hum
climbs climbs
to the very top of the tree
me expecting it to break
for him to fall down and bounce on the ground
get captured or killed at least

The police all stand around and watch too
as he swings back and forth
back and forth
high above the rooftops
in a circle of sun
framed by the sun
the orange sun
sun the color of the setting sun
see him swinging back and forth
and back and forth
and back and forth
with great swooshes of wind
reaching almost head first
down to the rooftops
on one side

then back over
way down
on the other side
the same way
framed by the sunlight
glowing gold in the sunlight
haloed in ecstasy
swinging with freedom
beyond death
knowing he will never get caught
knowing they will never get him
knowing that he is freeeee
freeeeeeeeeeee
freeeeeeeeeeeeeeeeeeeeeeeeeee

Omar Salinas

Listen To The King Of Spain... Cortez

Quetzalcoatle
            yawns...
        the temple
overrun by beaurocrats
a tired cockroach
brings the news
            the gods
on horses
have taken over

the sun
a woman burning
greetings from
Spain
a century
is ours
tell Cortez
to return home

we listen
to the applause
of roses
el mundo
será nuestro

Quetzalcoatle
sleeps
forever
(the quiet drums are hushed)
the Indian
maidens
are sweet
send more
missionaries
the rain,
sullen partner
of
god
falls
on the pink belly
of
christians

Untitled

The town became nervous
  after six months, then
    began to speak

  about my sister
    who combs my hair
      with the fingers
      my mother has given
         her

    about whimsical stars,
      aristocratic women

who make a blanket
   for my bed

the town is dead now
   it's ashes
   under my fingernails

   it appears in travel
      guides
     now and then
   in our nightmares

    the gentle utopia
      of haunted childhoods.

Jazz Through An Open Window

For Carlota

With hate
in the
back room,
children
avoid
silence.

Mestizo
jazz
through
the open window,
cognac and death
. . . a soft woman
blushes
on the street.

Horses pulled
by the wind
display
nobility.

There is noise in
an upper bungalow
in crisis
cheerful
happy bulls
a dancer's night
the plight
of the world
in a song

Walk with me Señorita
I too have
tears in my eyes.

from *Aztec Angel*

I

I am an Aztec angel
        criminal
                of a scholarly
                    society
        I do favors
            for whimsical
                    magicians
            where I pawn
                my heart
                    for truth
                and find
                    my way
                through obscure
                        streets
                    of soft spoken
                            hara-kiris

II

I am an Aztec angel
        forlorn passenger

```
        on a train
    of chicken farmers
        and happy children

    III

I am the Aztec angel
    fraternal partner
        of an orthodox
            society
        where pachuco children
            hurl stones
        through poetry rooms
and end up in a cop car
        their bones itching
            and their hearts
        busted from malnutrition

    IV

I am the Aztec angel
    who frequents bars
spends evenings
        with literary circles
    and socializes
        with spiks
niggers and wops
    and collapses on his way
        to funerals

    V

Drunk
    lonely
        bespectaled
    the sky
        opens my veins
            like rain
        clouds go berserk
            around me
        my Mexican ancestors
```

chew my fingernails
I am an Aztec angel
   offspring
   of a tubercular woman
   who was beautiful

Alfonso P. Santos

Santang Buds

Let me but see in dreams the santang buds
That in my absence blossom still besides
My window: Crimson buds, like crimson pearls,
Ever in faithfulness they bloom, unchanged,
Unfailing like the memories of home.
Now is the time, the season of their blooming...
An hour less, an hour more yet stays
Their crimson evermore, untouched, unchanged.
Let me but see in dreams the santang buds
That in my absence bloom in hope for one
Heart lost in foreign land, fated to share
No love, no fortune from the world, but born
     To suffer want and misery, decreed
     To live unknown, in pettiness and need.

Leslie Scalapino

from *The Woman Who Could Read the Mind of Dogs*

on itself. His red hair was standing up) "I just began to weep".

Much later, after I had ceased to know the man who had once
described to me how, driving his new car with its top down
   around and around the block (with his 1st wife in the car—
he said that he had been downtown with her drinking in a bar)

while he was looking for the entrance to the hotel parking lot,
he had collided, or rather, had grazed the sides of 3 parked
cars; as I said, it was much later when I was standing
on the jetty of a marina and watching a man standing up in
a motor boat, while he turned it around and around in circles.
"Well", (I remembered the man I had known saying about himself
—as I watched the man in the motor boat turning it slowly
on itself. His red hair was standing up) "I just began to weep".

from 'hmmmm"

"About the night on which a man said he would spend a 100 dollars
on me", a woman described, (and he did use up most of it
simply on taxi fares), "I was able to describe my feelings:

"About the night on which a man said he would spend a 100 dollars
on me", a woman described, (and he did use up most of it
simply on taxi fares), "I was able to describe my feelings:
by saying it was like being an insect who puts its feelers
out into the flowers of a plant, and sucks from them, as we were
(sucking) from the restaurants and bars of the city
to which the taxi took us. All night we were surrounded by lights.
As I lay back inside the taxi, just waiting for the man to make
arrangements for me (in regard to *that* part of my feeling,
I would describe the taxi as being more like a buoy), I had the
feeling (thru-out it) of rising slowly, and of floating along side
particular spots in the city. By morning, naturally, I was sated".

Ntozake Shange

My Name Means My Own & This Is For Me
not for but cuz a miz t.

somebody almost walked off wid alla my stuff
not my poems or a dance i gave up in the street
but somebody almost walked off wid alla my stuff

like a kleptomaniac waz workin hard & forgetting
while stealin this is mine / this ain't yr stuff
put me back & let me hang out in my own self
somebody almost walked off wid all a my stuff
& didn't care enuf to send a note home sayin
i waz gonna be late for my solo conversation
or two sizes too small for my own tacky skirts
what can anybody do wid my stuff / i know it waz
a niggah run off wid somethin of no value
on a open market / did you get a dime for my things
hey man / where are you goin wid alla my stuff
this is a woman's trip & i need my stuff
to ooh & ah abt / daddy i got a mainline number
from my own shit / wontchu put me back & let
me play this duet wid the silver ring in my nose
honest to god somebody almost run off wid alla my stuff
& i didn't bring nothin but the kick & sway of it
the perfect ass for my man & none of it is theirs
this is mine. 'ntozake' her own things'. that's my name.
give me my stuff. i see ya hiding in my laugh & how i sit
wif my legs open sometimes to give my crotch
some sunlight & there goes my love & my toes & my
chewed up fingernails / niggah wif the curlers in yr hair
mr. louisiana hot link / i want my stuff back
my rhythm and my voice / open my mouth & let me talk ya-'outta
throwin my things in the sewer / this is some
delicate leg & whimsical kiss i gotta have to give
to my choice / is not you runnin off wif my shit /
get this stealin & hoardin offa yr mine / you
cant have me / less i give me away / & i waz
doin alla that til ya ran off on a good thing
somebody almost ran off wif alla my stuff /
conyus knows / he saw me lookin for a $5
orchestra to play this sad symphony on market street /
jessica saw them wash my hair down a halloween nite
& where is my stuff / i know when i aint me
who is this you left me wif / some simple bitch
wif a bad attitude / gimme my things /
i want my arm wif the hot iron scar & my leg wif
the flea bite / i want my calloused feet & quik language

300

back / & sun-ra & joseph & jules / i want my own things
how i lived em / & give me my memories / what it waz
to be me / how i waz when i waz there / ya cant have it /
or do nothin to it / stealin my shit from me / dont make it
yrs / makes it stolen / somebody almost ran off wid all my
shit / & i waz standin there lookin at myself the whole time /
& it waznt no spirits took my stuff / waz a man whose ego
walked round like rodan's shadow / waz a man faster than
my innocence / waz a lover / a niggah / i made too much room for /
almost ran off wif alla my shit / didnt know i'd give it so quik
& i'm standin there wid no stuff / & the one runnin wid it
dont know he got it / & somebody almost run off wid alla my stuff
& i'm shoutin this is mine / & he dont know he got it /
my stuff is the anonymous ripped-off treasure of this year /
did you know somebody almost got away wif me / in plastic bag
under their arm / me / dangling on a string
of personal carelessness / i'm spattered wif mud
& city rain & didnt get a chance to take a douche
hey man / this is not yr prerogative
i gotta have me in my pocket to get round like a good woman shd /
& make the poem in the pot or chicken the dance / what i got to do /
i gotta have my stuff to do it to / why dont ya find
yr own things & leave this package of me for my destiny /
what ya gotta get from me / i'll give it to ya / give it to ya /
give it to ya / round 5:00 in the winter when the sky is
blue-red & do-city is gettin pressed / if it's really my stuff
ya got / ya gotta give it to me / if ya want it /
i'm the only one can handle it /

Rena Sheffield

The Artist And The Emperor

Ch'ung Ch'êng much prized a banquet hall
Hung round in cloth of gold;
He called Lin Hü to fresco there
A picture deftly scrolled,
And to the bidden artist said,

"If this I ban, off goes thy head.
And hark ye! ere the wild swans nest
Upon their reeds...seek thou no rest."

At twilight's fall returned Ch'ung Ch'êng,
Walked through his princely hall;
He saw pink sprays of budding plum,
Two doves atop a wall,
And, as he drew more close to view,
His broidered robe blurred out the two.
Lin Hü stood in alarm,
His hands outstretched to stay their flight
And counter further harm.
Then spoke Ch'ung Ch'êng in accents slow,
Lin Hü, all perfect things must go.
But hark ye! paint for me tonight
A scene on yonder wall,
For I would view thy work once more
Ere morning gilds my hall."

Pale Lin Hü took his palette up
Of teak inlaid with jade;
He mixed the dyes of grey and mauve,
And silver carp he made.
And when the dawn touched Omei's rim
Ch'ung Ch'êng stood there to judge of him.
He asked for palette and for brush;
While Lin Hü gave no sign,
The master painted out his work,
His glory of design,
For criss-cross went the pigment wet,
And when he finished...lo!
The fish were caught within a net
That held their silver glow.
And the artist heard his emperor say,
"Lest thy carp, Lin Hü, should swim away!"

Edward Rowland Sill

Lost Love

Bury it, and sift
  Dust upon its light,—
Death must not be left,
  To offend the sight.

Cover the old love—
  Weep not on the mound—
Grass shall grow above,
  Lilies spring around.

Can we fight the law,
  Can our natures change—
Half-way through withdraw—
  Other lives exchange?

You and I must do
  As the world has done,
There is nothing new
  Underneath the sun.

Fill the grave up full—
  Put the dead love by—
Not that men are dull,
  Not that women lie,—

But 't is well and right—
  Safest, you will find—
That the Out of Sight
  Should be Out of Mind.

Her Explanation

I am a lost illusion. Some strange spell
Once made your friend there, with his fine disdain
Of fact, conceive me perfect. He would fain

(But could not) see me always, as befell
His dream to see me, plucking asphodel,
In saffron robes, on some celestial plain.
All that I was he marred and flung away,
    In quest of what I was not, could not be,—
    Lilith, or Helen, or Antigone.

John Oliver Simon

North Country

we been making these bargains so long
it's a goddam conspiracy when the sun rises
smoke & platinum
somebody's fat white dog getting ready to
knock over the amanita muscaria again

up here you could spend all night dragging your
unborn children down the roads of the pygmy forest
until you try to make a fire with your teeth.
no use your silver bullets,
no use the funny crystals that you borrowed from the ocean.

these are the rules & there are no regrets. up here
they string their guitars with rattlesnake grass
& their violins with the feathers of an eagle.
the tombstones on the hill were all
handcrafted by jealous husbands.

Gino Clays Sky

Potatoes And Rosehips

There are icicles hanging from my beard, and my belt
is up two notches from the last hunt. My grandmother
is blind, and keeps asking for some meat. She could

live to be one hundred and twenty-five on potatoes and
rosehips and still have the sweetest smile in the valley.
These are lean years to eat, but fat years to dream.

The arrows that I'm making will soon be ready. My bow
is wrapped in deerskin tanned by my grandmother. Old
skills that are necessary for the hunt. The smoothness
of my walk, silence, and the beauty of being alone. One
deer can replace a shopping mall she told me in her eighty-
sixth year. These are lean years to eat, but fat years to
dream.

You must be able to hunt alone, and with the silence of
the falcon. Steal the wind and the colors of the sky, and
walk without tracks. Bring home the meat, skin out the
game, tan the hides, and prepare the meat for the smoker.
You can write your sonnets later she would say, but first
you must learn how to dream. With no meat in the pot your
eyes will become wall-eyed. Here, take this scent and
bring home our supper.

With my bow and arrows, my body covered with deerskin
rubbed with baylaurel, I move up the canyon. The wind
is blowing on my face, and I keep it there as a weather
vane. My grandmother is waiting. She has taught me everything, except how to kill. She is hungry, and doesn't
want to live to be one hundred and twenty-five eating
potatoes and rosehips.

Go for the heart, I hear her voice as I pull back on the
string, finding the tension point where release is lethal.
The doe is round and beautiful, and I see my grandmother
as a young woman riding her buckskin through the hills
chasing butterflies and eagles. The doe looks at me, and
I see my grandmother smile as I release the arrow.

Sitting close to the fire we eat the meat in silence. I
rub her feet, trim the dry, hard skin from her bunions with
my hunting knife, and rub them with oil. She is asleep,
and only now can I return to my fantasies. Sitting at my

pine desk reading books of other worlds—of poets who write
like rainbows and river. Tomorrow we will have a feast.
We will dance and sing, and tell great stories. And the
next day I will take down my bow and arrows, rub my body
with mysteries, and move out alone into the silence.

Genoveva Saavedra

In the Old Pueblo

WINTER COTTONWOODS

Bare Cottonwoods
Screen the parched bed of the river,
Spreading their fan of silver lace
Across a turquoise sky.

MISSION SAN XAVIER DEL BAC

"White Dove of the Desert"
In purest spun-gold nest,
A treasured bit of Spanish shawl
Upon her hallowed breast.

LATE SPRING

By a silver thread of a stream
Two dragonflies—
One, a needle of burnished copper,
The other, a stiletto of purest turquoise—
Play hide-and-seek
Among the water cress.

Martín Solis

Orgullo y Verdad

"Pride and Truth" is about a millionaire with no friends who lived alone and sick in a giant tower. He never helped the poor. He considered himself so rich and powerful that the tower would remain as an immortal symbol of his greatness after his death. But sadness overcame him when he realized that only the works of knowledge and talent are immortal.

¡Oh mis niños! . . . Sabed: un millonario
en gigantesco torreón vivía
sin amigos, enfermo y solitario.

Jamás al desvalido socorria
y al contemplarse rico y poderoso
con despotismo proverbial decía:

Yo . . . bajaré el sepulcro, presuroso . . .
¡Pero el sol immortal de mi grandeza
será esta torre, sin igual coloso!

Y devoróle pronto la tristeza
al clamar una voz solemnemente
No es del coloso tanta la firmeza.

Y el curso de los siglos, inclemente,
Ni huellas dejará de su cimiento
porque son immortales, solamente,
las obras del saber y del talento.

Alan Soldofsky

Poem For Sioux City

Whenever I come here
I find truck bodies grown over
with fur, the trailers unhitched

years ago, tied upright and still
to the rusted beds of flatcars.

In the rear-view mirror
I remember the jagged feel of
a broken nose, of hands torn
by a tow chain. The knife point
of the wind whipping through
the empty cattle yards.

At each intersection in this city
there is a cop whose face is so
small you could scrape it off
with a fingernail.

                I will say
nothing more of my in-laws,
or the meat packers committing
sabotage in the factories.

I will climb to a grave
above the river, where the bluffs
swing out steeply, where
during that famous expedition
of 1804 one man was buried

and the rest went on.

Gary Soto

Summer

Once again, tell me, what was it like?
There was a windowsill of flies.
It meant the moon pulled its own weight
And the black sky cleared itself
Like a sneeze.

What about the farm worker?
He had no bedroom. He had a warehouse
Of heat, a swamp cooler
That turned no faster than a raffle cage.

And the farms?
There were groves
Of fig trees that went unpicked.
The fruit wrinkled and flattened
Like the elbows
Of an old woman.

What about the Projects in the East side?
I can't really say. Maybe a child
Burned his first book of matches.
Maybe the burn is disappearing
Under the first layer
Of skin.

And next summer?
It will be the same. Boredom,
In early June, will settle
On the eyelash shading your pupil from dust,
On the shoulder you look over
To find the sun rising
From the Sierras.

History

Grandma lit the stove.
Morning sunlight
Lengthened in spears
Across the linoleum floor.
Wrapped in a shawl,
Her eyes small
With sleep,
She sliced papas,
Pounded chiles
With a stone
Brought from Guadalajara.

After

Grandpa left for work,
She hosed down
The walk her sons paved
And in the shade
Of a chinaberry,
Unearthed her
Secret cigar box
Of bright coins
And bills, counted them
In English,
Then in Spanish,
And buried them elsewhere.
Later, back
From the market,
Where no one saw her,
She pulled out
Pepper and beet, spines
Of asparagus
From her blouse,
Tiny chocolates
From under a paisley bandana,
And smiled.

That was the '50s,
And Grandma in her '50s,
A face streaked
From cutting grapes
And boxing plums.
I remember her insides
were washed of tape worm,
Her arms swelled into knobs
Of small growths—
Her second son
Dropped from a ladder
And was dust.
And yet I do not know
The sorrows
That sent her praying
In the dark of a closet,

The tear that fell
At night
When she touched
Loose skin
Of belly and breasts.
I do not know why
Her face shines
Or what goes beyond this shine,
Only the stories
That pulled her
From Taxco to San Joaquin,
Delano to Westside,
The places
In which we all begin.

The Firstborn

All day the Nina sewed in this room
The curtain pulled down
But where it was torn
The sun flared
On the wall
And on the wall
The fingerprints
Of the firstborn
Who drowned face-up
In the basin

That was weeks ago but still
She was frightened
When she washed
Or drank there
She thought of the baby
Coming up heavy
From the soapy water
His mouth open
on the cry
That did not reach
Humming she

Towelled and hugged
Her little one
Before laying him
On the kitchen table
Back in the room
She stood looking
At the basin
And did not understand
what she was looking at
Or why but then
Closing her eyes
Dipped her fists
in the water
And thought
Of her old town—
A rooster the winter wind sliced
Through a reed fence

Moving Away

Remember that you are moving away sister
From what was a summer
Of hunger
And of thorns deep in your feet
Prayers that unraveled
Like mama's stockings
At the day's end
When she came back from candling eggs

Those small things you knew on the old street
Have vanished a holly bush
And its bright jays
The rocks you scratched
From the yard
And were your dolls   blond dolls
Given heartbeats names legs
The sighs of those
About to cry

Remember that you have left
Grandpa nodding like a tall weed
Over his patch of chiles and tomatoes
Left a jar of secrets
Buried in the vacant lot
On a hot day
And our family some distance
From your life
Remember

Jay Roderic de Spain

I Heard Her Wings

The wind has whirring wings
and hums about my sill.
She pokes her slender bill
among the honeyed things
her fretful coming stirs:
the wind must be a bird.
I saw no form, but heard
her humming through the firs.

Richard Leon Spain

Plea

Lift singing towers of radiance from the earth
In dogwood tree and redbud tree, wild spring!
Let pristine hills be robed in emerald mirth!
Let creeks be joyous, and let chewinks sing!
Awake the rhododendron and allow
Its snowbank beauty to unfold for moth
And spangled butterfly ... Weave meadows now
Into an April-patterned kind of cloth ...

Let no dark thread of sadness stay, wild season!
Weave all the earth and sky into a flame
Of potent and tremendous joy! Let reason
Be gulfed within a peace too deep to name!
Lose me in joy, for I am one who goes
To sterner battles than a hill-tree knows...

Anna K. Spero

Lines To A Western Woman

An item in plate matter in this sheet
Of little consequence reads:—"Recently
A Pueblo princess died where she had lived,
Her pottery had found its way to all
The world's museums or to nearly all
Before she died at home." Her name is blurred.

Lone one—for every thinker is alone—
Did you draw patterns from the shadow-edge
The torn-topped terraces cast on the dust?
Or lolling lizards arabesqued? or dry
Sleek snakes green-bellied, backed with gold and black
Of banded intricacies and repeats?
Or crested thorny-spotted toads at home
Among the stones? or paws of grizzly bears?
Or from straight sticks and wrecks of mummied leaves
Blown into figures undesignedly
By scoriac winds? or from the rims of those
Ungainly cacti, fantasies, which bloom
When the Moon-mother looks beyond her waste—
Out of the world—to yours—out of the world?
Or from red narrow lightning jagged sharp?
Or clouds from which the rain gods pour on drouth?

Or were they symbols decorate, art-speech
Your lineage had of origins of worlds
And men, and gates souls use, their meanings clutched

From image-breakers or, it may be, lost
To Indians riding tragedy's long trail
From lands the Earth has called beneath the seas?

While others slept, dreamed not when dark came down,—
Unless of longer sleep, of food, of ease,—
You dreamed awake, and your large genius grew
The perfect of its kind, to all the world
A marvel as emergent from your race.

You are both seer and princess, royal twice,
Through lines of thought and action.
                              Did you wear
No topaz, Princess, on your forehead crowned?
No ruby-light as royal women wear?
And did you scorn the trader's trinketry,—
His filching beads,—let art and nature make
Your difference plain?
                              Your supple fingers, were
They brown as script they traced, enriching art
By humble clay? The clay your fingers touched
To form was art's thenceforth though scattered shards.

My sister, had we met, I would have laid
My heart to yours. You knew the rapture of creative mind!

Your isolation, set in life, to us
Indelicate, unthrilled, and visionless,—
A void,—was not, for you, disaster. Out
Against it moved your palpitant unrest,
Divine, co-operate with His who thought
The universe and marked it with His hand.

Jack Spicer

No love deserves the death it has.   An
        archipelago
Rocks cropping out of ocean.   Seabirds

shit on it.   Live out their lives on
        it.
What was once a mountain.
Or was it once a mountain?   Did Lemuria,
        Atlantis, Mu ever exist except in
        the minds of old men fevered by
        the distances and the rocks they saw?
Was it true?   Can the ocean of time claim
        to own us now adrift
Over that land.   In that land.   If
        memory serves
There (that rock out there)
Is more to it.

The country is not very well-defined.
Whether they are bat-people or real people.   The sea-
Coast of Bohemia.   The in-
Visible world.
A man counts his fingers in these situations.
        Whether there are five or ten of them or
        udders as we might go sea-bathing in
        dream.
But dream is not enough.   We waking
        hear the call of the
In-
Visible world
Not seen.   Hinted at only.   By some
        vorpals, some sea-lions, some scraggs.
Almost too big to get used to, its
        dimensions amaze us, who are blind to
        Whatever
Is rising and falling with us.

Gertrude Stein

A Poem

I

Believe me when I tell you what I think.
But believe me.
It is not easy to refuse to believe me when I tell you what I think.
Or rather it is not easy not to believe me.

II

They like to hear others cry out loud.
And they like to stand and see others see and hear.
And they like to know that here.
They can know that they can not see and hear.
But anybody can.
And anybody does.
Does and was.

III

Does and was is very pretty.
Do and see is very she
Did and said is very easy
And they will for all of me.

IV

which they may with which they will.
Rest as well as all until
Yes they do not without sashes.
Added very well with clashes.

V

I did not see them near.
Not very near.
But just as near
As they were
One once with wedding made a glance with credit at once they

made it a present to the ones they were with. It was known as attending when they were attending to helping in accidentally never have to make it to them in their mistaken in. What is the difference if it is or is not made on purpose when then it will do. The better wider that they mind after the firm of which they might be seated as if they had loaned it until they were through.

Stanza LV

I have been thought to not respect myself
To have been sold as wishes
To wonder why and if and will they mind
To have it as it is and clearly
To not replace which if they as they do
Can they content can they be as content
For which they will if even be it mine
mine will be or will not be mine
Rather than mine and mine.
I wish to say
That it is her day
That it might be well
To think well of it
It is not often led or left
But whichever and whenever
Can they not only be
All mine.
I often think will I be thought to know
Oh yes of course I will be known to know
I will be here I will be here and here
It may not be that it is I am here.
I will not add it more and not
Not change which is a chance to leave it.
I can be often very much my own
I wonder why
Is it that is it here.
Can I but not to try
I can cradle not infancy but really

What I can.
They can collect me.
They can recollect me
They can if mine is mine.
Not even mine is mine.
Mine which is mine.
Nobody knows a name for shame.
Shame shame fie for shame
Everybody knows her name.

Stanza LVI

I could be thoroughly known to come again.
Often if I do
I come again.
As often if I do.
I could not change often for often.
Which I do.
Often for often which I do.

Stanza LVII

I have often been doubtful if yes or no
Annoys him.
Or is it only the setting sun
Or the chairs softening
Or the direction changing
In which they see why I do.
Might it not be only what they like.
I like what I like.
Can they not like what they like.
But very often he means nothing.

George Sterling

The Black Vulture

Aloof upon the day's immeasured dome,
  He holds unshared the silence of the sky.
  Far down his bleak, relentless eyes descry
The eagle's empire and the falcon's home—
Far down, the galleons of sunset roam;
  His hazards on the sea of morning lie;
  Serene, he hears the broken tempest sigh
Where cold sierras gleam like scattered foam.

And least of all he holds the human swarm—
  Unwitting now that envious men prepare
    To make their dream and its fulfilment one,
When, poised above the caldrons of the storm,
  Their hearts, contemptuous of death, shall dare
    His roads between the thunder and the sun.

The Young Witch

Elder Davenport Speaks

Cry bravely, O town crier,
  (And ye, young men, beware!)
How Yale Ratchford, the strong smith,
  Is gone God knoweth where!

Yea! the tall smith is gone
  And comes not home again.
Tho he had a shrewish wife,
  he was man among men.

He shall drink no more ale,
  Nor smoke at the tavern door,
Nor sing old songs at his forge,
  And wrestle young men no more.

320

This he got for being so strong,
  And this for being so bold
As to have in scorn the white witch
  Who slept in her hair of gold.

By the dark pond in the hills
  She lived when her dam died,
With a black cat which minded her,
  And a black dog at her side.

In pinewood and marshy places
  Her low song was sung,
Where long moss is, and toadstools
  The hue of a goblin's tongue.

Where got she her sullen mouth
  And where her swaying form?
Would she live on eggs and apples,
  When the blood of men is warm?

All the town people went shy of her
  When the Ratchford baby died.
Folk tell how she laughed that day,
  and no folk say she cried.

Yale Ratchford cut him a switch
  From a hickory at his door,
And he went up among the hills
  To see she laughed no more.

There were whispers of a hanging
  The day that he went forth,
As had been done by holy men
  At Salem in the north.

A bear was shot at Hadlyme
  With fur as soft as silk,
And Goodman Ames of Saybrook
  Found minnows in the milk.

That night the geese went over,

A-belling for the Pole.
Some say it was the dark hounds
    That bay a loosened soul.

But saved, or damned forever,
    He comes back home no more,
And we who searched the witch's house
    Found grass against the door.

His wife is shrill in question,
    As she was shrill ere he left,
For all that she was well nurtured,
    A sayer, and right deft.

Now shall be heard much rumor,
    And talk at the tavern door;
And if a stranger come from Boston
    They'll tell him o'er and o'er.

It was not wise to go hillward
    With hand shut on a switch;
It is not given to young men
    To rid the land of a witch—

Not with eyes so wide apart,
    And in a face so white!
Not if she wander naked
    By a shrunk moon's light!

What shall he do her of service,
    As they strong do for the fair?
Shall he forge her an iron marriage ring,
    Or shoes for the Devil's mare?

For they ha' gone forever—
    Vanished, as men say true,
In blue sky or blue water
    Or the wind between the two.

Priscilla Stewart

A Voice From The Oppressed
To The Friends Of Humanity
(Composed by one of the suffering class.)

Written shortly after the passage of a bill demanding that all Free Negroes leave the State, at which time the Governor or Ruler of British Columbia sent his Harbor Master to San Francisco to extend an invitation to the Negro people to come to Canada to make their home.

Look and behold our sad despair,
   Our hopes and prospects fled,
The tyrant slavery entered here
   And laid us all for dead.

Sweet home! When shall we find a home?
If the tyrant says that we must go,
   The love of gain the reason,
And if humanity dare say "No,"
   Then they are tried for treason.

God bless the Queen's majesty,
   Her sceptre and her throne,
She looked on us with sympathy
   And offered us a home.

Far better breathe Canadian air
   Where all are free and well,
Than live in slavery's atmosphere
   And wear the chains of hell.

Farewell to our native land,
   We must give the parting hand,
Never to see thee any more,
   But seek a foreign land.

Farewell to our true friends,
   Who've suffered dungeon and death.

You have a claim upon our gratitude
   Whilst God shall lend us breath.

May God inspire your hearts,
   A Marion raise your hands;
Never desert your principles
   Until you've redeemed your land.

Charles Warren Stoddard

A Rhyme Of The Old Year

Who killed the Old Year?
   "I," said Sparrow time;
   "So put me in the rhyme—
I killed the Old Year."

Who saw him die?
   "I," said the Morning Star;
   "While watching from afar,
I saw him die."

Who caught his blood?
   "I," said each Man and Maid;
   "I caught a drop that will not fade,
For it is his blood."

Who'll weave his shroud?
   "I," said Memory;
   "Of flowers fair to see
I'll weave his shroud."

Who'll dig his grave?
   "I," said Oblivion;
   "For, sure, it must be done—
I'll dig his grave."

Who'll be chief mourner?
   "I," said Sad Regret;

"As I am fittest yet,
I'll be chief mourner."

Who'll come and sing?
    "We," said Hope and Trust;
    "We'll sing above his dust—
We'll come and sing."

Who'll toll the bell?
    "I," said the Broken Heart;
    "I can toll—it asks no art;
I'll toll the bell."

And so the service
    Is sung and said
Over the pitiful
    Year that is dead.

J. Anthony Stowers

The Natives Abroad

I must have a culture
Somewhere.
In some forgotten land
Blackness must have rolled
From the mind of God
To give me woolen hair
And thick warm lips—and
Eyes that were dark—wise
and free.
Oh, before the horrors came
My ebony soul must have
Uncoiled in tropic flare
To create the drum and
Dance, uncaged by white
Hands.
I must have a culture

Lost in the forgotten
World of my jet soul,
Where long ago I threw
A spear in childish play.
But the horrors came
With gin and holy words
To take my magic and
tongue—to crush my Gods
And rape my mountains
and bush.
And brought me unknown
To the gates of Cain,
Where death and blood
Sank me even deeper in
Rancid slush and tepid mire.
I must have a culture
Beside the housing projects,
The wasted lives, the crowded
rooms reeking with darkness and
Ignorance, the dry smell
Of pot and hissing dope
Spikes.
There must be more to
Remember!
More to love from my
Conquered history than bowing
Black faces of Africa.
More to this virile, ancient
Body that keeps rising from
The dust of America with
A powerful song to tremble
The earth.
I must have a culture
That is not madness or
Anger.
That is not a content
Nigger alley cat who loves
white women and long-toe
Shoes.
Somewhere I left a proud

Black man to become a
Feeble white nigger with
White ideas of success, power
And degenerate behavior.
I must find my culture
On the faces of the melted
Tribes dying hopelessly in
The gutters,
Laughing on broken steps
And cooking in greasy kitchens.
I must watch the old folks
Shout in church
And the sweating musicians burn
Their hip tunes
And the big rump sisters flirt
Their sensual dark eyes.
That's my culture! My love!
My country!

Barbara Szerlip

The Winery

It's said there were two brothers, having travelled great distances, across an ocean, a continent, to this valley. Cuttings swathed in their luggage that would be vineyards. Fruit so at home here the origins would be lost. And there were two houses built, one of mahogany and crystal, one modest of white clapboard, but the same stars overhead, the same birds at dusk. Then the Chinese came to hollow the mountain, cool grey tunnels for storing a pressed harvest they would not drink. Oak casks taller than four men on each other's shoulders.

Chenin Blanc. Zinfandel. Cabernet Sauvignon. "Drop everything," he wrote his brother, who'd gone as far as New York, happy with his publishing business. "Drop everything, we're tunnelling the mountain."

He came. His was the clapboard house. One wonders where the
Chinese were buried, or if their spirits enjoy the cool passageways,
their bodies feeding each season's shoots.

Genevieve Taggard

With Child

Now I am slow and placid, fond of sun,
Like a sleek beast, or a worn one:
No slim and languid girl—not glad
With the windy trip I once had,
But velvet-footed, musing of my own,
Torpid, mellow, stupid as a stone.

You cleft me with your beauty's pulse, and now
Your pulse has taken body. Care not how
The old grace goes, how heavy I am grown,
Big with this loneliness, how you alone
Ponder our love. Touch my feet and feel
How earth tingles, teeming at my heel!
Earth's urge, not mine—my little death, not hers;
And the pure beauty yearns and stirs.

It does not heed our ecstasies, it turns
With secrets of its own, its own concerns,
Toward a windy world of its own, toward stark
And solitary places. In the dark,
Defiant even now, it tugs and moans
To be untangled from these mother's bones.

Tauhindauli

The Man Who Travels

The man who travels
speaks to mountains
in his region

In the north
a snow peak

In the valley
buttes above the fog

In the south
a mountain by the ocean

The man who travels
speaks to mountains
in his region

Each peak receives
begins the journey
of the dead

And speaks of shadows
where death
is not death

And the path
from earth
is real

The man who travels
speaks to mountains
in his region

The man who
travels mountains
travels
and speaks of death

Hands Tell

Hands tell
of stories and directions
of the wind and breathing times

Like the screech
and grinding of an earthquake
coming first by sound

The sacred fire
made in a
way of thinking
has bubbles rising
from the flame

Cover the earth
again with fire
and death show symbols
travelling in a hall

Red Pond

Comes the morning
when the blood of dead
lay silent
floating in the
red red water

Where prancing
hoofprints creased
the edge of dreams
and ran down
unarmed people

The bodies cold
were running
northward
headless in the
snow fed waters

Mountain fed
yet blood
blood red pond
water pond
on Bloody Island

Rabbit Crazy

Rabbit laughed and slapped his knees
Oh lord you're really something
and mouse laughed back

They were talking how rabbit
got so many girls and what it takes
to keep them happy

It must be something real good "Yeah
for a ninety year old . . . he's saying
but he's really sixty two
which ain't bad for a rabbit

"They are from eighteen to old . . . .
He's talking of his women
I wonder who "they" are
and what he means by "old"

One time, rabbit to show
his friendship offered to
let mouse use his name
for one of rabbit's children

Mouse's wife said
she would beat him
if that happened
and mouse and rabbit laughed

They laughed as they talked
of women and babies
and what it takes to be
a crazy rabbit or a lover man

Untitled

The ceremony of flying
between bodies
blessed clean
in death

Birth and death
is not superstition
death's separation
is healed by smoke

The sacred fire
made in a
way of thinking
has bubbles rising
from the flame

And hands tell
of stories and directions
of wind and breathing times

One time I asked my uncle
for a name and he told me
our family name is a good
Indian name. I think of
myself by that name. It
has nothing to do with the
names used to sign things
It has to do with love

Untitled

Death is a sure thing
patterned after seasons
and changing forms of light

If you do not understand

yourself listen to
others and learn

I have been given
this lesson about
death and love

I sat beside an elder and
he introduced me to God
this is my nephew God
he was sitting up and had my hand

I still remember how nice
a day it was and how clear-eyed
and good his mind was

I sat by the bed
and listened to my uncle
introducing me to God

This is my nephew God
he was sitting up and had my hand
I want you to meet
my nephew
and I understood

Joyce Carol Thomas

Where Is The Black Community?

Where is the Black community?
holding down the corner
where 3rd street meets B

sitting in the second pew
at Double Rock Baptist Church

Where is the Black community?

at Bob's Barber Shop
busting jokes about the man

at the Delta sisters
fashioning J. Magnin and new hairdos

Where is the Black community?
Scrubbing chitlin grease
off a kitchen stove eye

and hawking Muhammad Speaks
on a Stanford campus

Where is the Black community?
transplanting kidneys
in a university hospital

and plowing cotton
in a Mississippi dawn

Where is the Black community?
teaching English
at Duke and Purdue

and arranging 4 kids
in a twin sized bed

Where is the Black community?
living in two story houses

on Poplar Street Drive

and swilling Old Crow
out of a crystal flask.

Quilting Bee

If the Oklahoma cotton fields
Didn't stop me
What you think I want
To sit down now for

You ain never seen no
Roadblocks like the ones
I done sperienced
You better get up from there and do it

A quilt is made the same
Way now
As they stitched them
then
a patch of color here,
A Dutch boy there,
Maybe a checkered square

Why, I used to straddle baby
Brother on my hip and
Run from the gray pack dogs
Somebody be frying fat back and
Taters on a ground stove fire
Sat my skinny self
Down on a cracker sack pallet and dined
Never oncet forgot to feed the baby

I seen the Oklahoma river rise
And peoples crawl up the hill
Like crawdads crawling up a river bank
Eighteen folks bedded down at our house
We thought it was fun
Inconvenience?
Chile, you ain never seen none

A quilt makes a fine pallet

My cousin stab my brother
And my mama a mile away
Raised up out of her pregnant bed
And screamed and screamed and
Screamed
Before she knew
She knew
Mystery to me
O yeah, you can do it

And when the welfare peoples come to the house

And look at us all with razor eyes
My mama say never mind
And we ate beans and she scrubbed floors
And the same peoples that helped her
Killed her
You better do it

Don't say nothing to me bout
No inconvenience
Please get out of my face

                                    it's amazing how you can
                                    Make beauty from scraps

Din't nobody never give me nothing
I worked for what I got
And if they take it away today
I still got a lot

                                    No, you couldn't buy
                                    one of these quilts in the
                                    store. They don't sell them.

Do it, she said, do it

John Thorpe

Untitled

Our Lady of No Defense
blue light of the fields
of the farthest sea
release your care
   Stay loving
welfare or bad work
freeloader, & those gone mad
w/ desire, w/
   holes in thin shoes.

        Hold to yourself
to hell, ever

    loving children abide
Remember that love
even you could not make real
in each man / as in
the vision destroyed in yr eyes.

        Yr majesty
        to whom Curtis Mayfield & all men
        have talked at night
        Queen without a King

Or mother, lover, stranger
Seen going down the street
infant to adore, home to share
joy. Welcome the wanderer
        dignify the
broken heart & mind, nerves
& muscles.
Bless the south for the bums
And the leader of the birds flight
in the broken mind
wch is yr lord

When our need comes, feed us
from the life in closed eyes.
You are the preparer of the world.
My lady, my head is no hole, nor
                        tender.
There are cats all over begging & stealing.
Don't leave me in cities & dripping tents.

I see a kerosene lamp moving across
the world at night. A flare led by a
sick child. The trees are a statue of all
future war, billowing w / the indifference of
amassed rebirth in the mountain winds.

Sotère Torregian

Aztlán.

We take up our fight with the Elements of this State, our home,
Aztlán. Poetry wears the clothes of a Zapatista of Orozco, reflected
in the sun by day and the moon by night. An Aztec heart beats in this
soil, — I feel its pulse as I walk over the terrain. And the white beard
of Quetzalcoatl appears reflecting its own imminence upon the shore.
All in the rhythm of working mothers. All in a caress as they caress
their hair bleached by the sun of their young. Theater of comets and
meteors beyond my understanding . California, regal misnomer of
its personage in an iron mask whose real identity is — *Aztlán !*
Genius of Aztlán ! I have no idea what time it is I know only that I am
grafted unto you; I don 't know if it 's time now for the rescue. *Je te
salue.* Aztlán I live in Aztlán. I know nothing of ecology schedules
but what the aborted mariners tell me of their coming out of the
desert sand-storm of mirrors reliving their lives only when I stop to
smile at a child whem I roam about still talking to myself not recognizing anyone who recognizes me. Like Pierre Vidal my wolf-suit
skin chased by the dogs of chivalry — because landscape you become
the landscape of a kiss. Salamis has enthroned you grandmothers !
manic husbands ! quagmires ! beached minotaur-shadow boxing
heraldries take us up and arm us with your becoming ! Taut as the
drum of your horizon, my heart is wild now with rising echoes. *Je
vive ici toujours pour le premier fois.*

January , 1977

Ernesto Trejo

To The Child Dead In My Larynx

Since morning I've been at a burial
I dressed this boy like an angel
and took away his name. Cussed him

and took his parents. Kicked him in the ass
to prove that I'm here.

I would spill off his shoulders like grease,
he would be a zoo staring me down.
and what do we share? He gave
birth to me: I buried him
with fresh dirt and spit.

He's always shooting rings of smoke,
promises floating to heaven.
I'm tundra where he wanders
carrying flesh under his arm.
Would he let me break in like light
through his eyelids? Would he be
a story to feed my big bones?
Would he come around to show me
the lint in his pockets?

Quincy Troupe

A Day In The Life Of A Poet

Woke up crying the blues:
bore witness to the sadness of the day;
the peaceful man from Atlanta
was slaughtered yester/day.
Got myself together
drank in the sweetness of sun/shine,
wrote three poems too the peace/ful lamb
from Atlanta; made love
to a raging Black woman
drank wine
got high: saw angels
leading the lamb to heaven?
the blues gonna get me
gonna get me for sure!
went too the beach/too forget

if only eye can
about the gentle soul of Georgia;
ate clam chowder and fish sandwiches;
made love in the sand
to this same beautiful woman:
drank in all her sweetness:
lost future child in the sand,
saw the bloody sun falling
behind weeping purple clouds;
tears fell in rivers for this gentle lamb
who eye can't forget.
The bloody star sinking
into the purple grave: blackness falls.
Go out into the decay of day;
copped three keys;
the key of happiness,
the key of creative joy,
the key of sadness.
Came back, watched the gloom on the tube
at her house; which was disrupted.
Kissed her, went home by the route
of the mad space ways: dropped tears in my lap
for the lamb from Atlanta.
Home at last
Two letters under the door;
a love letter from the past
grips at the roots of memory
at last another poem published!
good news during a bad news' weekend!
lights out;
drink of grapes;
severed sight closes
another day
in the life.

Red Bone Pot Lunch

California / L.A. sun people
beating down my black singing days

into the blood fusion
comes the rhythm of their poems
wheeling far-out over wide
spaced days come the
image-song blending
sun / sea-salt spray

the music in salt waves

where days pass when one thinks
the entire beautiful world of long
legged bikini-clad super-bad ladies
tan their black
brown / yellow / pink bodies
beneath an eye-balling sun
on the burning shifting sands
of Malibu Beach

& the days burn drifting
piling years, as freezing Wyoming snow
drifts during winter; as snow-cold death
of Big Foot, at the battle
of Wounded Knee
way back in 1890
during the last bloody
days of that december

Dee Brown has told the story
as many people have told true stories
as Malcolm X was a teller of true stories

as long days burn flash / bone for fuel-wood

but there are many sorry specters who will
                                        tell you

that all the bleeding days passing through
their sick sterile worlds, are as beautiful

as all the beautiful ladies
tanning on Malibu Beach

Estelle Beasley Turner

The Devil's Garden

The devil has a garden, too,
  To which he gives much care,
And weeds that spring from planted seed
  He sows in abundance there.

As a gardener he's a wizard true.
  He begins first with the soil;
He digs, he plows and harrows;
  He is not afraid of toil.

He fertilizes well with hate,
  He pours on selfish pride,
A goodly portion of discontent,
  And stirs in strife beside.

Of victory he is doubly sure,
  He works both night and day,
And never goes vacationing
  Although he could — with pay!

Feet

Perfect feet are much admired
When in fitting boots attired;
They may bring fame, fortune, too,
But be careful where they carry you.

Father

This indispensable fellow
    Stands up today for his share
Of honor which he so well deserves
    For his labor, his love, and his care.

It is he who has laid the foundation
　　Then builded the house for the home.
This indispensable fellow
　　Gives all he has for his own.

His arms, too, have carried the baby,
　　Pressing it close to his heart;
Helped to guide its little steps.
　　In all he shares a part.

Pity, when pity is needed;
　　Chiding, when chiding is due,
And yet like his heavenly Father,
　　His love for his children is true.

He Is On The Job

I will shut my door and stripe it well
Against the noisy vendor's yell;
Of his putrid wares I want no part,
He wheels the propaganda cart.

Look out, he is headed toward your way.
Unleash the dog, keep him at bay.
You'll find him trying to sell his goods,
Even in restricted neighborhoods.

Ecstacy

I like to hang my wash outside
　　Then swing the line up high
And watch the clean things sway
　　　　in rhythm
　　Beneath a blue, blue sky.

I like to hang my wash outside
　　With sunshine all around,
Then watch the playful magic in
　　Their shadows on the ground.

When comes a rowdy, romping wind
   To make of them a whip,
I like to see them whirl and swirl,
   To rise and fall and dip.

I like to hang my wash outside,
   then swing the line up high
And watch my banners flying gay
   Beneath the blue, blue sky.

Mark Twain

Lines

Mark Twain, on his Wife's Tombstone

Warm summer sun,
   Shine kindly here.
Warm southern wind,
   Blow softly here.
Green sod above,
   Lie light, lie light.
Good night, dear heart,
   Good night, good night.

Victor Manuel Valle

Police Magazine

January 30, 1975.

Among those waiting for buses,
or at break time
in the shop
among the cloth and the thread

          two gray pages open,
          two tongues find themselves
          naked

344

The tongue of the wind
goes numb in your veins,
silenced
the tongue of fire
in the language of hands and tools,
and then the tongue of theft speaks,
the black gloves and the prisoners tongues
that never finish speaking,
of seeing their lives opened to hopelessness,
of the blind and bloody vengeance
of Juan Ortiz that blossoms on the page;
the murder of his father and two brothers

The police and the photographers
send him to his jury:
they ask him to demonstrate
the murder, the stabbing.
                    "I came in at night.
                        The arid moon illumined
                        a flock of crows,
                        the horns of goats
                        and the palo verde fence
                        There was only the sound of the
                        knife, of bones,
                        of piercing, of mute anguish...
that speaks from eyes
                    ojos
                eyes that watch us from brown and grey
painful dream images,
the mournful images of *Alarma   Impacto   Magazine de policia*
                    the popular crime of gutted buses,
their lives strewn over rocks
in the land of the crucifixes,
land of bank robbers and kidnappers,
                    of the old woman and the ancient child of
                    the trash heaps in the cathedral
                    begging for alms,
                    of the castrated lover on the open page,
of Juan Ortiz
and his unblinking black eyes,

piercing nails of rancor
without fear of death
nor guilt for his bitterness—
an inheritance of shacks,
an abandoned dry earth,
of the hours in the sun
spending his strength on the journeys of dust
on the plains of a flat sky
with hooves of clay hills...

and to always work for the same master,
the one that robs
blood from the rivers of Sinaloa,
that slices the flesh of his earth,
who steals the purity
of flowers and clouds
in the bales of cotton...

and live to die impaled
on the claws of a border:
wedge that divides a people

Now his eyes speak to us;
the multiplied deck of eyes
that look from the pages of death:

There can be no display of suffering,
no lie,
no border fence
that can stop the flame of our knives:

two hands that seek to unite

Paul Vangelisti

Event 24: John the Baptist

Lately, however, there is only watching grandfather,
the predictable and helpless scenarios of life with
the old man. Grandfather having trouble with stairway
grandfather dizzy rising from dinner grandfather
sleeping later and later. For example, Las Vegas
police report that man calling himself John the
Baptist may be responsible for four fire bombings of
area churches within the last two weeks. The man,
telephoning a local newspaper, takes full responsibility for the fires and vows to continue burning
the city's churches. On the other hand, the best
living american novelist is also a man of brains.
Seasoned reader, veteran talker, he handles ideas
with the same juggling ease that he tells stories.
Not given to thinking small, he recently urged
both the third world and the industrial rich to put
aside petty grievances over narrow issues and concentrate on nothing less than a global compact to eradicate
poverty by the end of the 20th century. In fact, the
reporter who took the call claims that the Baptist
sounds very serious and is adamant about getting his
message printed in the newspapers. Steeped in the
skepticism of Chicago but still responsive to the war
cries of ideology, this great writer also proves to
be a great listener. Like every other visitor to
Israel, he soon tumbles into a gale of conversation.
He loves it: it makes him feel at home. But don't think
whaling different from any other American industry.
The first men in it are workers. The money and the
glory comes later, on top with the exploiters. And the
force goes down, stays where it always does, at the
bottom. So very little is said about the dreams themselves,
traces of childhood where events revolve in the most
gratifying and terrible of orbits where questions are
carefully asked of bystanders who look like none of the

family. Then as now the trick remains to reduce labor
costs lower than worker's efficiency— during the
1840s and 1850s it cost the owners 15¢ to 30¢ a day
to feed each crew member— and combine inefficient
workers and such costs by maintaining the lowest
wages and miserable working conditions. Of course,
one tries to be representative, the selector says,
including poets who are established in a more steady
way— who have a body of work and have embarked on
a direction that's profitable and not a dead end. The
result is that by the 1840s the crews on the whale-
ships are the bottom dogs of all nations and all races.
Of the 18,000 men, one-half ranked as green hands and
more than two-thirds deserted every voyage. One mistrusts
oneself as much as one endorses onself, says the
selector. While one moves among one's biases as consciously
as possible, the primary test, though, must remain the
intrinsic merit of the poem. Oddly enough, Americans
still fancy themselves such democrats. But their triumphs
are of the machine. It is the only master of space
the average person ever knows, oxwheel to piston,
muscle to jet. It gives trajectory. In fact, even with
her it is hard to talk about dreams of grandfather, a
man eighty years-old and in perfect health. She simply
replies that the man must be at least eighty and, after
all, what does anyone expect. Finally a try at changing
the subject, claiming how death surrounds them in that
place, the Porsche in the rear view mirror all the way
to work, the immobility the strange comfort found easing
into bed late when she is already asleep.

Roberto Vargas

on a plane to new york
3 am feb 21 1977

        mountain for november
carlitos...

november faded crimson into
the mountain canto of your
man / limbs   emaciated / stilled
              in struggle
november of the forest loras
that winged echoes to your carlos
footsteps   carlos   in your militant
stride towards nirvana   left each
print on the prolonged / feathered
clock of our history (of novembers)

birds   clocks   and struggle delicately
collaging the hard novembered-khaki
of your murder with 3 more words
                        toward freedom...
              (carlos fonseca amador)
3 months of haydee's besos to blanket
                    your solitary dreaming
3 deaths of the moon   counting cadence
                        in your stilled eyes
3 pages of   "el caledario del pueblo"
                flapping RED / BLACK
                in the face of verdugos
november to february

november to february
still fills *these words*
with the unsilenced blood
of our martyred brothers / sisters
they are strapped across
our chest   3x3
              as bandoleers
across our hearing   3x3
              as castanets
these words pregnant
              with minutes and powder
from november to new york...
    there is no difference
    in time nor space
              nor NICARAGUA........

A

i imagine building you a crestless mountain
of wordfeathers   beautiful and black as the
stroked plumes between your cinnamon crevices ⸰
your look at me is 100 years ago standing
anywhere   in your mestiza eyes /
              we are thinking "i love you / te quiero"
our mouths not in tune
                        with our music . . .

B

if i multiply the 8 years by almost 365 moons
that i'm sure my love found its soft glowing
head inside *you* in one form or another or another
or another x another x another x another   we
would have only two thousand nine hundred and
twenty revolutions of loving to go back to
where we started   *that night!*

Moonsong 6

U draw my smile
    (a line)
from a love poem
1 continent long.
All the pain
    in between
like teeth
too dull
        to eat!

Moonsong 5

Diana
        What absurd
        motions of
        my hand

350

```
        these
    to say
    "I love you"
        en inglés /
```

Pedro Ortiz Vasquez

Oh Sister

Wheatfields along the graveyard are almost
empty. It is the hour of the bull. Near-sighted
lizards blow trumpets. A cuckoo sings
in the blue mist. Under the wings of the jasmine
a newborn woman sleeps. Her breasts hang from the tips
of the moon. Her thighs are rooted to the darkness.
On her belly centipede dancers whisper secrets.
Salamanders burn on her hips and the cold silver
of the bull's eye runs through her hands

Inside the graveyard headstones crumble. Messenger bats
deliver roses. Earthworms gather stones. A black
stallion gallops through the fields. It is the hour
of the bull. No riders are approaching.

W.G.

Angeles

Soft o'er the vale of Angeles
   The gale of peace was wont to blow
Till discord raised her direful horn
   And filled the vale with sounds of woe.

The blood stained earth, the warlike bands,
   The trembling natives saw with dread,

351

Dejected labor left her toil,
    And summer's blithe enjoyments fled.

But soon the avenging sword was sheathed,
    And mercy's voice by "Stockton" heard
How pleasant were the days which saw
    Security and peace restored.

Ah think not yet your trials o'er;
    From yonder mountain's hollow side,
The fierce banditti issue forth,
    When darkness spreads her curtains wide.

With murd'rous arms, and haggard eyes,
    The social joys away they fright;
Sad expectation clouds the day,
    And sleep forsakes the fearful night.

Now martial troops protect the robbed,
    At distance prowl the ruffian band;
Oh confidence! that dearer guard,
    Why hast thou left this luckless land.

We droop and mourn o'er many a joy,
    O'er some dear friend to dust consigned,
But every comfort is not fled,
    Behold another friend we find.

Lo "Stockton" comes to grace the plan,
    And friendship claims the precious prize;
He grants the claims nor does his heart
    The children of the vale despise.

Derral de Ronda Wagers

Solano Hills

Torn shreds of ocean mist stream o'er the crests
And fold the upper glades in silvery gray.

The glowing brush of Dawn roughs in the ground
Of sun-kissed tawny ridge and khaki grass;
And all between, with bold and noble strokes,
Lays in the purple shades of clust'ring oaks
And close-wove chapparal.

Sleep

Oh, Sleep!   Thou blessed gate!
Thru which, a little space each day
From out this racking world we stray
To hold the hand of God;
To wander with Him
Along the margin dim.
And then return,
Filled with new life,
To face again the strife.

William Ross Wallace

Columbia

Columbia stands forth as the Queen of the Nation,
With the diadem of Freedom radiant with stars flashing
From her spotless brow.
Look up with proud and solemn joy unto our Flag,
That for the deathless right of man
Blazed over Freedom's threatening crag
When slavery's bolts were hurled,
For a million heroes made its stars
The hope-lights of the world.

Oh, see we not amid the joy
Now where the battle's o'er,
Our dear, great country, greater yet
On shouting chainless sea and shore,

All state hates from us hurled,
For a million heroes made our stars
The hope-lights of the world.

Gloria Watkins

Janie

her man done gone
left her
she just be
sitting on the
porch rocking
hands holding
each other
she got nothing
to say
to nobody
some folks
say she
never moves from
that chair
that she always
be waiting
other folks say
her mind been
slipping
ever since
the day
he left
me I say
she be just like
a dead person
someone should
walk up on that porch
and shut them eyes.

Marie de Laveaga Welch

Words

Minds are like silent towns and words
Are eager boastful men who haunt the street
And pass from town to town telling long tales
Of hills and towers and avenues of trees,
Of curling alleys and glimpses of the sea,
Loudly they tell the beauties of their towns;
But subtler loveliness evades their powers,
Only the frigid streets are theirs to praise.
The stolid walls of houses bar them out;
They cannot know the books on friendly shelves
Nor what strange fires burn on hidden hearths.

Littératrice

She lives too much in literature, too much
  In the recording of her ecstasy;
To her all joy of vision or of touch
  Is the crude stuff of prose or poetry.

She has indulged in voyages and dreams,
  Braved storms, responded to a lover's kiss,
But always with the thought of finding themes
  For exposition or analysis.

She exists in inspiring episodes,
  Not earth nor ash nor blood her pen would clog,
On her death-bed she'll compose burial odes,
  And quit the grave to write an epilogue!

Jazz Dancers

The rhythm interlaces with their bones;
Their blood grows thin and eager to complain
With the absurd wail of the saxophones;

Their blood grows thick and wild again
Under the heavy stirring of the drum;
And there are curious metal strings that hum
Beneath the muscles of their knees and thighs.
Rhythm devours reason out of their eyes;
Rhythm has eaten them, left them heartless, tongueless;
They are all pulse. The music quivers, grows louder,
And stops, and frees them from tormented jungles.
"Some dance, Big Boy!" The girl applies her powder;
The boy grins thirstily, wiping his wet
Palms on his coat, and lights a cigarette.

Camp Corcoran

*Written after a visit to a camp of striking cotton pickers, a majority of whom were
Mexicans, in the San Joaquin Valley in California*

This is the camp of the strangest workers,
Yesterday in the cherry orchards,
Today in the cotton fields,
Tomorrow in the vineyards.
This is the camp of the nomad harvesters.

                    *

Tonight, this a strikers' camp,
Tonight, this is a fort.
Around the field there is a strand of wire;
That is the wall.
Only workers pass here.
The sentinels watch.

Keep out disorder!
Pride is beginning here,
And dignity, and command.

Maybe of these four thousand
Only a dozen or a hundred men
Have more than hunger and patience,
More than a warm country's lazy habit

To wait with,
To take it almost easy,
Even the war of starving.

Maybe only a hundred of four thousand
Slowly, seriously,
Have won dignity, have accepted command.

But it begins.

The sentinels are unarmed.
The single wire is not barbed

        *

We walked through, in worried darkness,
In the camp of sullen war. In the silence
We stumbled into shallow pools of mud.

We are not used to walking in so much shadow;
We are not used to little fires like stains on the dark.
These are strange roads between the huts of sack and brush.

The little fires emphasize the dark;
They add confusion to the simple dark.

We are not used to this stirred broken dark.
We do not walk back a thousand years every evening.
We did not know the camps there are in the world.
We did not know the wars of the unarmed

        *

We are starving!
They need not starve.

They live in mud.
"They have always lived in mud."
Why should they live in mud?
"They need not starve
If they'll just live in mud."

We cannot answer.
In this argument, death
Goes round its circle.

*

There is a ring of men,
And one man singing,
On the ground.

There is a ring of men,
And one man talking,
On the ground.

Like their fires, like their mud,
On the ground.

Not many—the rest are sleeping.
Days are long;
Waiting is the only deed, and sleep
Is almost the only food.
A few children are tireless, their noise
Is sharp as light.
They laugh like screaming.

*

There's no beauty here.
Make no mistake.
This is the dust of human ground.
they work, it has not made them beautiful.

This is humanity. It does the work.
It is not beautiful.
Make no mistake.
This is humanity, it is not gentle.
This is humanity, it is not clean.

This is humanity, this is your world.
This is humanity, this is your work.

This is your kind, this is yourself.
Make no mistake.

*

But see here—beginning.
The stirring, not the form.
It is soft, it is without bones.
It is slow, it is without muscles.

The bones of pride,
The muscles of anger,
The fine nerves of love
Form slowly in the mass.

This is not the form.
This is not the power.

But see here—beginning.
Faint, like the first stir in the pregnant womb.
The body is not torn, only half-tense.
The move is little and deep.
Until passion, until danger, until birth
There will be a long time.

*

The leaders are fibre of this:
They know what is here.

Forget their courage;
Any man facing danger
Has courage.

They know what is here.

Forget their strength.
The others, even the arguers for death
Have strength.

The leaders are fibre of this.

I'll tell you what the leaders said:
They said, "You have it!"
I'll tell you what the leaders said:
They said, "It's yours!"

Life.
You have it.
It's yours.

I'll tell you what the leaders said:
They said, "Men!"

Lew Welch

The Song Mt. Tamalpais Sings

This is the last place. There is nowhere else to go.

> Human movements,
> but for a few,
> are Westerly.
> Man follows the Sun.

This is the last place. There is nowhere else to go.

> Or follows what he thinks to be the
> movements of the Sun
> It is hard to feel it, as a rider,
> on a spinning ball.

This is the last place. There is nowhere else to go.

> Centuries and hordes of us,
> from every quarter of the earth,
> now piling up,
> and each wave going back
> to get some more.

This is the last place. There is nowhere else to go.

> "My face is the map of the Steppes,"
> she said, on this mountain, looking West.

> My blood set singing by it,
> to the old tunes,
> Irish, still,
> among these Oaks.

This is the last place. There is nowhere else to go.

> This is why
> once again we celebrate
> the great Spring Tides.

> Beaches are strewn again with Jasper,
> Agate, and Jade.
> The Mussel-rock stands clear.

This is the last place. There is nowhere else to go.

> This is why
> once again we celebrate the
> Headland's huge, cairn-studded, fall
> into the Sea.

This is the last place. There is nowhere else to go.

> For we have walked the jeweled beaches
> at the feet of the final cliffs
> of all Man's wanderings.

This is the last place.
There is nowhere else we need to go.

Philip Whalen

Absolute Realty Co.: Two Views

1

THE GREAT GLOBE ITSELF

I keep hearing the airplanes tell me
The world is tinier every minute
I begin believing them, getting scared.
I forget how the country looks when I'm flying:
Very small brown or green spots of cities on the edges
        of great oceans, forests, deserts

There's enough room. I can afford to be pleasant & cordial to you
    . . . at least for a while . . .
Remembering the Matto Grosso, Idaho, Montana, British Co-
lumbia,
New Hampshire, other waste places,
All the plains and mountains where I can get away from you
To remember you all the more fondly,
All your nobler virtues.

7:v:64

2

Vulture Peak

Although my room is very small
The ceiling is high.

Space enough for me and the 500 books I need most
The great pipe organ and Sebastian Bach in 46 volumes
      (I really NEED the Bachgesellschaft Edition)
      will arrive soon, if I have any luck at all.

Plenty room for everybody:

362

Manjusri and 4700 bodhisattvas, arhats, pratyekabuddhas,
disciples, hearers, Devas, Gandharvas, Apsaras, kin-
naras, gnomes, giants, nauch, girls, great serpents,
garudas, demons, men, and beings not human, flower
ladies, water babies, beach boys, poets, angels, police-
men, taxi drivers, gondoliers, fry cooks and the Five
Marx Brothers

All of us happy, drinking tea, eating *Linsertorte,*
Admiring my soft plum-colored rug
The view of Mt. Diablo.

James M. Whitfield

To Cinque

*Joseph Cinque was one of fifty odd newly enslaved Negroes aboard the Spanish
schooner L'Amistad, which sailed in June, 1839 from Havanna for Puerto Principe,
Cuba; but, at sea, Cinque, a Mendi-speaking prince, led a revolt, killed the captain,
set the white crew adrift, and commanded the Spanish owners to steer the ship to
Africa. Instead of so doing, the two wily owners had the ship to sail North until, some
sixty-three days later, it drifted to the shore off Long Island, where it was spotted and
convoyed by the United States brig, Washington, to New London, Connecticut, the
Africans being charged by the circuit court at New Haven for the murder of Captain
Ferrer, and being claimed by the Spanish minister as reclaimable as property rescued
from pirates. Gaining increasing admiration from ever mounting demonstrations by
zealous abolitionists, the Africans eventually secured the services of seventy-three
year old, ex-president John Quincey Adams, who argued for eight-and-a half hours
for their freedom, in 1841, to return to Africa. The surviving Africans sailed for
Sierra Leone in 1842.*

All hail! thou truly noble chief,
    Who scorned to live a cowering slave;
Thy name shall stand on history's leaf,
    Amid the mighty and the brave:
Thy name shall shine, a glorious light
    To other brave and fearless men,
Who, like thyself, in freedom's might,

Shall beard the robber in his den;
Thy name shall stand on history's page,
    And brighter, brighter, brighter glow,
Throughout all time, through every age,
    Till bosoms cease to feel or know
"Created worthy, or human woe."
    Thy name shall nerve the patriot's hand
When, 'mid the battle's deadly strife,
    The glittering bayonet and brand
Are crimsoned with the stream of life:
When the dark clouds of battle roll,
And slaughter reigns without control,
Thy name shall then fresh life impart,
And fire anew each freeman's heart.
Though wealth and power their force combine
    To crush thy noble spirit down,
There is above a power divine
    Shall bear thee up against their frown.

J. Rutherford Willems

Animals in the Fields

At first, when coming
upon them
while on the tractor
i would stop
so as not to crush them.
They were toads, mice, and rabbits.
As the tractor moved
up and down the long furrows
they would be surprised
and then terrified
they would respond
to the crushing death
the green tractor meant.
But they only ran down

364

the furrows
away from me
never crossed away
out of the line of progress
and i was always faster
than they were
and had to stop
continually
to let them run ahead
away from their death.
Then i could no longer stop
and their death filled me
with a deeper terror
than theirs
until one day
i saw the rabbit
leap out of the way
correctly
to live.

Daryl Wilson

Our Leaders

In Chile they led the tattered poor
    to the long grave
    dug by the huge machines

. . . and, while holding guns upon them
    with full automatic control
    said,
        "Now, tell us who your leaders are!"

The poor answered, "Our leaders are need and hunger."

When they deliver me to the long grave
    let them know that my leader is freedom

and that I have agreed
with my leader
never to compromise our private and healthy respect for each other

no matter what the threat
no matter what the odds
no matter what the situation . . . .

Reflection

Long ago
    as winds over mountains and hills and plains
    of Pit River Country
    moved through mountain darkness
Grandmother sat with our bright eyes
    around murmuring fire and spoke over its warmth:

      "In our legends we say
          the dark eyes of our people
          as that of deer and squirrel and weasel
          is how we look into the spirit

      "Here all things may be seen
          good
          thoughts
          dreams
          emptiness

      "This is our people

      "There is another kind
          that have different eyes

      "It is as though looking into a mirror
          knowing mirror is able to reflect only . . . . "

Grandmother sleeps the long sleep
    but I have met those she spoke of over the fire long ago.

      "Humanity, in the form of the civilized, attacks nature

as if it were an enemy that did much harm and needs
revenge . . . for the Civilized do not know nature is life . . .

"Nature does not lash back because nature is a constant
and a forever

"Nature is life – all living things are of nature

"Civilized thinks of death

"Their God told them that death is a foreverness and life
is just a moment

"Nature is a constant and forever

These words passed over my thoughts again and again
as I sat by the stove in the schoolhouse
in my infant youth
having no desire to open the books or think in the way of the
Civilized

Teacher
seeing this
sentenced me to an hour outside *alone*

I listened
to the birds sing of nature and
brother sun whispered over winter's sky to me
the course of the universe

I smiled
as teacher punished me with a viciousness I did not understand . . . .

Civilized

At the foot of Grandfather Mountain
under stars dancing in vastness
near whispering waters by fire
Old One sat listening to chatter coming from my spirit
for so long I believed he slept . . .

When world was again quiet
    Old One swayed in shadows

With eyes dimmed with white clouds
    he looked long upon circling universe...

    "Small one
    you ask many questions
    'Why civilized is in conflict with nature'
    is your real question

    "You have been taught the proper way and know
    that nature walks upon mountain meadows and through deep
    quiet forests of soft foreverness

    "Swims through laughing waters of rainbow canyon and
    caresses blood of all life

    "Grows in deep canyons and upon distant stars

    "Looks over mountains at first light and makes our people sing

    "Dwells upon vastness and holds close dancing with our
        happy people and unfolds and unfolds and unfolds

speaking. The shade was good. As is the Indian way we waited
for Grandfather to speak. He was silent.

But his heart was pounding like the life of earth. His heart
listened to the gathering of nations. His heart listened to the
thunder of thousands of running buffalo. And his heart heard
the soft moccassin walking upon Indian land....the buckskin, the
Indian Spirit, the earth – again.

... And Grandfather's feelings were in our hearts also!

Listen!   The Beating Drums of the Gathering Nations
Memorial Day 1970

In the moving winds of early morning, in the coming of first light,
our hearts listened to the soft thundering of the gathering nations.

368

Great Spirit that makes the flight of the eagle, the clouds cover
the forest and the mountains, and the salmon return to the thundering waters, is speaking to many hearts. The time is ripe, like
the earth is ripe in the spring, to gather all people together.

In the shade of the hanging branches of the weeping willow tree,
Grandfather of all Indians spoke:

"The time now is as the time long ago
    when we gathered in the peaceful valley
    to prepare for the hunt
The land was young
Standing on a small mountain
    the eyes could see rivers of buffalo
    across the wide gold of the grassland
The heart knew much excitement

"In the darkness of evening arrowheads were made
By the light of the speaking fire
    dancing in the darkness of the tipi
    the lance was sharpened
    knives were honed
    bows were tested for strength

"Through the night there was much dancing
    and much speaking of the heart to
    Great Spirit

"Into first light there was much excitement
    and the excitement grew as the sun
    came over the mountain
    and looked at the people gathered in the valley

"The pony was prepared
Soon we mounted and moved out to the black buffalo
The hunt was good
Arrows came back
The Great Eating lasted for many suns

"That was long ago

That is what my heart remembered
My heart thought that the times of excitement were forever lost

"My eyes are dim
My heart is old
... But my heart is excited as before the hunt
For the time is good
The land will belong to the Indian again
    just as it was long ago

"I am prepared
I will stand with my people!
I will walk upon Indian land
I will glide across the valley
    like the shadow of the eagle
    upon my pony
On my land I will be
    again
    an Indian!"

Sun-God looked strong upon the land when Grandfather finished

The Shadow of the Castillian
The Tongue of the English

Who is this "Chicano"
... our brother and sister
that walks during the day
in the shadow of the Castillian

And by night
    in the light of the wisdom
    and the dreams
    of the Original Peoples
    The Natives of the Earth

Who is this "Chicano"
    that has had only
    the culture altered
    and not the blood or the spirit

370

Who thinks the thoughts of the "Indian"
    and speaks these dreams
    with the tongue of the
    Castillian?

You are the same as the "Indian" who
    thinks thoughts of the "Indian"
    and speaks these dreams
    with the tongue of the
    English

Who has had only the culture altered
    and not the blood or the spirit

Who stands in the light of the wisdom
    and the dreams
    of beautiful Ancestors
    of the earth

And walks during the day
    in the many shadows of
    the Anglos
    who roam without principle
    and do not understand the earth they roam upon

My brothers and sisters
    It is time that the Original Music
    of the drums around the fire
    beat with the tempo of our hearts
    and to the tempo of the hearts of our people

William J. Wilson

The Coming Man

I break the chains that have been clanging
Down through the dim vault of ages.
I gird my strength, mind and arms

And prepare for the terrible conflict.
I am to war with principalities, powers, wrongs,
With oppressions — with all that curse humanity.

I am resolved;
'Tis more than half my task;
'Twas the great need of all my past existence.
The gloom that has so long shrouded me
Recedes as vapor from the new presence.

And the light gleams. It must be life
So brightens and spreads its pure rays before
That I read my mission as 'twere a book.
It is life; life in which none but men,
Not those who only wear the form, can live
To give this life to the world;
To make men put off the thews and sinews of oppressed slaves.

Faracita Wyatt

A Myriad of Images

the future is without focus;
The past is drenched in delusions.
A myriad of images disturbs these reflections.

A young man shed his blood
That others could live in confusion.
He was but a face;
The void of the graveyard was beside him.

Winds tried tossing earth fumes skyward;
Many reluctant to rise
Remained to choke
The morrow's promises.

Men returned from battle
Bent and burned beyond belief,

Seeking the solace of security
In a world ensnared in violence.

Vacuous space diminished—
Clogged with useless clutter;
Men and women escaped responsibility
With complacency.

Denuded and uprooted,
consumed by careless flames,
Trees of the forest
Were prostrated.

The test of the strength of a bomb
Lashed the soil—
Defiled life.

Weighted with sludge
The waters barely succeeded
In catching the rays of the sun.

Astronauts orbited in space;
Many watched in awe—
Some with comprehension—
Others without feeling
Except for their own inescapable need.

Out of the mist
A meditation—
Old concepts thwart the new;
The new are shrouded in mysticism.

He Is Black

He lives with laughter and with tears,
but he is black,
or so they say.

He captures beauty through the years,

but he is black,
or so they say.

He feels the surge of love;
his eyes speak hate,
but he is black,
or so they say.

He smothers pain and is afraid,
but he is black,
or so they say.

His blood flows from an open wound,
but he is black,
or so they say.

He knows the crush of death and sorrow,
but he is black,
or so they say.

He dares to see the future in tomorrow,
but he is black,
or so they say.

Ile De Gorée

Off the shore of Dakar
On the Ile de Gorée
Stands the Slave House,
Dank and stark and still.

How much does it tell of human suffering?
How much does it reveal of human sorrow?

No communion here.
Men and women
Separated in silence and solitude.

Cells of thick, rough, windowless walls

374

Where hundreds of black males chained—and cowed in fearful
    dignity
Still echo the wails of supplication and deliverance.

The thick, rough walled enclosure for black females
Offered the only escape:
An opening in the wall to the sea
Where some hurtled their bodies on to the rocks and boulders below,
Choosing death rather than slavery.
The waters still resound in their cries
Of anguish heard centuries ago.

They were not savages
Those who were impressed here,
But men and women with pride of heritage.
Some could tell of ships and kings and empires and forest kingdoms,
Of wisdom at Timbuktu,
Of grassy savannas and burning dunes and great pyramids,
Of strength and dignity that follows triumph over the defiance of
    nature
    But - there was no one to listen
    No - they were not savages.

Off the shore of Dakar
On the Ile de Gorée
Stands the Slave House and its dungeons
Dank and stark and stilled by
The memories of torture and tragedy.

Karen Yamashita

Obasan

Oh my mother you are warm.
You are small in my arms.
I have returned to draw your
pain into my own.
Together we are ancient.

Your loose skin is my skin,
your shriveled breast
your sunken lip.
Our tears dribble downward
salty and tepid;
we are foolish.

Our pride has made us rich
in things we did not know
we did not need
such gilded arrogance
to shore up all our fears
that we might seem
the lesser in the race.
I have traveled distances
to buy pretension for that pride
and sent you piece by postcard
a portion of my gains,
and did you then survive?

I returned to find you sleeping
and talking in your sleep.
Your dreams embarrassed me;
impatiently I turned to go
and grew angry when you woke
and found me standing,
staring there,
bedecked in jewels and fine brocades
and armoured with a hundred
precious gifts.
Your lip quivered.
You smiled shyly.
You opened up your arms
to hug and hide
the aging face that came
to mock your own.
Still, you did not know
that I had heard
the selfish silence of your dreams.

376

Oh, I stayed a day
inventing tales like
an entertaining clown,
catering exotic food and drink and
spilling my opinions to show how
I could think.
Disgusted by my own smug
mug, I left
to be alone like you,
away from you,
independent and
responsible.

Now I am a shriveled child
wasted by that dream
I mumble to my children in
my sleep.
My scorn is now their sneer,
their eyes narrowed to polished pins,
their mouths hang blasé
oh,

My mother you are warm
I have returned empty—
handed with my life
cradled in my arms.

Al Young

In Marin Again

for Arl

Again we drift back to these mountains,
divine inclines our son could scale now.
Your blouse bends as you lean in your jeans
making it easy, a breeze to picture breasts
underneath, long legs, time's salty hello

still free flowing after years of rainfall.
Smoothly we slip into this renewed night
of jagged crossings & softened dark peaks.
Love growing wild is wondrous with its way of
bringing back meaning like rivers that move.

Michael at Sixteen Months

Ball	His whole world revolves around light dark
Bird	things sailing thru the air around chairs
Dog	the mystery of rising & falling & getting
Cheese	up again in the morning at night / scratching
Shoes	at windows to get out bananas oranges a
Cat	step / stepping down stepping up / keep the music
Juice	going / TV theme songs / walks on stones, dancing
Baby	on manhole covers, anything circular, objects
Daddy	that hang & flap in the breeze / the wind as
Mama	it foams into a room making the skin cool
Boat	puffing out curtains / baths / water / legs / kiss
Mama	Here we go into the rain turning sunlight
	Here we go down the slide into sandpiles
Mommy	Here we go clapping our hands as blocks fall
	Here we go running from Mama Mommy Mimi baby
No	crashing into Daddy dozing on the floor, a
	world is shooting out of rubber tree leaves
Nose	The window is a magic mirror / sad to see time
	flowing throwing itself thru flesh electric
Hot	that hard months ago was only a flash in
	a sea of possibility / the suffering afloat
Car	The meanness he will have to endure is only
	life ungathered in the eye of no world / is light
Book	pure & not so simple after all is living life

alive alive O!

One West Coast

for Gordon Lapides

Green is the color of everything
that isnt brown, the tones ranging
like mountains, the colors changing.

You look up toward the hills & fog—
the familiarity of it after so many years
   a resident tourist.

         A young man walks
toward you in vague streetcrossing denims
& pronounced boots. From the pallor of
   his gait, the orange splotch twin gobs of sunset
in his shades, from the way he vibrates
his surrouding air, you can tell, you can tell
   he's friendly, circulating,

      he's a Californian: comes to visit,
     stays for years, marries, moves a wife in,
  kids, wears out TV sets, gets stranded on
          loneliness,
      afternoon pharmaceutica,
  so that the sky's got moon in it by
  3 o'clock, is blooo, is blown—

        The girls: theyre all
     winners reared by grandmothers & CBS.

   Luckier ones get in a few dances with
    mom, a few hours, before dad goes back
in the slam, before "G'bye I'm off
    to be a singer!" & another runaway
     Miss American future drifts
       over the mountain &
       into the clouds.

    Still
    there's a beautifulness about California.
It's based on the way each eyeblink toward

the palms & into the orange grove leads backstage
    into the onionfields.

Unreachable, winter happens inside you.

Your unshaded eyes dilate at the spectacle.

You take trips to contain the mystery.

Intimacy

Right up under our noses, roses
arrive at middleage, cancer blooms
and the sea is awash with answers.

Right here where light is brightest,
we sleep deepest; ignorant dreamers
with the appetites of napping apes.

Right this way to the mystery of life!
Follow your nose, follow the sun or
follow the dreaming sea, but follow!

Connie Young Yu

Yours Truly, in Struggle

Has it been two years since you left this coast?
Forgive these belated words.
I want to tell you I saw our comrades,
Waiting in line at a movie
They send their love.

A bank is digging a base
In the square where we were nearly killed,
Truncheons whizzing above our heads
As we showed solidarity

With fellow Asians cornered on a map,
Zapped, napalmed and body-counted
Wherever the pointer fell.
We carried unseen wounds like stigmata,
Barricaded in basements,
Whispering in tight rooms of strange houses.

I remember how
Before your exile
You sent us to our outposts
With voice churning from your soul
And we sang our dreams
Dodging captors in the dark.

Everyone is reading now.
Reading.
Some have taken to eating no meat.
I think and think.

I remember you like a burning season
And how we feverishly fed the flames,
Trying to forge something
That could stop planes and trains and ships of state
Without filling out forms
And waiting for a permit.

Bernice Zamora

Mountain Goat in San Francisco

The face of a mountain goat
with serpentine horns
coiled on each side,
etches its form above
San Francisco.
The face towers over towers,
then withdraws itself to the sun
and melts the hearts of all

who believe that visions
are for the self-exiled
servants of the hollowed self,
or who believe that mountain goats
are found in San Francisco.

Prelude

Acts of stealth
stole in the brown cliffs
of Aztlán and caused
the cliffs to crumble
under the weight of hate
for the color brown.

The Brown Race faced
annihilation as did the Red;
and so it was decreed
that after the salmon leave
the river dry
bows, arrows, and darts
were to be buried
in the seventh bank
near the seventh hill
on the seventh day.

Three small women
were then to dig
the lime hills for chests
containing *una colcha*
y tres jarros de ronrones.
Uncovering the jars *y*
esperando lo mero ogro,
the three were then to release
hornets, wasps, and snakes
through the fields of
wooden scarecrows.

The blanket was to be
left unrolled until

the jaguars, the pumas, and the eagles
came to claim brown imprinted claws
on cloth woven for these acts of stealth.

Agustín Juan Vicente Zamorano

To The Beautiful Sex ("Al bello secso")

The Employees of the Maritime Customs

REFRAIN
To dance, and dance,
Is a duty wise:
Let's dance, my friends,
Until sunrise.

O beauteous nymphs,
Your prettiness,
Carriage and grace,
Who could withstand?
That gentility
Which in you is found
Brings all things aground
Under its command.
To dance, and dance &

Beauty does charm
With its own reign,
And the coldest swain
Is made to throb.
Two shining eyes
Glancing gracefully,
How effectively
Hearts of sighs will rob!
To dance, and dance &

A shape slim, adorned,
A body proud and free,
Moving airily

In rhythmic bliss,
　　Features the delight
Of love-tyrant blind—
Which, always unkind,
Deprives man of peace.
　　　　To dance, and dance &

　　The dance does render
Beauty more seducing.
The features suffusing
With placid allure.
　　When a beauty whirls
Her color will rise,
Lovelier than a sunrise,
With a glow demure.
　　　　To dance, and dance &

　　Veteran ensemble
Of beauteous femininities,
Dancing you are divinities
Of Love's wild unrest.
　　In the dance you triumph;
Courage is displayed
As bravely, till break of day,
You dance with full zest.
　　　　To dance, and dance &

　　As unto the wars
Soldiers sally out
To combat and rout
The powers that be
　　You damsels come forth
Showering grace-darts,
Wounding many hearts,
Dancing to victory,
　　　　To dance, and dance &

　　Every Montereyan
And Mexican maid
Comes here unafraid,
Polished and gay,

To dance with pleasure
In happy display,
Much as the winds sway
The roses in May.
          To dance, and dance &

California Venus
With allures profuse,
In the dance imbues
The heart with love's might.
     And the music lends
Its harmonies to express
That all is happiness
And finest delight!
          To dance, and dance &

All the fascination
And charms on this gay day
A wealth of love portray—
Pleasure without end;
     Here we are at last
Gathered and at ease,
Where frolic and surcease
Our many angels lend.
          To dance, and dance &

So much rich display,
Such excellent grooming,
Our desires consuming,
What shall we not see?
     Happy Monterey
Where proud beauty rages!
In the future ages
Famous it will be!
          To dance, and dance &

Monterey
July 17, 1836

Cyn Zarco

o

san francisco slow & cold
i have taken up smoking
& drinking
jamaican rum & coffee
walk reggae
in multi-colored ragamuffin chinese brocade
downstreets
of uptight korean landlords
in my straw borsalino
at night
white shades drawn
in the daytime
eyes peeking out of peking
at paradise
across the street
we meet
eyes cross
lips thin
to full
brown
blowing songs
of alto & soprano saxophone palm trees
they surreptitiously nod
to no one
in particular
building railroads
crossties
to
nowhere

Untitled

lolo died yesterday.
 they called him bill

short for villamor
i called him lolo
lolo doming
grandfather
even though he was my mother's uncle
even though he wasn't my real
grandfather
i called him lolo
star barber at the star barber shoppe
on 6th & mission
he talked about the navy
the american navy
he showed me the calligraphy
on his silver lighter
he showed me his diploma
from cosmetology school
lolo
lolo doming
hung out w/ the boys
at the mabuhay gardens
gambled in reno
got drunk
w/ the pinoys kumpadres
mga kasamahan
died dancing
on treasure island

Jake Zeitlin

Dirt Farmers

There'll be a wind
    blowing over a tomb-stone,
    cutting through the branches
    with a whining sound.

His hands are dry and cracked
    and his face beaten and hungry.

Bury him in his working clothes.
There'll be a pine board for a bed
And a pine coffin for a house:
The coyotes digging for bones
And a tar-paper shack
      stripped
      and falling.

Biographies

KEITH ABBOTT's "What You Know With No Name For It" was originally printed in a chapbook by the now defunct Cranium Press formerly of San Francisco, and is reprinted here with the permission of the author. Mr. Abbott is currently living with his family in Albany, California.

A.G.'s untitled poem appeared in the newspaper *La Voz de Méjico*, San Francisco, on August 28, 1862.

CHARLES ALEXANDER, better known as Prof. Charles Alexander, edited and published the (Los Angeles) *Citizen Advocate*, an early 20th Century black newspaper. He was a veteran journalist and the author of several books.

ALTA is the founder and editor of Shameless Hussy Press, one of the first national feminist presses. A native of Reno, Nevada, she moved to California when she was twelve and now resides in the Bay area. Alta's published works include *I Am Not A Practicing Angel* (Crossing Press) and an autobiographical novel, *Mamma* (Time Change Press).

ALURISTA has authored three collections of poetry: *Floricanto en Aztlán*, UCLA Aztlán (1971); *Nationchild Plumaroja*, Tolteca (1972); *Timespace Huracan*, Parajito (1976; a collection of children's stories, *Tula Y Tonan*, Tolteca (1972); a play, "Dawn," Chicano Drama and Chicano Theatre; and several literary essays of literary criticism. He is widely anthologized, has edited poetry collections, and has taught and lectured in colleges in the U.S.A. and Mexico.

JEAN ANDERSON has a book, *Poems* (SF: Neal, Stratford & Kerr, 1932), in the Bancroft Library.

MARIE BATHA ANDERSON is a native of New York who took up residence in Berkeley, California in 1961. After receiving her A.B. from the University of California, she taught Spanish for seven years and developed an Ethnic Studies program. At present she has a retail business, which occupies most of her time, but continues to enjoy reading, studying and doing research.

MAYA ANGELOU is the internationally acclaimed author of *I Know Why The Caged Bird Sings, Oh Pray My Wings Are Gonna Fit Me Well*, and other bestsellers.

JAIME DE ANGULO's "Indian fields over uplands" and "Land of many hues" is drawn from *Coyote's Bones*, a selection of the poet's poetry and prose, and is reprinted here with the permission of the publisher. A legendary California figure, Mr. de Angulo died in his home in Berkeley in 1950.

ANONYMOUS: The Anonymous poets wrote about the bad food, the risks of perishing on the coast, the perils of crossing the continent on the back of mules, on California Stage, only to reach a tentative land where disputes were settled by gun. On the other hand there were the "California Venuses," sunsets, a fresh start with pick, pan, and shovel, if you were a lucky fool. The anonymous poets spoke for Fools of '49 past and present. Who else would dwell in a place that might, at any moment, mudslide into the ocean?

JUANITA DE ARRANA's "Candle Flame" was published in *Poems from the Kernel* (LA: The College Press, 1939) and "Semele" was published in *Westward* V. 8 nos. 9-10, Oct. 1939.

ANNE HARLEY AVILA's "Song From A Brown Throat," is from *Land of Gold*, edited by James Neill Northe, 1934.

HERBERT BASHFORD (1871-1928). Born in Sioux city, Iowa. Author of such works as *Northwest Nature Stories*, 1899, *Tenting of the Tillicums*, 1903, and the book of poems *At the Shrine of Song*, 1909. He contributed to magazines such as the *Atlantic Monthly*, and also wrote essays, biography, plays, and poetry. He was on the editorial staff of the San Francisco Bulletin from 1909-19, and lived in Piedmont, California.

ROBERT BARLOW's "Tepuzteca, Tepehua" is drawn from the poet's *View From The Hill*, privately printed in Mexico in 1948. A leading figure of the Activist Movement, and Carl Sauer's teaching assistant, Robert Barlow became a pre-eminent authority on Aztec pre-history before his death in Mexico in 1951.

LESLIE BATES' poems, "Premonition," and "Out of Chinatown," appeared in *California Poets*, an anthology of 244 contemporaries, edited by the house of Henry Harrison, 1932.

JAMES MADISON BELL's "'Poem' was written and recited by the author...on the occasion of a great public meeting by the colored people in Sacramento, California, commemorating the death of the Martyred President, Abraham Lincoln, on Tuesday evening April 18, 1865. The poem afterward was published in the daily papers and also the colored papers." Delilah L. Beasley, *The Negro Trail Blazers of California*.

BILL BERKSON's "Election Day Fog" and "To Lynn" were submitted to the anthology by the poet. Mr. Berkson is the editor of *Big Sky Magazine*, and the editor/publisher of *Big Sky Books*. Mr. Berkson lives with his family in Bolinas.

DUANE BIGEAGLE: "Of Osage Sioux descent, I was born in 1946 at Claremore, Oklahoma. I attended the University of California at Berkeley on a Santa Fe Railroad Indian scholarship. My first book of poems, *Bidato, Ten Mile River Poems*, was published by the *Workingmans Press* of Berkeley in 1975. Currently I live on a sheep ranch in Mendocino County, California."

BLACK BART: For seven years, beginning with 1877, robberies and stage holdups were committed in the mountain regions of California by Black Bart. Never taking a life or firing a bullet, his bluff was to use an unloaded gun to his victim's head. Twenty-seven times he was successful; the twenty-eighth led to his capture and jailing. In 1888, he was released from state prison early, for good behavior, and was never heard from since.

JAMES WASHINGTON BLAKE grew up in Los Angeles. Educated at Contra Costa College, San Francisco State University and Stanford where he took his M.A. in English, he is the author of *Behind the Mask*, a collection of poems published by Julian Richardson Associates. He has taught at San Diego State University, UC Santa Barbara and Hartnell College. Born 1933.

PETER BLUE CLOUD: "I'm from Kanawake (Caughnawaga) Mohawk Nation. Currently living in Sierra foothills and working as carpenter, brush-clearer. Have had three books published: *Alcatraz Is Not An Island* (1973); *Coyote & Friends* (1976); *Bear & Wolf* (1976)."

ARNA BONTEMPS (1902-1973) spent his youthful, formative years in California, graduating from the Pacific Union College in 1923. Poet, novelist, scholar and editor, his distinguished works include: *God Sends Sunday, Black Thunder, The Story of the Negro, American Negro Poetry, Personals,* and *The Poetry of the Negro* (with Langston Hughes). For close to 30 years before his passing, he served as director of the Fisk University Library.

NATASHA BOROVSKY-HIDALGO: "I was born in in Paris in 1924, daughter of the Russian pianist, Alexander Borovsky, and a Russo-Polish émigrée. I grew up in France, Poland and Germany, went to boarding school in Lausanne, Switzerland. After the Nazi invasion of France, I was brought to California. I attended Sarah Lawrence College in Bronxville, New York, and worked for CBS as a foreign news monitor. With my ex-husband, of Venezuelian origin, and our two children, I settled in the Bay Area in 1951. I have written several novels and plays. I began to write poetry during a long illness. I am now at work on a collection of poetic sketches in Spanish and English based on my recent visit to Spain."

LILLIAN BOSS's poem was found in *Continent's End: An Anthology of Califor-*

nia Poets edited by George Sterling, Genevieve Taggard and James Rorty. San Francisco: Printed for the Book Club of California by J.H. Nash, 1925.

JAMES BROUGHTON's "I asked the Sea" and "I heard in the Shell" were submitted to the anthology by the poet. In addition to his accomplishments in literature, James Broughton is one of the country's finest independent film-makers. Mr. Broughton is currently living in Mill Valley.

EVA CARTER BUCKNER was a popular black Los Angeles poet in the early 1900s.

CARLOS BULOSAN (1913-1956) was born in the Philippines. He came to California in 1930 where he worked as a fruit picker. After travelling around the United States on freight trains, he returned to California and became a labor leader. He is the author of several collections of poetry and short stories, *Letter From America* (1942), *The Voice of Bataan* (1943), and *The Laughter of My Father* (1944). He published an autobiography, *America Is In The Heart* in 1946. Bulosan died of tuberculosis in 1956 and four years after his death his letters were published under the title *Sound of Falling Light: Letters in Exile*.

FRANK GELETT BURGESS (1866-1951) was a poet, critic, illustrator, painter, designer of furniture, member of *Les Jeunes*, and on the staffs of *The Wave* and *The Lark*. A part of a brilliant circle at the turn of the century Bohemian Club, he said of San Francisco of those days: "I found Romance. I found Adventure. I found Bohemia."

ROBERT LOUIS BURGESS's poem was found in *A Day In The Hills* edited by Henry Meade Bland. San Francisco: for Edwin Markham Chapter of English Poetry Society held at Villa Montalvo, Saratoga, Santa Clara, California, 1926.

EDWARD CAIN's "Forget-Me-Not" was found in Delilah Beasley's *The Negro Trail Blazers of California*. The poem was written in the nineteenth century.

SADIE H. CALBERT, born 1885 at Roaring River, North Carolina, moved to California at the age of one where her father, a schoolteacher, obtained work as a clerk for the Gerwin Co. at 27 California Street in San Francisco. A resident of Oakland, she is chipper and as clear as a bell. *My Thought, My Faith, My Dreams* is her only book of poems and appeared in 1975. She describes herself as a "compulsive scribbler," and is the oldest living Afro-Californian whose work appears in this collection.

BOB CALLAHAN's "Faith" and "The Dream" were submitted to the anthology by the poet. Mr. Callahan is the Editor of the *Turtle Island* publication series and is currently living in Berkeley.

EILEEN CALLAHAN's "A torn shard of hair" and "The Shape of the Body, Earth" were submitted to the anthology by the poet. Ms. Callahan is the editor/publisher of Hipparchia Press, and is currently living in Berkeley.

RAYMOND CHANDLER (1888-1959), an American, is the author of hard-boiled detective stories with American city settings that include *The Big Sleep* (1939), *Farewell, My Lovely* (1940), and *The Long Goodbye (1954)*.

"CHANTECLER" ("Chanticleer") was the pen-name of a poet who was frequently published in El Heraldo de Mexico, a Los Angeles newspaper. The name means "rooster." The Middle English and Old French meaning of the word was "sing clear." "Chantecler" was also one of Chaucer's characters.

AMANDA M. CHASE's poem, "Broken Rhythms," appeared in the anthology, *West Winds*, published in 1925.

BURIEL CLAY II, founder of the San Francisco Black Writers Workshop, edited the Glide Publications anthology, *Time to Greeze!* His plays have been successfully produced and his poems and other writings are staples in the California little magazines.

ROSADA CONSUELO COLTON's "Like Ocean Waves," was found in *The Poinsettia. California, 1945-46, Peace, Power, Praise,* published in San Diego.

CONYUS: "Poet/Writer/Visionary Mayombero. Son of an alchemist and conjure Louisiana Mother. Born on the back of a donkey in a Detroit steel mill. Raised on the teat of a full moon. Friend of Olukun, Dada, Oggun and Oasin. Last seen with Oke, (the God of mountains and protector of those who live in high places) running over far mountains buck naked and very black."

INA COOLBRITH (1841-1928) was born in Illinois of New England stock of English and Scottish origin. She was the first white child to enter California by way of the Beckwourth Pass, making that journey perched in front of the saddle of the famous Black scout and Chief of the Crow Indians, Jim Beckwourth. In 1915 the State Legislature named her first Poet Laureate of California. Her home, whether in Oakland, San Francisco or Berkeley, was a "salon"—the meeting place of the famous men and women of her time.

ANTONIO C. CORREA's "To an Ex-Soldier," and "For Peddlers, Solicitors, and Agents" were found in magazines published in 1941.

JAYNE CORTEZ was born in Arizona and grew up in Los Angeles Calif. She is the author of four books of poetry: *Pissstained Stairs And The Monkey Man's Wares* (1969), *Festivals And Funerals* (1971), *Scarifications* (1973), *Mouth On Paper* (1977)), from which the poem "Rose Solitude" is reprinted, and a recording *Celebrations And Solitudes* (Strata East Records 1975). Her works have been published in numerous literary magazines and anthologies. She has lectured and read her poetry throughout the United States and West Africa.

ANNA ROZILLA CREVER is a California poet published widely in literary journals. She is the author of *Variant Voices*, S.F., Harr Wagner Publishing Co., 1925, and *Lyrics of Life; an Offering of Verse*, Campbell, Calif., The Keesling Press, 1931.

STANLEY CROUCH: "Born in Los Angeles, December 14, 1945. Grew up there, a marginal bad boy and fugitive scholar (you know the early embarrassments of being caught *reading*!). Taught state and private colleges for six years, led bands and moved to New York in the fall of 1975. Published or known of as literary artist, critic and musician over a few continents and in the plaintive wilds of contemporary Japan. First child, Dawneen Scott-Crouch, born September 4, 1977. Greatest achievement thus far."

EUSEBIO HOWARD Y CRUZ's "Disenchanted" was published in *Poets of the Western Scene; Poems from Westward*, A National Magazine of Verse, San Leandro, 1937.

VICTOR HERNANDEZ CRUZ was born in Puerto Rico; he now lives in San Francisco. He has published three books of poetry: *Mainland* and *Snaps* from Random House, and *Tropicalization* from Reed, Cannon & Johnson.

ARTIE CUELHO: "I was born in Fresno, California on May 20th, 1943 to Portuguese parents. My grandparents on both sides were from the Azore Islands. I was raised in Riverdale, a small farming community 25 miles south of Fresno. My father pioneered the alkali, slough-ridden, sagebrush land 13 miles west of my hometown at Wheatville, which burnt to the ground in the thirties. I am the only living legacy the dead town now has. It was located in what is now called the Westside area; north of Linda Vista Farms two miles at Howard and Cerini Avenue. The poem, *Wheatville Trucking Blues*, was written about my brother Gene, who has a trucking business, and who had his shop headquarters on the family farm for years. I mention this because the valley of my birth, the San Joaquin, and its people has been a large part of my art, not only in poetry, but in short story and novel form too."

BEVERLY DAHLEN's "The Occupation" is drawn from the poet's *Out of the Third* published by Momo's Press of San Francisco, and is reprinted here with the permission of the poet. Ms. Dahlen is currently living in San Francisco.

BETSY DAVID's "A Field of Pumpkins Grown for Seed" and "4th November Rain Dance, With A Difference" were submitted to the anthology by the poet. Ms. Davids lives in Oakland where, with the artist-photographer Jim Petrillo, she edits, designs and publishes the collective workings of the remarkable Rebis Press.

MICHAEL DAVIDSON's "I am watching the vanguard move in" was drawn from the poet's collection *The Mutabilities* published by Sand Dollar of Berkeley, and is reprinted here with the poet's permission. Mr. Davidson is currently living in San Diego.

WINIFRED DAVIDSON's poem, *Irish*, appeared in the anthology, *West Winds*, published in 1925.

DIANE DI PRIMA's "Revolutionary Letter #61" is drawn from the author's *Selected Poems*, published by North Atlantic Books, and is reprinted here with the permission of City Lights. Ms. de Prima is currently living with her family in Marshall.

RALPH DICKEY (1945–1972), poet and musician, leaves one published volume, *Leaving Eden* (Bonewhistle Press).

HESTER DICKINSON's poem, "How Shall It Be?" was published in *Book of Verses*, Oakland, California: Press Club: Alameda County, 1910.

EDWARD DORN's "California Landscape" and "A variation on Vallejo's III" were drawn from the poet's new collection of verse *Hello La Jolla* (Wingbow Press: 1978), and are printed her with the poet's permission. Mr. Dorn is currently living with his family in Boulder, Colorado.

ROBERT DUNCAN's "Nel Mezzo Del Cammin Di Nostra Vita" was drawn from the poet's *Roots and Branches* (Poems 1959-1960), published by New Directions, and is reprinted here with the permission of the poet and publisher.

JOE ECKELS (aka Askia Akhnaton), poet, professor, minister, Ph.D. Stanford University, student C.G. Jung Institute, Zurich, Switzerland, author of eight books of poetry and one book of critical essays, *Pursuing the Pursuit— The Black Plight in White America*: listed in *Who's Who Among Black Americans*, 1975-76 and *Drum Voices* by Eugene Redmond—believer in Liberation, Humanigation, Imagination.

CLAYTON ESHLEMAN's "For Milena Vodickova" was submitted to the anthology by the poet. Editor of the now defunct *Caterpillar Magazine*, Mr. Eshleman is currently living in Los Angeles.

WILLIAM EVERSON was born in Sacramento in 1912, and grew up in Selma, Fresno County. He converted to Roman Catholicism in 1949, entered the Dominican Order in 1951, taking the name of Brother Antoninus. He left the order in 1969, before receiving his final vows, and currently lives in Santa Cruz, where he is poet-in-residence at Kresge College, University of California. He has published 25 books of poetry, including *The Residual Years* (1948), *The Hazards of Holiness* (1962), *The Rose of Solitude* (1967) and *Man-Fate* (1974).

SARAH WEBSTER FABIO: Poet, critic, educator, M.A. Degree in Creative Writing/Poetry at San Francisco State University, 1964, and was a San Francisco Poetry Center younger poet the same year; pioneer of Black Studies at Merritt College—1966 and '67, and University of California, Berkeley, 1968-71. She has published a seven volume of poems *Rainbow Signs* (1973); a volume *A Mirror: A Soul* (1968); four LP folkways records of poetry—often with musical back-up—between 1972 and '77. She is the subject of a biographical film, *Rainbow Black* (1976). Her work appears in numerous anthologies including *Poetry of the Negro*, edited by Langston Hughes and Arna Bontemps, and *Understanding New Black Poetry*, Stephen Henderson. Her work also appears in magazines such as *Black World* and *Black Scholar*.

JOAN LENT FALCK: "I was born in Bishop, California in 1952, I am a Paiute Indian. I am now in my fifth year at San Diego State University, majoring in Liberal Studies and a credential in Elementary Education."

GRANT FISHER's "July 4, 1976—A Comment" was submitted to the anthology by the poet. Mr. Fisher is currently living in San Francisco.

REYMUNDO GAMBOA: "I received my Ph.D. in Barriology at the age of six when hit in the face with a chair; since then I have granted reprieves in forms of art." His work has appeared in various anthologies. *The Baby Chook and*

Other Remnants, with Ernesto Padilla was published by Tempe: Other Voices Publishing House, 1976.

VIRGINIA GARCIA's "Pompeii" was found in a Scripps College publication, *First the Blade*, V. 3, 1930.

BARRY GIFFORD's "Bohemian Cigar Store, San Francisco" was submitted to the anthology by the poet. Mr. Gifford is currently living in Berkeley.

GLAUCO's 'La Gaceta de los Estados Unidos,' was published in Los Angeles, 24 August, 1918.

LAWRENCE GRACIA's "The Sabre's Song" was published in *Westward*, V. 1, no. 3 in February, 1927 in San Francisco.

JOANNA GRIFFIN's "Song" and "Gnosis: Instertice" were submitted to the anthology by the poet. Ms. Griffin is currently living in Berkeley.

JESSICA TARAHATA HAGEDORN was born in 1949 in Manila, Philippines and came to San Francisco in 1962. She has published a collection of poetry called *Dangerous Music* (Momo's Press, 1975). In 1973 her work appeared in *Four Young Women: Poems* (McGraw-Hill). She has recently completed an erotic novel called *Pet Food*. She has also been working with her new band, The West Coast Gangster Choir, which specializes in poetry and music.

STEVEN HALPERN: "I was born in 1953 at Aberdeen, Md., but lived most of my life in San Diego, California. I attended high school there, and colleges all over California. I live and work in Santa Cruz now. I am a turtle clan Cayuga; one of the six Iroquois Nations."

BRET HARTE (1836–1902): Through his stories and poetry, Bret Harte gave California's Gold Rush the romantic image that became its mythic history. He arrived in California lin 1854, and moved to San Francisco in 1860. A book of verse, *Outcroppings*, appeared in 1865, and in 1868 he became editor of the *Overland Monthly*. In 1871 he went East, traveled to Europe in 1878, where he died in London.

JANA HARRIS: "In 1975 I decided to rent a poetry office space—someplace where I could escape the domestic influence of my house and 2000 years of tradition, someplace where I couldn't do anything else but write, rewrite, or conduct 'the business of poetry.' I found a garden room in a Victorian office building at 1708 Shattuck in Berkeley and hung a 'JANA HARRIS, POET' sign out on the street alongside the Transcentury Realty sign, the Homefinders sign, and the Timco, Inc. sign—not to advertise for business, but as a political statement. In a culture where there is so much emphasis on 'what you DO,' the political statement here is 'I am a poet, I am serious, I am a vital component in this society.'"

WILLIAM J. HARRIS has taught at Cornell and UC Riverside. He is the author of two poem collections: *Hey Fella Would You Mind Holding This Piano A Moment* and *In My Own Dark Way*, both brought out by Ithaca House.

SADAKICHI [CARL] HARTMANN (1869?-1944): Born in Japan of a Japanese mother and a German father, Hartmann was early brought to the U.S. and naturalized. He was influenced by his friendship with Walt Whitman, of whom he wrote *Conversations with Walt Whitman* (1895). He was also active in the bohemian circles of Greenwich Village and later of Hollywood. Among his other works are poetry, prose plays, and historical works.

BOBBIE LOUISE HAWKINS' "Branches and leaves" and "A wet day long ago" were published in the poet's *Fifteen Poems* published by Arif Press in 1974, and are reprinted here with the permission of the poet. Ms. Hawkins is currently living in Bolinas.

DAVID HENDERSON, a native New Yorker, emigrated to California many years ago. Widely published and admired, he is the author of *Felix of the Silent Forest*, and *De Mayor of Harlem*. He is at work on a book about Jimi Hendrix.

LYN HEJINIAN's "Beginning wih the Local Boys" and "Song" were submitted to the anthology by the poet. Ms. Hejinian is currently living in Berkeley.

JUAN FELIPE HERRERA: "I was born in Fowler, California, on the way north where my family was heading for field work. After a while we did head north and then south again. Somehow Escondido, Ramona and San Diego were the last stops. I will never forget those days. During the last seven years I have traveled in Mexico and Central America. I believe in nature and arte humano."

JACK HIRSCHMAN's "And" is from the author's chapbook, *The Cool Boyetz Cycle / And*, published by Golden Mountain Press in 1975. The poem is reprinted here by permission of the poet. Mr. Hirschman is currently living in San Francisco.

PATRICK HOLLAND's "Horses in November" and "Red Dakota" originally

400

appeared in the author's *Horses in November* published by the Cranium Press of San Francisco. The poems are reprinted by permission of the poet. Mr. Holland is currently living in Bolinas.

LAWSON FUSAO INADA is a Sansei born in Fresno in 1938. His collection of poetry, *Before the War: Poems As They Happened* (William Morrow Co., 1971) is the first collection of poetry ever published by an Asian American in America. He is a co-editor of *Aiiieeeee! An Anthology of Asian American Writers* (Howard University Press, 1974).

KENNETH IRBY's "Homage to Coleman Hawkins" is drawn from the poet's most recent collection of verse, *Catalpa*, from Tansy Press of Lawrence, Kansas. Mr. Irby is currently living in Lawrence.

HENRY JACKSON is a poet whose previous works appeared in volumes IV and VI of Yardbird Reader. He is also a political scientist in the Department of Afro-American Studies, University of California, Berkeley, and is author of the political science analysis, *The FLN in Algeria: Party Development in Revolutionary Society* (Westport, Conn: Greenwood Press, 1977).

ELSIE JANIS (surname Bierbower) 1889-1956, was an American actress who appeared in vaudeville (1898-1903). She starred in *The Belle of New York* (1904), *The Fortune Teller, The Vanderbilt Cup* (1906-08), *The Hayden, Elsie Janis & Her Gang* (written by herself) etc.; entertainer to A.E.F. (1917-1918).

ROBINSON JEFFERS (1887-1962): Jeffers was born in Pittsburgh, Pennsylvania, but settled in Carmel, California after his marriage, where he built a stone tower overlooking the Pacific and began to write poetry. He published over 19 volumes of poetry and drama.

RONALD JOHNSON's "Letter Picture" and "Obelisk" are drawn from the poet's *Eyes & Objects*, published by the Jargon Society, and are reprinted here with the permission of the poet. Mr. Johnson is currently living in San Francisco.

JEANNETTA JONES' "Christmas 1976" and "Duck Hunting in North Beach" were submitted to the anthology by the author. Ms. Jones is currently living in Berkeley.

BUNICHI KAGAWA published two collections of poetry, *Silent Intimacy and Other Poems* (193?) and *Hidden Flame* (Stanford, California: Half Moon Press, 1930). Hinkel and McCann *Biographies* (Vol. II, 118) states: "born

November 4, 1904 in Japan to Mr. Shoichi Kagawa. No formal education, honorary member of the English Club (Stanford University); lived in Palo Alto for ten years (1921-1931); no data for later."

LENORE KANDEL's "Woman Chant" and "Dead Billy" were submitted to the anthology by the poet. Ms. Kandel is currently living in San Francisco.

IWAO KAWAKAMI was born in 1907. Grew up in Berkeley and San Francisco. In the early Thirties he became the first editor of the *Pacific Citizen* newspaper. He joined the staff of the *Nichi Bei Times* in San Francisco in 1946. Iwao Kawakami died in San Francisco in 1976.

BOB KAUFMAN is the legendary proto-Beat surrealist bop poet whose books, *Solitudes Crowded with Loneliness* (New Directions) and *Golden Sardine* (City Lights), have been translated into French. His influence on contemporary poetry is inestimable.

ANDREA J. KELSEY (Hupa / Yurok / Karuk) was born and raised on the Hoopa Valley Indian reservation in Humboldt County, Northern California. She has published in the newspapers *Coyote, Awkwasasne Notes, Davis Daily Democrat, San Diego Indian Center Newsletter* and the magazines *Suntracks, As Long As The Grass Shall Grow*, and *Songs of Liberty*.

EDWARD C. KEMBLE was editor of the newspaper, *California Star*, beginning in April, 1847. The *Star* was the first paper published in San Francisco (or as the town was then called, Yerba Buena). He was an Argonaut of the Argonauts.

ED KISSAM's "Riding the Thermals" and "Moving On" were submitted to the anthology by the poet. Mr. Kissam is currently living in Sonoma County.

STEVE KOWIT presently lives and writes in San Diego. He translated Neruda's *Incitement to Nixonicide* (Quixote, 75) and is completing a version of Cardenal's *Canto Nacional*.

GERALDINE KUDAKA, a controversial lady, lives and writes in San Francisco. She belongs to an Asian American writers' collective, RENGA, and has been published in *Third World Women* (TWC), *Time to Greez!*, (TWC / Glide), and *Third Women* (Houghton Mifflin). *Exiles & Passages of Return*, a book of poetry, will be released through Greenfield Review. She is presently working on a manuscript of short stories, and editing a magazine, *Beyond Rice*.

JOANNE KYGER's "September" and "In this endless dream of parties" are drawn from the poet's *All This Every Day*, published by Big Sky, and *Trip Out & Fall Back*, published by Arif Press. The poems are reprinted here by permission of the poet. Ms. Kyger is currently living in Bolinas.

PHILIP LAMANTIA's "The mermaids have come to the desert" and "The talk of the gods" are drawn from *The Touch of the Marvelous*, published by Oyez Press, and *Ekstasis* published by the Auerhahn Press. The poems are reprinted by permission of the poet. Mr. Lamantia is currently living in San Francisco.

BERYLE LAROSE lives in the Bay Area. She works with Native American Women's groups.

ALAN CHONG LAU is a San Francisco legendary poet because a few years ago he was seen leaving for Japan by Greyhound Bus. Years later he returned from a trip around the world with a wife, and he and his wife now live in Santa Cruz, California. Alan was born in Paradise, California in 1948. Young Asian American poets are always quoting from his widely circulated but unpublished collection of poetry.

JOAQUIN LEGASPI was born in 1896 in the Philippines. Immigrated to California at the age of 21. He was director of the Manilatown Multi-Service Center, a social service agency serving the Filipino community in San Francisco. He received an award at the first Asian American Writers Conference at The Oakland Museum in 1975 for pioneer writing. He died in San Francisco in 1976.

LULU DELMA DE LEON's "Fearless" was published in *Westward,* v. 13, no. 2, 1945.

GEORGE LEONG is a poet, a musician, and the organizer of the Writer's Workshop at the Kearny Street Workshop which constitutes an Asian American Art Collective in Chinatown, San Francisco. This work comes from *A Lone Bamboo Doesn't Come From Jackson St.* (Isthmus Press, 1977).

PHILLIP LEVINE's "Saturdays in Heaven" and "Making it New" were submitted to the anthology by the poet. Mr. Levine is currently living in Fresno.

JACK LONDON (1876-1916): Born in San Francisco, he lived the life of a sailor, a waterfront loafer and hobo (1891-94). Became Socialist. made soap-box speeches; went to the Klondike and back (1896-97). His first collection of stories was published in 1900. In the next sixteen years he produced 43 books and miscellaneous works. Served as war correspondent in Vera Cruz, Mexico (1914).

WALTER RALEIGH LOVELL's poetry is selected from *Lyrics of Love & Other Poems*, privately printed in 1921.

L. CURTIS LYLE was born in 1944 in Los Angeles, California. He was one of the original members of the Watts Writers Workshop. He has been widely published in anthologies, and literary magazines, and has released a recording of some of his poetry called, "The Collected Poems of Blind Lemon Jefferson" (1972). This work was found in a Beyond Baroque Foundation publication of his work, *15 Predestination Weather Reports* (1977).

LEWIS MACADAMS, a native Texan, settled in Bolinas in the late sixties. After several years of traveling around the world, he returned to Bolinas when he was named director of San Francisco State University's Poetry Center in 1975. He has published several books, including *The Poetry Room* (Harper & Row), *News from Niman Farm* (Tombouctou), and most recently, *Live at the Church* (Kulchur).

NATHANIEL MACKEY: "Born October 25, 1947 in Miami, Florida (Sun degree symbol: "From a broken bottle traces of perfume still emanate.") Mother from Georgia, father from Panama. Moved to Rodeo, California in 1952, from there to Santa Ana, in 1958. College at Princeton and Stanford. Taught two years at University of Wisconsin, now teaching at University of Southern California and am Director of Black Studies. Have published only in magazines and journals so far, but have a booklength selection of poems, *The Various Burning*, in search of a publisher." While at Stanford, Mr. Mackey was editor of the legendary *Hambone*.

GERALDINE SEELEMIRE MACLEOD's poems "Native," and "Night Mountain" appeared in *California Poets*, published in 1932 by Henry Harrison.

ALVIN MANOOK: "My Christian name is ALVIN MANOOK, and I was born in the Yukon River village of Nulato, Alaska. I am Athabascan, with a quarter Russian in my veins. My grade school education was at the parochial schools of Holy Cross, Alaska, and Pius X Mission, Skagway, Alaska. I served six years in the United States Navy as a Hospital Corpsman, and after discharge, I spent a few years working as an X-ray technician. In 1976, I received my Bachelors degree in English, with Creative Writing emphasis. I am currently working toward a Masters in the same major. Both will be earned at San Diego State University."

PAUL MARIAH's "Let me call this pine" was submitted to the anthology by

404

the poet. Mr. Mariah currently is living in San Francisco where he edits *Manroot Press.*

EDWIN MARKHAM (1852-1940): An Oregon-born poet, Markham lived in California from 1857-1901, where he grew up and worked as a farmhand and sheepherder. He then became a schoolteacher. His *Man with the Hoe and Other Poems* (1899) were quite popular at the time, as was *Lincoln, and Other Poems* (1901). He was a frequent lecturer on poetry and on social and industrial problems.

JIM MARKS is a poet and drummer who has worked with Dexter Gordon and John Handy, among others. His most recent books are *Jazz, Women, Soul* (Celestial Arts) and *I Am What I Am* (Ashanti Publications). His popular "Jazzoetry" program is aired weekends over KRVE-FM, Los Gatos.

WALTER ALFREDOK MARTINEZ: "I was born in Honduras, Central America, on an United Fruit Co. plantation on the Atlantic Coast. I began reading and writing at a very early age. When I was 12 years old my family moved to Los Angeles, where, like everyone else in similar predicaments, I lost my Spanish and never quite learned English. The linguistic and cultural shock was of a magnitude that, literally, made deaf, dumb and mute. I have, however, somehow recovered. I am now writing, publishing and, in general, expressing all I can no matter the odds. I have two beautiful children who are part of a generation in a particular situation, that deserves the best I have to offer and demands that I not rest."

BEULAH MAY's poem was found in the anthology *Land Of Gold*, edited by James N. Northe, Ontario, California, 1934.

FRANCISCA CARRILLO VALLEJO MCGETTIGAN: Francisca Benicia Carrillo was the wife of don Mariano G. Vallejo. One of their grand-daughters, Francisco Carrillo Vallejo McGettigan, was born July 18, 1875, in Vallejo, California. She later because a well-known San Francisco poet. In 1956 she published a book of poems entitled *San Francisco Souvenir*. "Ballad of California" is from an earlier work, *Along the Highway of the King*, published in San Francisco in 1943.

DAVID MELTZER's *Grandmother Sarah* is drawn from the poet's *The Eyes, the Blood* published by Mudra Press and is reprinted here with the permission of the poet. Mr. Meltzer is currently living in Richmond.

ANNA BLAKE MEZQUIDA was born in San Francisco and lived in California all her life. She died March 13, 1965. She is author of *A-Gypsying*, a book of poems published in San Francisco in 1922 by Marvin Cloyd.

JACK MICHELINE currently lives in San Francisco. His poems and short stories have been widely published in literary magazines. His latest work, *Last House In America* is due from Second Coming Press.

JOAQUIN MILLER (1841 (?)-1913), whose real name was Cincinnatus Heine, lived among the Indians, was a gold miner, pony express rider, edited a paper, wrote poetry, dramas and novels. He lived in the Oakland hills, where he built a home and planted thousands of eucalyptus trees. "I am Francis of Assissi, Novalis, Plato, Swedenborg, Porphzy and Buffalo Bill. I fill myself with asceticism, get drunk on abnegation, recite my own poems and dance a 2-step inspired by self-sacrifice. I am touched with madness, but sane enough to know it. I have a good time on nothing."

EDWARD MONTEZ, "Wintun/Shoshone, was born and raised on the Cachil Dehe Rancheria on the Sacramento River, near Colusa, California. He attended University of California at Davis. Both poet and actor, he has given poetry readings throughout Northern California. "The American Indian has been characterized as many different things, either stoic, romanticized, hero of literature, with or without regard to his inner world that he grapples with daily in his will to survive. Poets try to penetrate that inner world, and point to the familiar—this is what I know—this is what is in my inner world, and often forgotten or too controversial is the struggles of the skid row bum, the losers, the forgotten, the unromantic, whose inner world is as real to him as is the heroes of literature, and whose existence marks a graphic battlefield from which there is no truce, no victories, and fleeting alliances serve only to make one vulnerable. It is about these war-torn, non-heroes of survival that I write, with no other authority except having lived among them, been one of them, and grappled with that same inner world."

JOSE MONTOYA was born in Escaboza, New Mexico in 1932. He moved with his family to Sierra Vista Camp No. 8 at Delano, California, then going from one labor camp to another. Presently, he teaches at Sacramento State University. He calls himself "Veteran Chicano Poet."

ALEJANDRO MURGUÍA was born in California, 1949. Raised in Mexico City, returned to the U.S. of A. while still at an impressionable age. Has lived in San Francisco's Mission District nearly ten years. Presently Editor of *Tin-Tan* Magazine. Taught Latin American Literature and Creative Writing at San Francisco State for three years.

HAROLD NORSE: "I was born and raised in New York City. Published 10 books of poetry. Contributed poems, short stories and reviews to countless magazines in the U.S. and abroad. Spent 15 years in Europe and North Africa and have been living in San Francisco where I edit and publish

BASTARD ANGEL, a literary magazine. Have taught Creative Writing at various times, most recently at San Jose State University. To earn a living I write sexy stories for HUSTLER Magazine. I have recently received several grants such as a Creative Writing Fellowship, 1974, from the National Endowment for the Arts and two grants for my magazine, *Bastard Angel*, from the NEA and the De Young Museum of Art. Have also given readings widely, including one at Zellerbach Auditorium with the late Anaïs Nin and The Beat Generation Reading at the De Young Museum with Ginsberg, Snyder, Ferlinghetti, McClure, Duncan, et al."

WILLIAM OANDASAN: "My tribe is the Yuki of the Round Valley Reservation of Northern California, approximately 160 miles north of San Francisco. We are often thought the oldest culture in existence on that section of the west coast. We have no cultural traces nor linguistic stock but our own and, like the famous California redwood which has for the longest time been considered the oldest continuing life form in that region of the world, we have appeared as if to spring directly from the California earth. I have often thought with much pride how long my ancestors must have lived in that region with those redwoods to know that they were their own oldest representation of their species, human and botanic, and to choose the redwood as our name and emblem." Mr. Oandasan has published *Earth & Sky* (A Press Ltd.), *Taking Off* (A Press Ltd.), and *Raindrops* (Sun-Lotus Books), and is the editor of *A, a journal of contemporary literature*.

GEORGE OPPEN's "And Their Winter And Night In Disguise" is drawn from the author's *Collected Poems* published by New Directions, and is printed here with the permission of the poet & the publisher. Mr. Oppen is currently living in San Francisco.

SIMON ORTIZ (Acoma Pueblo): "I've been a journalist, teacher, for a very short time baker's helper, clerk, soldier in the U.S. Army, college student, laborer, public relations director, and other things. I am mainly writing now, using that language, and giving readings and lectures." His most recently published work is *A Good Journey* (Turtle Island, 1977). He currently resides in San Francisco.

ERNEST PADILLA: "Born: Las Cruces, New Mexico. Raised: Tulare, California. Taught writing and literature in high schools and university. Currently finishing Ph.D. in American and British literature at University of California at San Diego. Published one book of collected poetry: *The Baby Chook and Other Remnants*. Currently, I am an associate editor of *Citybender* poetry broadside publishing out of San Diego."

MICHAEL PALMER's "The Library is Burning" & "Without Music" were submitted to the anthology by the poet. Mr. Palmer is currently living in San Francisco.

KENNETH PATCHEN (1911-1972) was born in Niles, Ohio. He received the Guggenheim Memorial Award in 1936, the Shelley Award in 1954, and the National Foundation for the Arts and Humanities Award in 1967. He had a one-man show of work, graphics, paintings and books at the Corcoran Gallery, Washington D.C., 1969.

OSCAR PENERANDO was born in 1944 in Barvgo, Leyte, Phillipine Islands. He lives in San Francisco, teaching at San Francisco State. His short stories have been anthologized in *Asian-American Authors* and *Aiiieeeee!* His poetry has appeared in various literary magazines.

TOM RAWORTH's "Entry" and "9:00 PM May 1st 1970" were drawn from the author's *Moving* published by Cape Goliard Press and are printed here with the permission of the author. Mr. Raworth is currently living in England.

EUGENE REDMOND, native of East St. Louis, Illinois. Professor of English and Poet-in-Residence in Ethnic Studies at California State University, Sacramento for the past seven years. Attended Southern Illinois University and Washington University (St. Louis, Mo.). Author of *Drumvoices: The Mission of Afro-American Poetry*, five books of poetry, and has edited two anthologies and the posthumously published works of Henry Dumas. He is the Director of Henry Dumas Creative Writing Workshop of Sacramento, and has released one LP reading poetry to music. He also writes ritual dramas and directs stage and television plays.

ISHMAEL REED's latest novel is *Flight to Canada*. Nok Publishers recently issued *Secretary to the Spirits*, his fourth collection of poems. *Shrovetide in Old New Orleans*, a book of essays, was published by Doubleday in 1978.

WILLIAM NAUNS RICKS was, from the early 1900s to mid-century, a highly popular black California poet who resided in the East Bay.

AL ROBLES was born in 1944 and lives in San Francisco. Al Robles is one of the spirits of Chinatown, Japantown and all of San Francisco. Grew up in Nihonmachi (Japantown), in the Fillmore, Chinatown. He has published poetry in dozens of newspapers, magazines and anthologies, and is a member of Asian-American Writers Workshop. Mr. Robles is presently working on a book of the Manongs (1st Pilipino immigrants to America), *Rapping With Ten Thousand Carabaos In The Dark*, songs, myths, stories, history, tales, and visions. Forthcoming, 1978.

FLOYD SALAS lives in Berkeley, has taught in colleges and correctional institutions throughout the Bay Area, and acted as Greater California Coordinator for Poetry In The Schools. His published work includes *Tattoo the Wicked Cross*, a novel (Grove Press); *Lay My Body On The Line* (Y'Bird Publishing Co.); *What Now My Love*, a novella, (Grove Press); and poetry published in "Transfer," "Hyperion," and "The San Francisco Bark."

OMAR SALINAS: "I was born in Robstown, Texas, 17 miles from the Gulf of Mexico. As a child attended Catholic schools and wanted to be a singer, came to California in 1949. Attended several colleges and taught for a year at Fresno State University. Wrote *Crazy Gypsy*, a book of poems, and co-edited *From the Barrio* Chicano Anthology. Lives presently in Lindsay, California and working on another book of poems."

ALFONSO P. SANTOS' poem was found in *Westward*, International Magazine of Verse, edited by Hans A. Hoffman. San Leandro, CA: v. 8, nos. 9-10, October, 1939.

LESLIE SCALAPINO's "On itself" & "About the night" are drawn from the poet's *The Woman Who Could Read The Minds of Dogs* published by Sand Dollar, and are printed here with the permission of the poet. Ms. Scalapino is currently living in Berkeley.

NTOZAKE SHANGE has written for *Black Scholar*, *Yardbird Reader*, *Invisible City*, *Third World Women*, *Time to Greez!*, *Margins*, *Black Maria*, *West End Magazine*, *Broadway Boogie*, *APR* and *Shocks*. She received a B.A. from Barnard College and an M.A. in American Studies from UCLA. Her Choreopoem, *For Colored Girls Who Have Considered Suicide When The Rainbow Is Enuf* was produced on Broadway.

RENA SHEFFIELD's poem "The Artist and the Emperor" was found in *Land of Gold*, edited by James N. Northe, 1934.

EDWARD ROWLAND SILL, pseudonym Andrew Hedbrooke, arrived in California in the early 1860's after graduation from Yale, and remained until 1883. A member of the Bohemian Club's literary circle, Sill assumed the role of a cultural missionary to California's "Cimmerian darkness."

JOHN OLIVER SIMON's "North Country" was submitted to the anthology by the author. Mr. Simon is currently living in Berkeley.

GINO CLAYS SKY's "Potatoes and Rosehips" was submitted to the anthology by the author. Mr. Sky is currently living in Idaho.

GENOVEVA SAAVEDRA's poem was found in *First the Blade,* an Intercollegiate Anthology of Student Verse, V. 9, 1936. She was then a student at Mt. St. Mary College.

MARTÍN SOLIS' "Orgullo y Verdad" was taken from *Algo, Versos de Martin Solis,,* published in San Francisco in January, 1917, by the poet himself.

ALAN SOLDOFSKY's "Poem For Sioux City" is drawn from the poet's *Kenora Station,* published by Steam Press, and is printed here with the permission of the author. Mr. Soldofsky is currently living in Oakland.

GARY SOTO, born in 1952, was raised and educated in Fresno, California. After graduating from Fresno State University, he went on to earn an MFA from the University of California at Irvine. His work has appeared in many periodicals, including *The New Yorker, Paris Review, The Nation, Partisan Review,* and *Poetry.* He compiled the anthology *Entrance: 4 Chicano Poets* (Greenfield Review Press, 1976). His first collection *The Elements of San Joaquin* received the U.S. Award of the International Poetry Forum for 1976, and was published by the University of Pittsburgh Press in March of 1977. This past Spring he was a visiting lecturer in poetry and fiction at San Diego State University.

JAY RODERIC DE SPAIN was born in Illinois; came West at a young age. Was a miner, woodsman, painter, farmer and teacher. He wrote his first poem in 1911. "I Heard Her Wings" appeared in the magazine, *Poets of the Western Scene* in 1937.

RICHARD LEON SPAIN's poem "Plea," appeared in the magazine, *Poets of the Western Scene,* edited by Hans A. Hoffman, San Leandro, 1937.

ANNA KALFUS SPERO's poem "Lines to a Western Woman" was published in *West Winds, A Book of Verse,* copyrighted 1925 by the California Writers Club.

JACK SPICER (1925–1965), legendary poet and pin-ball wizard, is best represented in the poet's *Collected Books* (Black Sparrow: 1975) from which "No love deserves the death it has" and "The country is not well defined" are drawn.

GERTRUDE STEIN (1874–1946): Stein grew up in Oakland and San Francisco, California. She settled in Paris, where her salon became the center for the expatriate writers of "the Lost Generation." She also championed avant-garde painting. Much of her writing was considered experimental, and

410

appealed to a limited audience. Her influence on following generations of writers is inestimable.

GEORGE STERLING (1869-1926) was born in Sag Harbor, Long Island, and came to California in his teens. He became a symbol and center of the San Francisco Bohemian revival. "To a generation he embodied the life lived for art." (Kevin Starr) He published many volumes of his own work, anthologies of other poets—but he is mostly remembered for his lifestyle.

MRS. PRISCILLA STEWART was a 19th Century black pioneer about whom little is known. According to Delilah L. Beasley's *The Negro Trail Blazers of California*, her poem "A Voice from the Oppressed to the Friends of Humanity," was written shortly after passage of a bill demanding that all Free Negroes leave the state, at which time the Governor or Ruler of British Columbia sent his Harbor Master to San Francisco to extend an invitation to the Negro people to come to Canada to make their home. Mrs. Stewart recognized the call as coming from Queen Victoria.

CHARLES WARREN STODDARD (1843-1909) was brought to California from New York as a boy of twelve. One of the great personalities of San Francisco's Bohemia, he helped edit *The Overland Monthly* with Bret Harte and Ina Coolbrith. He traveled far, always returning to California, until his death at Monterey.

J. ANTHONY STOWERS was a resident of the Bay Area for most of his life. His only published work is *The Aliens* (White Rabbit Press, 1967). He died in 1977.

BARBARA SZERLIP's "The Winery" was submitted to the anthology by the poet. Ms. Szerlip is currently living in San Francisco.

GENEVIEVE TAGGARD (1894-1948) was born in Waitsburg, Washington and lived in Hawaii during her childhood and youth. The Hawaiian setting had a strong influence on her poetry. Her life was spent writing, editing, and interpreting poetry, and she published numerous collections of poetry such as *For Eager Lovers* (1922) and *Origin Hawaii* (1942). She also taught English, founded and edited a poetry journal called *The Measure* (1920-26), wrote a biography of Emily Dickinson (1930), edited several anthologies, and wrote lyrics for composers.

TAUHINDAULI (FRANK LAPENA): "I was born on Oct. 5, 1937 at 2:32 A.M. in San Francisco, Calif. of Asian and American Indian parents. There were three children in the family. I was the oldest. My mother could not support us after my father died. Because we were enrolled tribal members we were put in Government Indian schools. I attended Stewart Indian school in Nevada and Chemawa Indian School in Oregon. My mother passed away. Working my way through college I finally got an A.B. degree after nine years and later got a lifetime teaching credential, but my most meaningful education has been from the medicine people, singers, and elders of my tribe as well as other Northern California Indian tribes and other Indian people. My wife and children are important to me. When I write I am always thinking of familiar *people*, those before us, the present time and those yet to come. *TRADITION TEACHES HOW THE CONNECTION IS* made and how the spiritual world and "reality" are one. *Tribal elders are the teachers and examples of the experience of this land.* Writing sometimes helps explain the experience."

JOYCE CAROL THOMAS resides in Berkeley. Her books include *Bittersweet*, 1973; *Crystal Breezes*, 1974; *Blessing*, 1975; and plays produced: *A Song in the Sky*, (1976); *Look What a Wonder!* (1976); *Magnolia* (1977). She has been a teacher and administrator in Bay Area colleges and universities since 1968.

JOHN THORPE's "Our Lady of No Defense" originally appeared in *Io Magazine* and is reprinted here with the permission of the poet. Mr. Thorpe is currently living in Bolinas.

SOTERE TORREGIAN: "b. 25 June 1941; of Middle Eastern ancestry (traces to Moors, Armenians, Greeks, Turks, & Arabs). Associated with Surrealist tendency in poetry. Resident in California since 1966. Divorced; single parent, two daughters, Tatyana (10) and Janaina (8½)." Politically active since age of 15, in movements for Social Justice, Torregian has been active with Third World Liberation; worked as Assistant to Dr. St. Claire Drake, Afro-American Studies, Stanford, 1968-1973: teacher, Santa Clara U., poetry, art, and politics in Third World. Author of *The Golden Palomino Bites the Clock* (Angelhair, 1966); *The Wounded Mattress* (Oyez, 1968); *The Age of Gold* (Kulchur, 1976); *The Little Bird From Eric's AMTRAK Trek* (Telephone: 1977); *A Nestorian Monument in Cathay* (prose) in preparation.

ERNESTO TREJO was born in 1950 in Fresnillo, Mexico. He grew up in Mexicali. Later, he attended universities in California and Iowa. At present he makes his living in Mexico City as an economist. A chapbook, *The Day of Vendors* (Calavera Press) was recently published in Fresno, California as well as his first book in Spanish, *Instrucciones y Señales* (Máquina Eléctrica, 1977) in Mexico City. He translated the poetry of Tristán Solarte, *The Rule of Three* (U. of Iowa, 1976) and co-translated, with Philip Levine, a collection of *The Poetry of Jaime Sabines* (Twin Peaks Press, 1978).

412

QUINCY TROUPE, one of the original Watts Writers Workshop participants, founded and edited *Confrontation*. He is the author of *Embryo* and co-editor of *Giant Talk*, the important anthology of Third World writing published by Random House.

ESTELLE BEASLEY TURNER's poems were selected from a mimeographed pamphlet prepared by the Rev. William A. Harris, Associate Minister of Beth Eden Baptist Church, Oakland, 1947. She was born in Shreveport, Louisiana and moved to Oakland in 1918. Her poems have been published in the *Oakland Tribune* and *Woman's Day* magazine.

MARK TWAIN (1835-1910), born Samuel Langhorne Clemens in Florida, Missouri. Clemens worked as a journeyman printer in the East and Middle West (1853-4) and became a steamboat pilot on the Mississippi. When the Civil War began and the riverboats were no longer used, he went to Nevada with his brother. He describes this trip West and his adventures as a miner and journalist in *Roughing It* (1872). After he joined the staff at the Virginia City Territorial Enterprise (1862), he adopted the pseudonym Mark Twain and began his career as a journalist dealing with humorous frontier subjects. He is famous for *Huckleberry Finn* (1884) and *Tom Sawyer* (1876), nostalgic tales of boyish adventure, and for his humorous narratives which challenge the genteel and established.

VICTOR MANUEL VALLE: "I'm 26 years old, a Mexicano born in Califas and long-time resident of Los Angeles, mas bien un pueblo de animas y demonios. Am presently working with the magazine *Chismearte*. Have just finished an M.A. in Comparative Literature. My thesis consisted in translating six short stories of the late Peruvian novelist Jose Maria Arguedas. One of these stories has just been published in Beyond Baroque's *New Magazine*. Have also been published in *Tin Tan*. Won second place in the Third Chicano Literary Prize sponsored by the Spanish and Portuguese Department at U.C. Irvine.

PAUL VANGELISTI's "Event 24: John the Baptist" was submitted to the anthology by the poet. Mr. Vangelisti is currently living in Los Angeles where he edits *Invisible City* magazine.

ROBERTO VARGAS was born in Managua, Nicaragua, a Pisces (Feb. 24, 1941). He currently resides in the Mission district, San Francisco, where he is active with Nicaraguan Liberation Front.

PEDRO ORTIZ VASQUEZ: "I was born in Lerdo, Durango, México and now make my home in Escondido, California. I have published in various small

413

presses and currently am an associate editor of CITYBENDER, a poetry broadside published out of San Diego. I am employed by Community Arts as an artist-teacher conducting poetry workshops throughout San Diego County."

W.G.'s poem appeared in a California periodical, *Californian*, November 14, 1846. In the first conquest of Los Angeles nobody was hurt; the poet was fooled by a fake report of the conquest. Commodore Stockton's army took possession of the city without firing a shot.

DERRAL DERONDA WAGERS' "Solano Hills" and "Sleep" appeared in *Westward*, Internation Magazine of Verse, V. 1 No. 1, San Francisco, 1927.

WILLIAM ROSS WALLACE' "Columbia" was published in Delilah L. Beasley's *The Negro Trail Blazers of California*. The poet lived in the 19th century.

GLORIA WATKINS: "I was born in Hopkinsville, Kentucky and lived there nineteen years. With me in Hopkinsville were my great grandparents, my grandparents, parents and numerous aunts, uncles, cousins. This simple rigorous loving rural background influences my poetry. Many of the poems I write express the desire for a 'home' a place to put down roots. I've recently completed a book of poems, *Legacy*."

MARIA DE LAVEAGA WELCH was a life-long California resident and was active in a literary way from a fairly young age. In 1925, while a student at the University of California in Berkeley, she was one of the editors of "The Dumbook," a journal of California letters published in Mill Valley. During that period she was writing poetry and reviewing books. "The Dumbook" later became the "San Francisco Review." Among her published books are: *Ways of Earth* (San Francisco, 1932); *Poems* (N.Y., Macmillan, 1933); and *This is our own* (N.Y., Macmillan, 1940).

LEW WELCH (1926-1971): "The Song Mt. Tamalpais Sings" appeared in a number of editions, most recently the author's *Collected Poems*, and is reprinted here by permission of the publisher, Grey Fox Press.

PHILIP WHALEN's "Absolute Realty Co: Two Views" is drawn from the author's *On Bear's Head*, published by Harcourt Brace, and printed here by permission of the poet and the publisher. Mr. Whalen divides his time between Tassajara and San Francisco.

JAMES M. WHITFIELD (1823-1878) was born in Exeter, New Hampshire, and spent much of his life in Buffalo, New York working as a barber. He probably died in California, while making an expedition to Central America, which he proposed American Negroes colonize. His most widely known published work was *America and Other Poems* (Buffalo, 1853). Another work, *Emancipation Oration* was published in San Francisco, 1867.

J. RUTHERFORD WILLEM's "Animals in the Fields" was submitted to the anthology by the poet. Mr. Willems is currently living in San Francisco, and was the founder and editor for many years of *Isthmus Press* and *Isthmus* magazine.

DARYL WILSON. "Lumberjack. Poems published here and abroad. Readings throughout California."

WILLIAM J. WILSON's poem, "The Coming Man," was written in the nineteenth century and found in Beasley's *Negro Trail Blazers Of California.*

SHAWN WONG was born in 1949 in Oakland, California, raised in Berkeley, the islands of the Pacific, and in the Sierra Nevada Mountains. He co-edited a special issue of the *Bulletin of Concerned Asian Scholars* on Asian America, *Yardbird Reader* No. *3*, and *Aiiieeeee!*, an anthology of Asian-American Writers (Doubleday). He has published poetry, essays and reviews in various periodicals and anthologies and is presently working on a novel, *Homebase.* He lives in Seattle where he is a co-director of the Combined Asian-American Resources Project, Inc.

FARICITA WYATT, a native of Bakersfield, has been based in Berkeley since the mid-1920s. Educated at San Jose State College and at UC Berkeley, she served in the Women's Army Corps during World War II, has worked as Executive Secretary to Congressman Cohelan and as an English instructor at Skyline High School, Oakland.

KAREN YAMASHITA was born in 1951. She is a graduate of Carleton College and winner of a Watson Fellowship. She has studied in Brazil, and in 1974 won the *Amerasia Journal* Short Story Contest.

WAKAKO YAMAUCHI was born in 1924 in the township of Westmoreland, California in the Imperial Valley. Recently her play, "And the Soul Shall Dance," was staged at the East West Players in Los Angeles and received rave reviews. She is the recipient of the East West Players Rockefeller Grant in playwriting.

AL YOUNG's latest book of poems is *Geography of the Near Past.* Bill Cosby produced, directed, scored and starred in the First Artists movie version of his novel *Sitting Pretty.*

CONNIE YOUNG YU was born in San Francisco, California in 1944. She wrote and narrated a film on the Chinese in California called *Jung Sai* for public television. She lives in Los Altos with her husband and three children and is completing a novel.

BERNICE ZAMORA is a Chicano poet originally from Pueblo, Colorado. Her first book of poems, *Restless Serpents*, was published by Diseños Literarios, Menlo Park, Ca. A graduate student at Stanford Univeristy, published in Europe, Latin America and U.S., she is currently working on second book of poems, *After the Salmon Leave*.

AUGUSTÍN JUAN VICENTE ZAMORANO (1798–1842) was a printer by trade. The poem "Al bello secso" (copied from a reprint made by the Zamorano Club in 1953, as it appears in the Bancroft Library) has been attributed to him. Originally printed in Spanish, it is dated July 17, 1836, Monterrey. The translation is by Miss Haydee Noya of the Henry E. Huntington Library. "Al bello secso" is sometimes referred to as the "first original poetry known to have been written and printed within the territory of California."

CYN. ZARCO is a Pilipina-American poet/journalist who believes in erotic, political art. She has been published in anthologies and magazines throughout the United States and is currently working on a new genre of fiction, a musical noveletta, *MARBLES: An Affair Between A Piano & A Saxophone with a Guest Appearance by Miles Davis*. "cyn. has been in California since 1970."

JAKE ZEITLIN was born in Racine, Wisconsin, on November 4, 1902. A resident of Fort Worth, Texas from 1904 to 1925, he has lived in Los Angeles, California from 1925 to the present. Mr. Zeitlin is an antiquarian book dealer and a publisher with Zeitlin & VerBrugge.

NOTES ON RESEARCH: HISPANIC POETRY

The research for this project has been extremely challenging and exciting but I've come away from it with the feeling that the surface has barely been scratched. Many hundreds of hours were spent (most of them fruitless) in order to locate the material which is presented.

There is quite a bit of poetry in book form (individual poets as well as anthologies), journals and newspapers available in the libraries, but there must certainly be a great deal more in unpublished form to be found among the personal effects of many California residents.

Among the "Californios," English may have become the dominant language, but much of the hispanic culture and language remained as a major influence in their daily lives and in the arts.

Women poets in the Spanish-speaking community are well-represented. Even a few of the children were lucky enough to have teachers who took an interest in their creativity.

There is no doubt, however, that most of the California poetry which did get published was in the "mainstream" or "anglo" tradition. As in all other fields, the opportunity to be listened to and given recognition is never as great for the minority.

—*Marie Batha Anderson*